G.K.C. AS M.C.

BIBLIOPHILUS MAXIMUS
G. K. C. DRAWN FROM LIFE BY J. H. DOWD

G.K.C. AS M.C.
A COLLECTION OF 37 RARE
G. K. CHESTERTON ESSAYS

BY

G. K. CHESTERTON

SELECTED AND EDITED
BY
J. P de FONSEKA

WIPF & STOCK · Eugene, Oregon

Wipf and Stock Publishers
199 W 8th Ave, Suite 3
Eugene, OR 97401

GKC as MC
A Collection of 37 Rare G. K. Chesterton Essays
By Chesterton, G. K. and de Fonseka, J. P.
Copyright©1929 The Royal Literary Fund
ISBN 13: 978-1-4982-2411-6
Publication date 5/3/2016
Previously published by Methuen, 1929

TO E. V. LUCAS

My dear Lucas,

May I make bold to dedicate to you this patchwork of old prefaces, this awful aftermath of forewords; to you whose friendly advice has so often helped me in bringing something like order into the chaos of my articles, and especially in the most difficult task of all, in providing such a nameless anarchy with a name. It is time that the world was told that it was you and not I who invented the excellent title of 'All Things Considered'; probably the only really witty words in the book. Nor, I think, was this the only occasion on which the best phrase in the volume was to be found on the title-page. It was perhaps easier for you than for me to make the extravagant demand of 'A Shilling for My Thoughts'; and though the rise in prices has rendered the title ironic, it remains very apt in the abstract. I can claim little in that connexion except the invention of the one title of 'Tremendous Trifles'; which is only too magniloquent and is a mournful example of that taste for alliteration which is one of my worst vices. And as this collection is in its nature even more chaotic than the rest, I select it for the occasion of expressing my lifelong gratitude; selecting it because its disorder contrasts so much with your own exact felicity: a case (if you will excuse the horrid jest) of *Lucas a non Lucendo*.

He who introduces a speaker always declares that the introduction is unnecessary; and he who has introduced many writers may well look somewhat blankly at a whole pile of unnecessary introductions. The obvious criticism of such a collection is only too obvious. He will be as ready as any reader to cry from his heart, 'Would that we were allowed to have the books without the prefaces, rather than the prefaces without the books!' And indeed it would seem that the number of books that I have defaced with a preface would make, undefaced and by themselves, a very pleasant little private library. The only excuse I can advance for my friend, whose excess of enthusiasm has inspired this collection, is that the writer called on to introduce a book with prefatory remarks is generally driven in despair to write about almost anything except the book. The more he really appreciates the authors, the more he will wish to let the authors speak for themselves; and be driven in his turn to speak only for himself, and probably on some totally different subject. It may therefore be found that, in spite of occasional lapses into relevancy, these scraps of scribbling have something of the character of personal essays. Some of them must be judged, if possible leniently, with reference to different periods in a personal career. For some of them were written long ago, when some of my views, or at least the final deductions from my views, were not fully formulated, and they may contain elements, superficial in every sense, which would probably not be so presented now. On the whole, however, whenever I happen to come across one of these fortunately forgotten fragments from my stratified past, I may indeed shudder at their crudity of expression, but I am rather surprised to see how little my fundamental convictions have changed. For my final conviction, which was also a conversion, did not come to destroy but to fulfil.

At least I hope the bundle will serve to show that my taste was catholic with that small *c* that is considered more important than a large one. The notes at least are not all on one note, and deal with somewhat different subjects in so far as they deal with a subject at all. I am glad to see that I have written tributes to detective stories as well as to theological pamphlets, to drinking songs as well as to selections from the literary classics. Some talk of the vast mass of lighter literature as a torrent of trash pouring to mere oblivion; but I am not sure it is not the heavier rather than the lighter works that are and ought to be first forgotten. A man is much more likely to remember a drinking song or a detective story, that really rejoiced his youth, than all the huge lumber of official biographies and politico-economic analyses or books devoted to the description of new religions and party programmes, which have encumbered his working middle age. And it may be some excuse for such a mixed collection, if it sends back any casual reader to what seemed at the time an equally casual publication. In this matter also there is often a connexion between levity and humility, and some of the books that seem only to ask to be read once are those that are really worth reading again.

In any case, this introduction to introductions may well be brief. Its only object is to thank you, not only as so many have reason to thank you, for the classic grace and dexterity of your own work, but for your assistance in ordering and harmonizing the more Gothic barbarism of mine. And, feeling myself thus under both a public and a private obligation, I know of no method by which to repay it except to acknowledge it; as I do here.

G. K. CHESTERTON

PREFACE

ABBREVIATIONS, so far as this essay is concerned, are a lengthened form of saying a thing. And in regard to this abbreviated and dilatory manner there is no doubt that the dark and sinister mystery of the symbol G.K.C. (on which some very penetrating speculation has been made somewhere in the last paper of this book) is only matched by the harassing problem and puzzle of the term M.C. In no conceivable sense, of course, could G.K.C. be dismissed as an airy nothing; but, if not so dismissed, it would certainly be an exhilarating change for Gilbert Keith Chesterton (for as such has he been revealed by nothing less than an oracle in this book's sub-title in fear of a murky and all-pervading ignorance) to appear, not as usual in an atmosphere vibrating with his approach, but, if possible, as a complete and almost cataclysmic surprise. And to reciprocate, let every one else put aside that old newspaper notion of a familiar figure. For he himself has expounded the sacred duty of surprise, and praised dogs and other philosophers for their need of seeing the old road as a new road. Such a need for seeing the old thing as a new thing (which is the same virtue defined philosophically) would certainly mitigate the crime of these pages inserted here. And rising to the height of that argument, and by a precipitate and radical loss of memory, I should urge at once that all the writings extant supposed to bear the name of G.K.C. are probably phantoms of other people's brains, but that this book is the only one I am now aware of as the real product of his own.

As for the rest of the mystery, it may forthwith be imagined by some people that this is a book to commemorate the investiture of G.K.C. with the Military Cross for some notable deed of muckle valour; and, considering the extraordinary pugnacity and championship of Christian counsels which are associated with his name in mere rumour, the conjecture would be deeply reasonable. Then a school of thought which remembered hearing in floating legends how masterfully G.K.C. planned and carried out the strategy of the English Napoleon on Notting Hill might feel gratified that he had after all been gazetted as Master Commandant; while those who knew from vague hearsay of the transactions of the Club of Queer Trades and the League of the Long Bow could very plausibly rejoice that this was an appointment to be Member of the Council. But, while leaving each group of opinion full liberty of conscience, I should wish to put forward my own personal and partisan view—and perhaps the less satisfying explanation at that—that this is the book of G.K.C. as Master of Ceremonies. And, it should be added at once, not merely the Master of Ceremonies, but the Grand Master himself. For, during all this century, he has functioned in that dignified and picturesque office, and with due pomp and circumstance heralded the approach of contemporaries and the return of classics. In this aspect of the literary art I rather doubt if one could recall a longer or worthier record, nor could one think of a more diverse array of persons for whom the ceremonial services of introduction could have been performed. But the question at the moment is not the exquisite sense of ritual with which each has been presented, or the mastery of language with which the words of initiation have been spoken. Some of these introductions do indeed display rich veins of the refined gold of criticism; others, the sentimentality, chaste as a lily, of a rich poetic insight. But the question at the moment is (one which may be addressed to me with withering scorn), should there be and what is the ceremony for the induction of a Master of Ceremonies? And in a complete disregard of the wasteful excess of painting that lily and gilding that refined gold I may be taken to have answered.

It may now be said that, when G.K.C. arrived and wrote the first of the prefaces selected in this book, the last century was promptly rounded off and the present one begun. And in view of the determined agnosticism of this essay described earlier, it would be true to say that his achievement between the turn of the century and this moment has been a remarkable sequence of introductions contributed to various books by other people. They have shown a decided tendency to increase and crowd in the recent years, and all together make an impressive catalogue of some sixty-seven papers, of which thirty, for other reasons than that they were not valuable or important enough, have had to be left out. To this omission should be added also a series of introductory papers to a whole uniform library of Dickens, which stand too compact to be touched. If some cosmic revolution had occurred in the publishing business, followed by a general shaking-off of other people's rights, the course of true love, in the present undertaking, would have been so smooth as to have included all. But as this volume, in spite of that good intention, yet remains a selection, several doubts and difficulties may reasonably be brought up against it.

It may be questioned, for example, why anyone should select anything and serve up a patchwork of stray papers and pieces; and the answer can be collected from the first preface included here, that on Boswell. If it may be questioned how the excerpts have been ordered, the order is chronological; but no theory is to be advanced on it. In the history that G.K.C. understands, it has been remarked apocryphally, there are no dates, and even this book may be read backwards; and no countenance is to be given by me to the perverse doctrine that with time he progressed. By which is meant, not that G.K.C. is Peter Pan or the person unconscious of modernity known to some of his (purely hypothetical) critics; but that what he wrote yesterday might in substance have been written twenty odd years ago, and *vice versa*, a phenomenon which cannot be adequately described by a mere metaphor from the road. Accordingly, the apology for Boswell at the beginning of this volume, and the apology for his own weekly paper at the end, could well change places without any inward difference; because the essence of either apology would yet be the same. And for another reason, even a cursory comparison with Masters of Ceremonies in other walks would reveal that the whole worshipful company have been born majestic and remain. The third doubt would arise from critics with the contextual cast of mind as to whether these introductions could somehow stand alone. This may be resolved on two points, that any formal capacity could read them here with a footnote and the contextual mind could explore them in their original settings; if one breaks the other will hold, but if both break (in the noble phrase of Shakespeare) your gaskins fall. But of such a crisis, however, there need be no fear; for, to begin with, these introductions do read as independent essays and may well be as self-contained as those which popular imagination so credulously attributes to G.K.C. in the weekly issues of the *Illustrated London News*. Only, these essays boast a dignity which the spurious journalism alluded to does not claim. These essays are prefaces to which other people have fervently contributed excellent books.

There is a wise old proverb that it takes all sorts to make a Chestertonian world; and the proverb has been rather much in advance of its time, seeing that the only ground for its truth is the present volume. In the thirty-seven cases picked out here there is as varied a parcel of humanity as you could meet on a summer's day; but, unlike the comparative turmoil of a summer's day, the assembly compose and lie here in a peace and reconciliation with the great dome over all. Johnson's Boswell is in the same room as Dickens'

Forster; and only under a truce of God could Matthew Arnold refrain from turning round and proving the clear unhistoricity of H. M. Bateman, or the artist refrain from depicting in reply the tragic historicity of Matthew Arnold's whiskers. Perhaps nowhere else could there be seen so edifying a spectacle of interior concord and sympathy as when it is Jane Austen who would be found harbouring a raging volcano and William Cobbett who would be found nursing a shy vestal fire; or when at the same seat of interpretation are found gathered the Muse of Job harmonizing with the muse of Mrs. Elizabeth Turner, the fabled animals of Æsop consorting with the fantastic humans of Gilbert and Sullivan, and the sanctity of the saintly Curé d'Ars blending and communing with the lore of the Royal Society of Literature And it goes without saying, there must keep recurring, in no wise inaptly, the great English Johnson, as there must too the great English Dickens. Johnson, among other things, the most magnificent of the Masters of Ceremonies, and Dickens, among other things, the pre-eminent Chestertonian.

All these and the rest could certainly converge and commingle because they have come into a spacious and catholic philosophy, which can include and find a use of all, just as certainly as in many another philosophy they could not so

converge and commingle. In a Bolshevik order
of society, for instance, there could be no letter
written to a godchild, because there would be no
godchild, because there would be no God. The
Grandmamma who wrote moral rhymes for children would probably be summoned before the
Ogpu for corrupting youth with morality, and
that through the wicked and unbridled medium
of rhymes. The reference to a literary London
would have become quite unintelligible and obsolete, because by then the place would have been
renamed Leningrad, and that ancient testament
of Lud to Lyly and Lodge, Lamb and Landor,
Lucas and Lynd obscured for ever. Then in
the Pussyfoot scheme of the world there would
be no singing of the songs of the tap, if a man
may not even say when; and another form of
society would have banned the immoral and complex word, veal-and-ham-pie, because the world
had become at heart very, very Vegetarian. These
may be rather distant events. But there are also
the very near and living realities. There is a
reality called Ireland; and the question is whether
she has a soul. There is a reality called the
Catholic Church, and the question is whether she
is anybody in particular and big enough to write
her name in a *Who's Who*. There is a reality
called H. G. Wells, and the question is whether
his favourite Utopia is real. And there is a

reality called the English peasant, and the question is whether England has room yet for him or he must die. These questions have arisen casually, though they are far from casual, from the books which contained them, and G.K.C. has merely taken the cue. (A quite groundless report says he never declines.) And in that respect these prefaces open debate and are preliminaries; and some preliminaries answer to the name of principles.

In this way the introductions reprinted here could be made to yield up even other principles; but there is no need to extract them in this place. The prefaces will speak for themselves. They could also speak some other matter, which in view of the complaint voiced by so discerning and lucid a critic as Mr. John Freeman, may be referred to here. The complaint was that there is very little of what may be called autobiography in the writings of G.K.C.; to which I would answer that the complainant had no acquaintance with such an authentic work as this. This one *is* autobiographical. There could be nothing so true of our lives and so full of human kinship as that eternal hope of hearing a nightingale. G.K.C. had that aspiration, it is said, all his time at Battersea. It is said he relates stories to little boys. It is said he sings songs in the company of his friends. It is quite clear that he writes letters to his little god-daughters. To one in Germany there is included here a letter dated 1909, which carries a prophetic hint of war and is reminiscent (if G.K.C. will allow the reminiscence) of Johnson's letter to the little daughter of Bennet Langton, written large and round that the child may read. It is said in this letter that G.K.C. once played Father Christmas at a children's party, but on that occasion Father Christmas could not come down the chimney. Then somewhere else it is said that G.K.C. and his brother never quarrelled because they always argued; that is, as others would add, almost forgetting to quarrel because of the paradox. Then there is a prevailing belief that Belloc and G.K.C. have been friends from creation, a belief promoted by a noted picture in which the two are portrayed as perpetually holding ale-mugs in their hands (a delightful occupation) and perpetually denouncing the errors of Geneva (a comparatively dull business). But the sober truth is now available that they were once strangers; then they met and were translated into a quadruped.

Finally, as an excellent ending with a powerful moral, there remains the crux, whether literary introductions are any conceivable use. If it be roundly asked whether there is any earthly reason why anyone should introduce anyone else's work, the question would indeed fetch a hearty response from G.K.C. that there is none. But as to the suggestion that he himself has produced the most conspicuous and admirable work in our time in that superfluous form of activity—that, on the other hand, would be a topic for embittered controversy with him. But the explanation that introductions to classics are largely a matter of course, and those to contemporaries largely a matter of courtesy, does not explain enough; for if they were useless the course would not long run smooth or the courtesy be long sustained. So that the earlier example of Johnson, again to be resisted by G.K.C., needs to be recalled, that Johnson had his hand in the work of his contemporaries because his hand was wanted there, and as he had nothing of the bear except the skin, his contemporaries could be sure it would be a hand that he would extend, and a hand that could not maul. A similar word could, I think, be said by his friends of G.K.C. as a private person, but that should be a private word. But that he has introduced writings for a generation with nothing of a reserve of his genius but with a beautiful and splendid humility, depreciating himself but appreciating everybody else and rating the prologue as nothing but the play as everything—all that is and should be part of the public conscience. That is why the introductions really introduce, and the prefaces present not merely books but men. And verily there is a gentle art of introducing. If I suggested that that art also pieced out the imperfections of other people with his thoughts, bridging any hiatus of other people's thoughts and supplying any lacunæ in their philosophy, I should feel the tremor of a mountain flying shrieking, or even more dangerously, advancing against me. But it would yet be true to say that in that art, into a thousand parts, or somewhere near it, was divided one man. And whether his words have anteceded the classic masterpieces or the modern messages, at length or in brief, there have always been expressed his mind and character whole. That, I think, is, in a Shavian and, therefore, a humble and abstract phrase, the quintessence of Chestertonism. And I believe that that essence will still reveal an identity, even when the perfect cipher has been worked out in future academies and when a man's contribution has become a canon and the man himself conclusively proven to have been a myth.

J. P. de FONSEKA

Foreword to the 2016 Edition

NO one could adequately describe G.K. Chesterton in only a few pages. The newspaper columnist who only wished to be remembered, if remembered at all, as merely a jolly journalist also confected the best book yet written on St. Thomas Aquinas, at least in the opinion of the director of Pontifical Studies at the University of Toronto for some decades and, perhaps, the mostly highly respected Thomists of the twentieth century, Etienne Gilson (not to mention a strong second to Gilson's opinion coming from Jacques Maritain). The foremost reason Chesterton's reputation rose rapidly at the beginning of the last century was his mastery of comical prose outfitted in paradoxical garb, as well as his being recognized as an unsurpassed author of the short essay.

Within a few years, although his audience knew the gigantic man from Battersea was delightfully humorous, they only a touch more slowly realized that he was never frivolous. He always meant what he said, and not a clause of his writing was written for mere effect. Somewhere in Heretics he remarks that the opposite of being funny is not being serious, but rather, not being funny. He then launches into a number of reasons many intelligent people make the non sequitur of thinking the jokester trivial. Historically, those who have hated (and that is not too strong a word) Chesterton's ideas will point to his comedy so as to dismiss him as buffoon. GKC pointed out early in his career that this was a tactic of the purely ignorant.

The smiles in some of the circles where he was read began hanging slightly askew by the time Chesterton found at least part of his calling by hammering modern heresies. What he meant by a heretic at this time was anyone who deliberately allows himself to see the universe as meaningless or a holder of some political view that would become what later we were to call totalitarian. Usually the thought of the heretics examined in his book of that name were, simultaneously, advocated ridicule and tyranny when their own thoughts were revealed in the light of common day.

For a man so public with his opinions, he was remarkably quiet at this early period in expressing his own position. One of his adversaries whined that he would consider Mr. Chesterton's chiding only when he told us what he believed himself. For reasons that utterly escape me, this line of reasoning has from time out of mind been the refuge of those unwilling or unable to refute or to even discuss a topic.

Happily, Chesterton obliged his opponent by writing what many consider his masterpiece, Orthodoxy, and his defense of traditional religion is superb, although I would submit that one already needs to be somewhat on his wavelength to get the principle thrust of the argumentation. The discussion does not go in a straight line, which, although it temperamentally seems right at all times, does not conform to standard discursive argument. He discusses this in the book itself in the chapter right entitled "The Ethics of Elfland." Chesterton argues like a mystic at all times in that any topic will take us from that place where everything is really relative, but unlike the unhinged pragmatist, this relativity leads us directly to God, who is Truth itself.

His enemies, either real or simply confrontational had to admit his brilliance, and he even made a lifelong friend of one of the men given over to being the butt of his humor much of the time, and one of the heretics, George Bernard Shaw.

In 1909, Shaw dubbed Chesterton's study of him "the best book I have yet provoked." For nearly nine years Shaw prodded the fifteen stone knight until he squeezed a play from him somehow; and what a play it was! Magic still holds the stage well and has been successfully performed in the past few years in both St. Louis and in Nashville. Unfortunately only four full-length dramatic works issued from GKC's pen, and one of those was adapted from his own novel, The Flying Inn.

By 1914, he had issued five novels and that was to be followed by *The Return of Don Quixote* in 1928. His novels could all be turned into plays and they might well even gain from the transference, although a few would require elaborate staging. I saw a stage adaptation in Chicago a few years ago of *The Man Who Was Thursday*, easily his most popular novel. The director thought he was doing the work a favor by removing all that religious stuff from the play. To do that to Chesterton is to make his play diabolical, because if God is not watching over the world he creates, some one abominable is; which I understand is what the hapless instigator thought Chesterton was about in this intense nightmare of nature unleashed. Only asking what lies behind the nightmare can cure the questions and aching of the human soul. He came to Chicago that night as a demon from hell.

The protagonists he really created are all quixotic, almost always with miraculous elements implied, but supernatural intervention is never overt. In this way he is similar in his inventive tales to, of all people,

Alfred Hitchcock, especially the Hitchcock of the television series. Often a supernatural element was implied in that program, but a natural explanation invariably followed; yet the haunting atmosphere remained nevertheless. To my knowledge, Hitchcock never chose a Chesterton story for his program, probably because Chesterton dealt in mystery, whereas Hitchcock always gave the viewer information that lets him in on the true nature of the situation, which is the difference between mystery and suspense.

Mystery of some kind is the central element in Chesterton's short story collections, which run to about a score. In most of them, he relates the exploits of one character in a series of stories.

The most famous of these figures, of course, is Fr. Brown. Thousands of readers who otherwise never heard of Chesterton have read the Fr. Brown tales. The five volumes about the dumpy little Catholic priest who solves crimes because he had listened to so many confessions have remained in print at all times since they were published. The priest who many think a dunce, and who spends most of his time dropping parcels, solves crimes more to reform the criminal than to turn him over to the police. One example of his reformation even becomes his close associate in detection.

The year 1905 was something of an annus mirablis for Chesterton. Not only did he write *Heretics*, publish his first novel (*The Napoleon of Notting Hill*), and meet Shaw, but also he commenced his column for *The Illustrated London News*. Except for the six months he was in a life-threatening coma in 1914 (and therein lies a remarkable tale in itself), he wrote one essay a week for the periodical until he died in 1936. Older collections of his essays are culled from these pieces or from the *London Daily News*, for which he wrote numerous columns until 1913 when he was unceremoniously fired after he obliquely referred to his boss in this manner: "Cocoa is a coward and a cad." His boss was Lord Cadbury (the chocolate magnate), who did not back Chesterton during the Marconi scandal. (The short piece contained herein on Cecil Chesterton puts these probably actionable words of Gilbert into perspective.)

GKC As MC is a collection of thirty-seven prefaces Chesterton had written by 1929, when J.P. de Fonseka, a Ceylonese who wrote essays in something of a style reminiscent of Chesterton and Hilaire Belloc, collected the cream of Chesterton's prefaces into one volume. Another volume almost as good could have been culled from the leftovers.

Until rather recent times, especially in the U.K., publishers called the "preface" what is now rather universally known as the "foreword". Technically, then, the pieces gathered in this volume are the forewords to other books; thus the MC part of the title. Whether they are forewords or prefaces, Chesterton ranges over a good many topics including well-known figures such as Samuel Johnson, along with others who now require identification, such as Bernard Capes. In one case he writes of that poet of exquisite taste, Alice Meynell, who deserves being restored to the canon.

The reader need only a short acquaintance with Chesterton to be able to dip into this work from any angle; but much is now obscure because of the nearly hopeless mess of cultural Marxism dictated by effete arbiters of taste, a process already well on its way in Chesterton's time, but nearly pandemic today.

These essays themselves require a short essay (or is it a long annotation), for each of the thirty-seven prefaces. You hold in your hands that rare book, a collection of Chesterton that has not been reprinted since his lifetime. You are in for a special treat, but these annotations, positioned in order at the end of this volume, will provide food for thought about each essay.

Arthur Livingston
Chicago, Illinois
January 2016

CONTENTS

	PAGE
DEDICATION	v
PREFACE	ix
BOSWELL	1
OLIVER WENDELL HOLMES	11
MATTHEW ARNOLD	19
LITERARY LONDON	29
THE BOOK OF JOB	34
THE MAN IN THE FIELD	53
A LETTER TO A CHILD	59
DR. JOHNSON	63
THE BOOK OF SNOBS AND THACKERAY . . .	76
AESOP	83
DICKENS AS SANTA CLAUS	90
HILAIRE BELLOC	96
WILLIAM COBBETT	103
ERIN GO BRAGH!	108
CECIL CHESTERTON	113
BERNARD CAPES	124

	PAGE
MY NAME-VILLAGE	128
THE HUMOUR OF H. M. BATEMAN	133
JANE AUSTEN	139
DICKENS'S 'CHRISTMAS CAROL'	149
UTOPIAS	156
GEORGE MACDONALD	163
DETECTIVE STORIES	173
A STORY FROM THE GOTHIC	178
FRIENDS, ROMANS, COUNTRYMEN	184
GILBERT AND SULLIVAN	189
RASSELAS	196
THE MAN WHO WAS THURSDAY	202
WOMEN IN DICKENS	208
SOME FELLOWS	213
RHYMES FOR CHILDREN	224
THE ENGLISH PEASANT	231
DICKENS'S FORSTER	238
A SHROPSHIRE LASS	247
SONGS FROM THE SPIRIT	254
THE CURÉ D'ARS	259
APOLOGIA	265

CONTENTS

COMMENTARIES

BOSWELL	275
OLIVER WENDELL HOLMES	277
MATTHEW ARNOLD	279
LITERARY LONDON	281
THE BOOK OF JOB	283
THE MAN IN THE FIELD	285
A LETTER TO A CHILD	288
DR. JOHNSON	291
THACKERAY AND THE BOOK OF SNOBS	293
AESOP	295
DICKENS AS SANTA CLAUS	297
HILAIRE BELLOC	300
WILLIAM COBBETT	302
ERIN GO BRAGH	305
CECIL CHESTERTON	308
BERNARD CAPES	311
MY NAME VILLAGE	313
THE HUMOUR OF H.M. BATEMAN	315
JANE AUSTEN	317
DICKENS' 'CHRISTMAS CAROL'	320
UTOPIAS	322

GEORGE MACDONALD 325
ON DETECTIVE STORIES 328
A STORY FROM THE GOTHIC 330
FRIENDS, ROMANS, COUNTRYMEN 333
GILBERT AND SULLIVAN 335
RASSELAS 338
THE MAN WHO WAS THURSDAY 340
WOMEN IN DICKENS 343
SOME FELLOWS 345
RHYMES FOR CHILDREN 348
THE ENGLISH PEASANT 350
DICKEN'S FORSTER 353
A SHROPSHIRE LASS 355
SONGS FROM THE SPIRIT 357
THE CURE d'ARS 359
APOLOGIA 361
BIBLIOGRAPHY 365
ACKNOWLEDGEMENT 366

G.K.C. AS M.C.

G.K.C. as M.C.

BOSWELL[1]

NOBODY, it is to be hoped, can raise any objection to a republication of Boswell's *Johnson*, but there may be people who will raise an objection to a selection from it. Upon the whole the more cultivated people of the modern world have a tendency to protest against the practice of selecting from such masterpieces, and the phrases 'mangling', 'truncating', 'lopping' and 'torturing', are phrases, I imagine, which are kept set up in type in most newspaper offices. But how many people—I am not speaking now of professional literary men or the critics—how many of the ordinary, everyday people have read Boswell's *Johnson* in its entirety? It is a very bulky book—or series of books. Its very bulk, I venture to say, frightens many away from the attempt to read it; nay, it forbids them even to possess it. Here, at any rate, is some-

[1] Boswell's *Life of Johnson*, abridged and edited by G. Nugent Banks and Hinchcliffe Higgins. Isbister, 1903.

thing they *can* read. It is not all Boswell, certainly; but it is the best of him and much more than any man, having read, can remember. That for certain purposes, and those perhaps the largest, a complete text of any document is preferable, will not be disputed. But if it be maintained that no statement or narrative is of any value if it be fragmentary and selective, the consequences are interesting and alarming. For it is overwhelmingly probable that almost all the documents upon which we base our belief in the existence of Jesus Christ or Socrates have been mangled and edited again and again. The art of selection has not been invented by modern editors. It is a process which goes on by inevitable operation in all historic ages. Every great philosophy, every great religion is founded not upon a diary, but upon a scrap-book. If the world of the future knows nothing more of Boswell's *Johnson* than a selection of some of the most admirable passages, it will be knowing as much (and possibly a little more) than most of us know about the Greek philosophers, or the incomparable wit and wisdom of the medieval schoolmen. The act of making selections from a writer is simply the crown which awaits his fame; it is the proof of his immortality. If it is really useless for us to judge of anything in samples (and so the most artistic critics tell us), then, certainly, we are all in a most difficult position. There is that interesting object, the earth, for instance, we cannot see it in its entirety, except by going to the moon and then somewhat obscurely; we see as much of it as we can get hold of. The universe itself cannot show us its unity; we have to judge it in selections. If there is really no justification for dipping into a book, as is the habit of some of us, it seems really doubtful whether there is any justification for dipping into existence, as we all of us do. Whenever and wherever we are born, we are coming into the middle of something; at whatever time we first begin to take notice, we are reading the last chapter of some story first. Once establish the proposition that good things are useless, if they are fragmentary, and all our lives, religion, principles, politics and habits, become useless indeed. For whether they are good or bad, they are all fragmentary. I can therefore scarcely admit that a good thing is not good, even in a small quantity. I am prepared to maintain that if one cannot have too much of a good thing one cannot have too little. But it must be admitted that in the case of Boswell a certain extra difficulty arises.

That the book from which the following selections are made is the record of a very great man few will now dispute. The fact which it still requires a certain degree of positiveness and hardihood to maintain is another fact, the fact that it is the record of two very great men. One of these unique figures seems to fill the stage with his stature and the house with his voice; he is emphatic, overpowering, indisputable, a great genius; the other lurks in the background, subordinate, timorous and eclipsed. He is partly a super, partly a prompter, partly a scene-shifter, partly a carpenter. But when all is said and done he is the writer of the play. He is Boswell, the great dramatist who has made a figure live, like Shakespeare. And at last after a hundred years at the end of the last echo of Macaulay, he seems to stand some chance of being called before the curtain.

The explanation of Boswell's artistic success which Macaulay gives, to the effect that he gained this great eminence because of his deficiencies, because he was vulgar, and infantile, and pert, and mean, cannot be taken as serious. It is a legitimate rhetorical paradox: it stirs the blood as Macaulay's paradoxes do (and that is no small thing), and it has a certain loose, exaggerative truth if it is taken as meaning that some of Boswell's moral deficiencies fitted in with his mission; so did the frivolity of Congreve or the violent life of Mirabeau. But if it is to be taken as meaning that mere curiosity and impertinence can supply the place of insight and a power of portraiture; if it means that a man can become a great biographer by being a snob, the sooner such nonsense, and such evil nonsense, is dismissed the better. We have all known people who gossiped and fawned, who crawled into drawing-rooms and listened at keyholes, but we have not generally noticed that their conversation was a series of subtle and brilliant portraits. And if one of them comes in to talk to us at the moment that we are picking up Boswell's *Johnson*, we generally realize sharply which is the more interesting.

One of the chief indictments against that sodden and sulky realism which is too common to-day is that it does *not* give the true portrait of a man. It exhibits the things of which a man is ashamed, but the very fact that he is ashamed of them shows that they are not typical of the man or his class and age: it reveals that which is hidden, but if the hidden thing were natural and characteristic it would reveal itself, like a flower. It is really preposterous that Boswell should be explained simply as a brilliant eaves-dropper. For the fact is that Boswell succeeded in giving a most intimate and powerful picture of a human being without ever having recourse to these privacies and delicacies at all. He wrote nothing about Johnson except what half a score of other people heard; he only describes him as he is on the surface, but he reads that surface like a man of genius. He paints him in the street, but sees his soul walking there in the sunlight. The fact is in truth an almost inexhaustible evidence of the falsehood of the realistic or keyhole method. The truth about a man comes out much more truly when he is telling his dreams and standards, as Johnson does in the great conversations, than when he is scolding his cook or being scolded by his wife. From the great human Johnson here presented, with his moods, his transports, his odd tenderness, his odder ferocity, his humour, his humility, his vanity, his love of battle, we can deduce what he would have been like if his cook had been negligent or his wife captious. But from solemn realistic diaries by the cook and the wife we could learn nothing at all. Boswell, so far from being the keyhole snob of biography, is the great destroyer of that snobbishness: if men had been wise, he would have stopped up the keyhole for ever. Nothing could be more significant in this matter than a contrast between Johnson and Carlyle. Of Carlyle we have had all the parlour and bedroom details, and he is still a mystery. Every revelation only leads to antagonistic revelations. Facts always contradict each other. But Johnson was painted by a genius and according to the spirit, and there is no more mystery about him.

It would appear to be a singular misfortune of Boswell that people tried to accuse him of those particular biographical vices of which he was not guilty. As has been indicated above, it is not uncommon to speak of him as if he were an unsavoury gossiper and detailer of private things, whereas in truth he achieved a greater triumph of psychological analysis without using one private fact or one indiscreet word. In the same way, the very word Boswell has passed for some extraordinary and quite incomprehensible reason into a symbol for extravagant biographical admiration, and humiliating biographical servility. Even Macaulay, who enjoyed Boswell with the whole of the magnificent literary geniality which is to be set against all his errors, took it into his head to describe the tendency in biographers to a cringing eulogy as the *lues Boswelliana*. And all the time James Boswell simply towers above the whole eighteenth century, as the one man who had discovered that it was not necessary to praise a man in order to admire him. Further than that he was the first who discovered that in biography the suppression of a man's faults did not merely wreck truth, but wrecked his virtues: 'I will not,' he said, 'make my tiger a cat to please anybody.' Boswell's life is absolutely soaked with the weaknesses and vanities described with the clearness of an inspired affection. The thing is so artistic that it appears almost to be lifted out of the democracy of the real into the aristocracy of the fictitious. Johnson lives as Uncle Toby and Sir

Roger de Coverley live, and that is, no doubt, a very different sense from that in which Harley or St. John, or the Earl of Orford lives. The explanation of the whole is merely that Boswell was a great artist, and one of the great men of the eighteenth century.

In a certain sense the very merits of this great book have brought about the difficulties involved in it; the victory of Boswell is proved by his defeat, for he has made this daily and conversational life of Johnson so real that men tend to ask more of it than such a description can give; just as some art critics have maintained that if a statue were coloured and shaded so as precisely to reproduce a human figure, we should only be stricken with a sudden and insupportable sense of disgust that the figure did not move or speak. For it must be remembered that the Samuel Johnson, with whom the reader becomes acquainted in these pages, is a very different figure, by the nature of the case, from all the other figures of the eighteenth-century literature. The greater number of the ablest modern critics have sat down to argue with Johnson the views, the fascinating and aggressive views that he utters in this book, precisely as if they were discussing one of the speeches of Fox, or one of the minutes of Warren Hastings, Burke's *French Revolution*, or Gibbon's *Decline and Fall*. So brilliant and so dexterous are Johnson's utterances that they seem at once to the critic to be brilliant but fallacious essays, dexterous but insufficient Parliamentary speeches. It never occurs to any one that those polished but misleading demonstrations were poured out like remarks on the weather, or curses at a daily paper, and taken down by a man who happened to be listening. They are so good that men have paid to them the supreme and paradoxical compliment; they have not admired them as conversation; they have reviewed them as books.

Nevertheless, every reader should be warned that a certain danger goes with this conversational and over-solemn treatment of the great Johnsonian debates. The truth is that nothing is so delicate, so spiritual, so easy to lose and so difficult to regain as the humorous atmosphere of a social clique. Frivolity is, in a sense, far more sacred than seriousness. Any one who regards this as paradoxical can easily put the matter to a test. Let him ask himself how considerable a number of people there are to whom he would tell, if necessary, a family tragedy. And then let him ask himself how many people there are to whom he would recount, in all its solemn detail, a family joke. There is no bird so wild and shy as the grouse in the gun-room. And it is necessary even because of the wonderful success of Boswell's biographical art, to endeavour to realize to ourselves the peculiar uproar and frivolity of the table at Johnson's Club.

The extraordinary mistakes that have been made by ignoring this are too numerous to mention. For instance, ever since Johnson's time there has been a succession of solemn and eloquent and inane discussions about Johnson's great prejudice against Scotchmen, about whether he was right or wrong, wise or foolish in hating and excluding them as he did. It is perfectly evident to any one who reads the book with the ordinary sympathies of a human being, that Johnson did not hate or exclude the Scotch at all. Some of his best friends, including Boswell, whom he loved very warmly and very justly, were Scotchmen. It is, in short, perfectly evident that Johnson's hatred of Scotchmen was a standing joke in the circle, recognized as such by him as much as by every one else, and that, whenever an opportunity offered he braced himself for an attack on Scotland in the same way that a recognized humorist would for a comic recitation. Once a Scotchman said to him in what is obviously a waggish and provocative tone, that after all God made Scotland; 'you must remember,' said Johnson, 'that He made it for Scotchmen; comparisons are odious, but God made hell.' There do positively exist in the world people who can read that conversation and think it was serious.

OLIVER WENDELL HOLMES [1]

GENERAL and fantastic as was the characteristic writing of Oliver Wendell Holmes, there was at least one element in it which was really dominant and consistent, and that was the influence of his profession. A good doctor is by the nature of things a man who needs only the capricious gift of style to make him an amusing author. For a doctor is almost the only man who combines a very great degree of inevitable research and theoretic knowledge with a very great degree of opportunism. He unites, as it were, the exact virtues of a botanist with the wilder virtues of a commercial traveller. He is alone in combining those verbally similar but profoundly diverse things, a knowledge of the cosmos and a knowledge of the world. The result of this fusion is a certain quaint wisdom, a certain variegated experience and sudden synthesis which is pre-eminently characteristic of

[1] *The Autocrat of the Breakfast-Table*, by Oliver Wendell Holmes. Red Letter Library. Messrs. Blackie & Son, Ltd., 1904.

Holmes. This is pre-eminently characteristic of him, and it is characteristic of the one other man in literary history who bears a curious resemblance to him. Sir Thomas Browne was also a physician, he was also a fantastic, he was also a humorist and a devout philosopher. In him also we have the same bewildering ingenuity of allusion and comparison, the same saturnalia of specialism, the same topsy-turvydom of learning. We have even a similarity between them in such other matters as a certain unmistakable tinge of the aristocratic idea, the Cavalier tradition of manners and dignity, which is very noticeable in Holmes as compared with all other American writers. Holmes, again, has fully as much as Browne the notion that these scientific minutiæ and these physical ingenuities with which he has become acquainted as a doctor, are very solemn symbols of a certain rude and awful benevolence in the nature of things, a Providence that speaks like a candid doctor. Across all the bound volumes to which Wendell Holmes put his name might be written the general title or description 'Religio Medici'.

This scientific basis in Wendell Holmes has much to do with his most obviously characteristic quality, his power of startling and delightful simile. When he compares Shakespeare to an apple, and conversation to a garden hose, when he establishes his admirable parallel between natural poets and women with yellow hair, he is acting in a certain sense in the highest spirit of physical science. Physical science has everything in the world to do with fancy, though not perhaps much in the highest sense to do with imagination. Imagination as we have it in great poetry is concerned with the things that fall naturally into an harmonious picture; but fancy is concerned with things which conceal an intellectual affinity under a total pictorial difference. Imagination celebrates the stars and clouds together, but fancy and physical science alike see that a squib or a pipe-light, or perhaps even a humming-top, are more akin to the stars than a cloud is. The whole fascination of science lies in this disguised fraternity. Nature in this aspect seems made of secret societies in the darkest and most misleading costumes. No elf-land of the human fancy can offer a kingdom so preposterous as that in which a whale is nearer to a bat than a whale to a shark, or a bat to a bird. This general consciousness that the most perfect similarities exist in the most diverse examples is a thing that must have haunted the minds of hundreds of good-working physicians when they saw the same disease attacking an aspidestra in a fernery, and an old gentleman in his arm-chair. But of all these silent and fanciful men one was born with the magic and almost non-human power of saying what he meant, the power of literature. He wrote the line that sums up the whole matter—

> 'The force that whirls the planets round
> Delights in spinning tops.'

Holmes had another aspect in which his literature was the outcome of his work, the distillation from all his drugs and herbs. He found himself prominent both in the literary and scientific world at a time when science and the modern spirit were first making themselves felt to the modification of the ancient Puritanism of America. And he took, as will be seen from the pages of the *Autocrat*, a prominent and somewhat peculiar part in the fight. He was anything but a materialist, he was too much in love with a positive piety even to be described as an agnostic, yet he did not, like a large and growing part of the intellectual world of to-day, rise to a refuge in a luminous mysticism and cleanse deity of all materialistic notions, hanging it alone in the heaven of metaphysics. He took as his conception of God rather the happy father of the robust family of nature, a shrewd and benignant being, something between Jupiter and Æsculapius. His God was practically merciful, but he was mercilessly practical, and in *Elsie Venner* Holmes reaches the extreme point of this almost disdainful philan-

OLIVER WENDELL HOLMES 15

thropy, protesting against the cruelty of taking human freedom too seriously, and appearing in some sense to toss to the images of God the pardon which is due to puppets. There is very much of the doctor in this almost humiliating kindliness, this almost insulting acquittal. The orthodox churches, doubtless formal and fatuous in many things, and deserving Holmes' humanitarian satire, were nevertheless founded on a certain grand metaphysical idea which Holmes never quite justly appreciated, the idea of the dignity and danger of the human soul, the pride, and the peril of the *imago dei*. Doubtless this idea is transcendental, and in that sense unscientific in the orthodox creeds. But it is equally transcendental in the 'Declaration of Independence'.

It would be false and exaggerative in the last degree to speak as if Holmes' warm-hearted rationalism threw him into antagonism either with the Christian churches or with the 'Declaration of Independence'. But it is a singular fact, and suggestive of the close kinship between Christianity and the democratic sentiment, that Holmes stands in American literature as whitewashing aristocracy in the same airy, open-minded, half-laughing manner with which he pokes fun at the churches; in the same very light and tolerant sense in which he can be called an opponent of orthodoxy he can be called an admirer of oligarchy.

Of all American writers he is the least democratic; he is not only the doctor, he is very decidedly the professional man, the gentleman. In American literature, indeed, he may be said to be, not by actual birth or politics, but by spirit, the one literary voice of the South. He bears far more resemblance to that superb kingless aristocracy that hurled itself on the guns at Gettysburg or died round Stonewall Jackson, than to Hawthorne, who was a Puritan mystic, or Lowell, who was a Puritan pamphleteer, or Whitman, who was a Puritan suddenly converted to Christianity. No one can read *The Autocrat of the Breakfast-Table* without being struck chiefly by the incomparably delightful studies and maxims in the great philosophy of manners. The tabulation of all the signs of spiritual vulgarity, the chance phrases 'that blast a man's pedigree for three generations up and down', the coarse compliment, the unmeaning blush, the needless apology, the craven and unsteady features, the bombarding of a stranger with an insistent and tyrannical commiseration—

> 'Nor cloud his features with the unwelcome tale
> Of how he looks if haply thin and pale.
> Health is a subject for his child, his wife,
> Or the rude office that insures his life'.

This war of Holmes against everything that hurt that liberality and dignity of living which we summarize in the word 'gentleman' was really a fine thing finely done, a thing needed everywhere, especially in a new country. Still, the fact remains that the union in Holmes of a gay impatience with theologians and a gay impatience with cads is, looked at from another point of view, an evidence of that tendency of all fine naturalistic thought towards oligarchy, which can be seen from Aristotle to Hume and from Hobbes to Nietzsche. So good a gentleman as Holmes could not really understand the divine vulgarity of the Christian religion.

It was in *The Autocrat of the Breakfast-Table* that Holmes collected for the first time all this picturesque experience and frivolous wisdom, and embodied it in a form of which he rapidly became a dazzling master, the irregular monologue varied by conversations. How rich and admirable are those conversations no one who has read them will ever forget. They blaze with wit, but not after the manner of a novel of the 'smart set' in which the people are less important than their own trivial sayings, in which their vulgar souls are eclipsed by their own epigrams as their vulgar bodies are eclipsed by their own diamonds. At the breakfast-table there is something more important even than the amazing cleverness which is lavished upon it. There is a human atmosphere which alone makes conversation possible. The lamps of their brilliancy are not, like the electric sparks of *Dodo*, lit in a vacuum; they toss and flare in natural winds like the glorious naphtha jets that stream upon a booth in Ratcliffe Highway. In fact, there are characters in Holmes' books which, when recalled, make me think I have been too sweeping in my reference to the aristocratic flavour of his work. That sublime creature, the young man named John, was assuredly conceived by one who could feel the value of the everlasting ordinary man. Still, it is the ordinary man seen from without, not from within. Seen from within, his name is not John but 'Walt Whitman of Manhattan, a cosmos'. Holmes was the most large-hearted and humorous of philosophers, but he was not the democrat of 'the open road'. He was the Autocrat of the Breakfast-Table.

MATTHEW ARNOLD [1]

OUR actual obligations to Matthew Arnold are almost beyond expression. His very faults reformed us. The chief of his services may perhaps be stated thus, that he discovered (for the modern English) the purely intellectual importance of humility. He had none of that hot humility which is the fascination of saints and good men. But he had a cold humility which he had discovered to be a mere essential of the intelligence. To see things clearly, he said, you must 'get yourself out of the way'. The weakness of pride lies after all in this; that oneself is a window. It can be a coloured window, if you will; but the more thickly you lay on the colours the less of a window it will be. The two things to be done with a window are to wash it and then forget it. So the truly pious have always said the two things to do personally are to cleanse and to forget oneself.

Matthew Arnold found the window of the

[1] *Essays Literary and Critical*, by Matthew Arnold. Everyman's Library. Messrs. J. M. Dent & Sons, Ltd., 1906.

English soul opaque with its own purple. The Englishman had painted his own image on the pane so gorgeously that it was practically a dead panel; it had no opening on the world without. He could not see the most obvious and enormous objects outside his own door. The Englishman could not see (for instance) that the French Revolution was a far-reaching, fundamental and most practical and successful change in the whole structure of Europe. He really thought that it was a bloody and futile episode, in weak imitation of an English General Election. The Englishman could not see that the Catholic Church was (at the very least) an immense and enduring Latin civilization, linking us to the lost civilizations of the Mediterranean. He really thought it was a sort of sect. The Englishman could not see that the Franco-Prussian war was the entrance of a new and menacing military age, a terror to England and to all. He really thought it was a little lesson to Louis Napoleon for not reading *The Times*. The most enormous catastrophe was only some kind of symbolic compliment to England. If the sun fell from Heaven it only showed how wise England was in not having much sunshine. If the waters were turned to blood it was only an advertisement for Bass's Ale or Fry's Cocoa. Such was the weak pride of the English then. One cannot say that is wholly undiscoverable now.

But Arnold made war on it. One excellent point which he made in many places was to this effect; that those very foreign tributes to England which Englishmen quoted as showing their own merit were examples of the particular foreign merit which we did not share. Frenchmen bragged about France and Germans about Germany, doubtless; but they retained just enough of an impartial interest in the mere truth itself to remark upon the more outstanding and obvious of the superiorities of England. Arnold justly complained that when a Frenchman wrote about English political liberty we always thought it a tribute simply to English political liberty. We never thought of it as a tribute to French philosophical liberty. Examples of this are still relevant. A Frenchman wrote some time ago a book called *A quoi tient la superiorité des Anglo-Saxons?* What Englishman dare write a book called 'What causes the Superiority of Frenchmen'? But this lucid abnegation is a power. When a Frenchman calls a book 'What is the Superiority of Englishmen?' we ought to point to that book and say—'this is the superiority of Frenchmen.'

This humility, as I say, was with Arnold a mental need. He was not naturally a humble man; he might even be called a supercilious one. But he was driven to preaching humility merely as a thing to clear the head. He found the virtue which was just then being flung in the mire as fit only for nuns and slaves: and he saw that it was essential to philosophers. The most unpractical merit of ancient piety became the most practical merit of modern investigation. I repeat, he did not understand that headlong and happy humility which belongs to the more beautiful souls of the simpler ages. He did not appreciate the force (nor perhaps the humour) of St. Francis of Assisi when he called his own body 'my brother the donkey'. That is to say, he did not realize a certain feeling deep in all mystics in the face of the dual destiny. He did not realize their feeling (full both of fear and laughter) that the body *is* an animal and a very comic animal. Matthew Arnold could never have felt any part of himself to be purely comic—not even his singular whiskers. He would never, like Father Juniper, have 'played see-saw to abase himself'. In a word, he had little sympathy with the old ecstasies of self-effacement. But for this very reason it is all the more important that his main work was an attempt to preach some kind of self-effacement even to his own self-assertive age. He realized that the saints had even understated the case for humility. They had always said that without humility we should never see the better world to come. He realized that without humility we could not even see this world.

Nevertheless, as I have said, a certain tincture of pride was natural to him and prevented him from appreciating some things of great human value. It prevented him for instance from having an adequate degree of popular sympathy. He had (what is so rare in England) the sense of the state as one thing, consisting of all its citizens, the *Senatus Populusque Romanus*. But he had not the feeling of familiarity with the loves and hungers of the common man, which is the essence of the egalitarian sentiment. He was a republican, but he was not a democrat. He contemptuously dismissed the wage-earning, beer-drinking, ordinary labourers of England as 'merely populace'. They are not populace; they are merely mankind. If you do not like them you do not like mankind. And when all the rôle of Arnold's real glories has been told, there always does remain a kind of hovering doubt as to whether he did like mankind.

But of course the key of Arnold in most matters is that he deliberately conceived himself to be a corrective. He prided himself not upon telling the truth but upon telling the unpopular half-truth. He blamed his contemporaries, Carlyle for instance, not for telling falsehoods but simply for telling popular truths. And certainly in the case of Carlyle and others he was more or less right. Carlyle professed to be a Jeremiah and even a misanthrope. But he was really a demagogue, and, in one sense, even a flatterer. He was entirely sincere as all good demagogues are; he merely shared all the peculiar vanities and many of the peculiar illusions of the people to whom he spoke. He told Englishmen that they were Teutons, that they were Vikings, that they were practical politicians—all the things they like to be told they are, all the things that they are not. He told them, indeed, with a dark reproachfulness, that their strengths were lying neglected or inert. Still he reminded them of their strengths; and they liked him. But they did not like Arnold, who placidly reminded them of their weaknesses.

Arnold suffered, however, from thus consenting merely to correct; from thus consenting to tell the half-truth that was neglected. He reached at times a fanaticism that was all the more extraordinary because it was a fanaticism of moderation, an intemperance of temperance. This may be seen, I think, in the admirable argument for classical supremacy to which so much of this selection is devoted. He saw and very rightly asserted that the fault of the Mid-Victorian English was that they did not seem to have any sense of definite excellence. Nothing could be better than the way in which he points out in the very important essay on 'The Function of Criticism at the Present Time' that the French admit into intellectual problems the same principle of clearly stated and generally admitted dogmas which all of us in our daily lives admit into moral problems. The French, as he puts it in a good summarizing phrase, have a conscience in literary matters. Upon the opposite English evil he poured perpetual satire. That any man who had money enough to start a paper could start a paper and say it was as good as the *Athenæum*; that any one who had money enough to run a school could run a school and say it was as good as Winchester; these marks of the English anarchy he continually denounced. But he hardly sufficiently noticed that if this English extreme of a vulgar and indiscriminate acceptance be most certainly an extreme and something of a madness, it is equally true that his own celebration of excellence when carried past a certain point might become a very considerable madness also; indeed has become such a madness in some of the artistic epochs of the world. It is true that a man is in some danger of becoming a lunatic if he builds a stucco house and says it is as fine as the Parthenon. But surely a man is equally near to a lunatic if he refuses to live in any house except the Parthenon. A frantic hunger for all kinds of inappropriate food may be a mark of a lunatic; but it is also the mark of a lunatic to be fastidious about food.

One of the immense benefits conferred on us by Matthew Arnold lay in the fact that he recalled to us the vital fact that we are Europeans. He had a consciousness of Europe much fuller and firmer than that of any of the great men of his great epoch. For instance, he admired the Germans as Carlyle admired the Germans; perhaps he admired the Germans too much as Carlyle admired the Germans too much. But he was not deluded by any separatist follies about the superiority of a Teutonic race. If he admired the Germans it was for being European, signally and splendidly European. He did not, like Carlyle, admire the Germans for being German. Like Carlyle, he relied much on the sagacity of Goethe. But the sagacity of Goethe upon which he relied was not a rugged or cloudy sagacity, the German element in Goethe. It was the Greek element in Goethe: a lucid and equalized sagacity, a moderation and a calm such as Carlyle could not have admired, nay, could not even have imagined. Arnold did indeed wish, as every sane European wishes, that the nations that make up Europe should continue to be individual; that the contributions from the nations should be national. But he did wish that the contributions should be contributions, parts, that is, of a common cause and unity, the cause and unity of European civilization. He desired that Germany should be great, so as to make Europe great. He would not have desired that Germany should grow great so as to make Europe small. Anything, however big and formidable, which tended to divide us from the common culture of our continent he would have regarded as a crotchet. Puritanism he regarded at bottom as only an enormous crotchet. The Anglo-Saxon race most certainly he would have regarded as an enormous crotchet.

In this respect it is curious to notice how English public opinion has within our own time contrived to swing from one position to the contrary position without her touching that central position which Arnold loved. He found the English people in a mood which seemed to him unreal and un-European, but this mood was one of smug Radical mediocrity, contemptuous of arts and aims of high policy and of national honour. Ten years after his death the English people were waving Union Jacks and shouting for 'La Revanche'. Yet though they had passed thus rapidly from extreme anti-militarism to extreme militarism they had never touched on the truth that Arnold had to tell. Whether as anti-militarists or as militarists, they were alike ignorant of the actualities of our Aryan civilization. They have passed from tameness to violence without touching strength. Whenever they really touch strength they will (with their wonderful English strength) do a number of things. One of the things may be to save the world. Another of the things will certainly be to thank Matthew Arnold.

LITERARY LONDON [1]

THERE are many vices of large cities; but the worst of their faults is that they refuse to look at themselves; perhaps because the sight would be too disconcerting. The trouble about people living in a big city is not that they do not know anything about the country; it is not that they do not know anything about pigs or about primroses or about the cuckoo. It is that they do not know anything about houses or railings or lamp-posts or pavements. It is that they do not know anything about the great city. People say that the country is more poetical. This is not true. The town would immediately strike us as far more poetical if we happened to know anything at all about the town. If we applied to human traces the same vivid imagination which we apply to the traces of beasts or birds we should find not only the street, but any chance inch of the street more romantic than a glade. We say (when in a country lane): 'Here

[1] *Literary London*, by Elsie M. Lang. Messrs. T. Werner Laurie, Ltd., 1906.

is a nest,' and we immediately begin to wonder about the bird who made it. But we do not say: 'Here is a railing,' and then immediately begin to wonder about the man who made it. We regard such things as railings as coming by a kind of fate, quite unlike the most individual influence which we recognize in the growths of the countryside. We regard eggs as personal creations and molehills as personal creations. Such things as railings are the only things we think impersonal, because they are the only things that are really made by persons. This is the difficulty of the town; the personality is so compressed and packed into it that we cannot realize its presence. The smallest street is too human for any human being to realize. It would require some superhuman creature to understand so much mere humanity. This principle, which is true of the undistinguished in a human street, is even true of the distinguished. So intense and close is the presence of a million personalities in a great urban centre that even fame is in that asphyxiating atmosphere a feeble flame. Even glory is darkened and doubtful. Even the known are unknown. And it is this fact which renders necessary such a book as that which follows. The chances are a hundred to one that every man of us has almost as much ground for interest in his own neighbourhood as if he had a cottage on the plain of Waterloo or a bungalow erected in Runnimede. The only way to support such a general assertion is to take what is literally the first case that comes to hand. I am writing these words in Battersea, and a very little way off is the place where, by tradition, the brilliant Bolingbroke lived, and where (as some say) Pope wrote the *Essay on Man*. Across the river I can see the square tower of a church in which (it is said) the great Sir Thomas More lies dead. Right opposite me is the house of Catherine of Braganza. I could go on for ever. But these things are obliterated from the mind by their very multiplicity; it is as if twenty battles had been fought at Waterloo or all English political documents written at Runnimede. A street in London means stratum on stratum of history, poet upon poet, battlefield upon battlefield. This is partly the reason why we feel London to be unromantic: that it is too romantic to be felt at all; the other reason which arises from the first, is that it is never so closely and clearly described in the books that we read as is the country. Nearly all our books tell us what to look for in a field: it is the aim of this book to tell us what to look for in a street.

There are one or two definite mistakes to be cleared up. The suburbs, for instance, are commonly referred to as prosaic. That is a matter of taste: personally, I find them intoxicating. But they are also commonly referred to as new. And this is a question of fact, and reveals a very real ignorance of the trend of English history and of the nature of English institutions. The suburbs have real faults; but they are not modern. The suburb is not merely what the Germans call a 'colonie' (their most successful form of colony) —a group of houses which have really come into being owing to the needs of a central city. Some London suburbs are like this, but not Battersea or any of the rest. The proper London suburb is a tiny town that once stood on a clean hillside by itself, but has permitted the surge of growing London to sweep around it. These places are annexed, but they are, as it were, annexed nations. They are so far degraded perhaps that the empire of London has destroyed them. But they are not so degraded that the empire of London created them. I always feel when I pass through Wandsworth or Putney that I may find in the heart of it a wild beast or a memory of patriotism. This point is of enormous importance in connection with the question to which this book is devoted: the question of the tracks of great men across London. For many of these great men (if the Hibernianism is admissible) lived in London when it was not London. Camberwell is now one of the greyest spots in our present area; when

LITERARY LONDON

Browning lived in it, it may even have been of the greenest. Certainly he heard two nightingales at once (not one nightingale, to which we still aspire in Battersea)—two nightingales, and that apparently night after night. Let us then regard the important suburbs as ancient cities embedded in a sort of boiling lava spouted up by that volcano, the speculative builder. The whole charm and glory of London consists in the fact that it is the most incongruous of cities. Anywhere in London an American bar may be next door to a church built before the Crusades. A man may very well be exasperated with London, as he may be with the universe; but in both cases he has no business to be bored with it.

THE BOOK OF JOB[1]

THE Book of Job is among the other Old Testament Books both a philosophical riddle and a historical riddle. It is the philosophical riddle that concerns us in such an introduction as this; so we may dismiss first the few words of general explanation or warning which should be said about the historical aspect. Controversy has long raged about which parts of this epic belong to its original scheme and which are interpolations of considerably later date. The doctors disagree, as it is the business of doctors to do; but upon the whole the trend of investigation has always been in the direction of maintaining that the parts interpolated, if any, were the prose prologue and epilogue and possibly the speech of the young man who comes in with an apology at the end. I do not profess to be competent to decide such questions. But whatever decision the reader may come to concerning them, there is a general truth to be remembered

[1] *The Book of Job.* S. Wellwood, 1907; Cecil Palmer, 1916.

THE BOOK OF JOB

in this connection. When you deal with any ancient artistic creation do not suppose that it is anything against it that it grew gradually. The Book of Job may have grown gradually just as Westminster Abbey grew gradually. But the people who made the old folk poetry, like the people who made Westminster Abbey, did not attach that importance to the actual date and the actual author, that importance which is entirely the creation of the almost insane individualism of modern times. We may put aside the case of Job, as one complicated with religious difficulties, and take any other, say the case of the Iliad. Many people have maintained the characteristic formula of modern scepticism, that Homer was not written by Homer, but by another person of the same name. Just in the same way many have maintained that Moses was not Moses but another person called Moses. But the thing really to be remembered in the matter of the Iliad is that if other people did interpolate the passages, the thing did not create the same sense of shock as would be created by such proceedings in these individualistic times. The creation of the tribal epic was to some extent regarded as a tribal work, like the building of the tribal temple. Believe then, if you will, that the prologue of Job and the epilogue and the speech of Elihu are things inserted after the original work was composed.

But do not suppose that such insertions have that obvious and spurious character which would belong to any insertions in a modern individualistic book. Do not regard the insertions as you would regard a chapter in George Meredith which you afterwards found had not been written by George Meredith, or half a scene in Ibsen which you found had been cunningly sneaked in by Mr. William Archer. Remember that this old world which made these old poems like the Iliad and Job, always kept the tradition of what it was making. A man could almost leave a poem to his son to be finished as he would have finished it, just as a man could leave a field to his son, to be reaped as he would have reaped it. What is called Homeric unity may be a fact or not. The Iliad may have been written by one man. It may have been written by a hundred men. But let us remember that there was more unity in those times in a hundred men than there is unity now in one man. Then a city was like one man. Now one man is like a city in civil war.

Without going, therefore, into questions of unity as understood by the scholars, we may say of the scholarly riddle that the book has unity in the sense that all great traditional creations have unity; in the sense that Canterbury Cathedral has unity. And the same is broadly true of what I

THE BOOK OF JOB 37

have called the philosophical riddle. There is a real sense in which the Book of Job stands apart from most of the books included in the canon of the Old Testament. But here again those are wrong who insist on the entire absence of unity. Those are wrong who maintain that the Old Testament is a mere loose library; that it has no consistency or aim. Whether the result was achieved by some supernal spiritual truth, or by a steady national tradition, or merely by an ingenious selection in after times, the books of the Old Testament have a quite perceptible unity. To attempt to understand the Old Testament without realizing this main idea is as absurd as it would be to study one of Shakespeare's plays without realizing that the author of them had any philosophical object at all. It is as if a man were to read the history of Hamlet, Prince of Denmark, thinking all the time that he was reading what really purported to be the history of an old Danish pirate prince. Such a reader would not realize at all that Hamlet's procrastination was on the part of the poet intentional. He would merely say, 'How long Shakespeare's hero does take to kill his enemy.' So speak the Bible smashers, who are unfortunately always at bottom Bible worshippers. They do not understand the special tone and intention of the Old Testament; they do not understand its main idea, which is the idea of all men being merely the instruments of a higher power.

Those, for instance, who complain of the atrocities and treacheries of the judges and prophets of Israel have really got a notion in their head that has nothing to do with the subject. They are too Christian. They are reading back into the pre-Christian scriptures a purely Christian idea—the idea of saints, the idea that the chief instruments of God are very particularly good men. This is a deeper, a more daring, and a more interesting idea than the old Jewish one. It is the idea that innocence has about it something terrible which in the long run makes and re-makes empires and the world. But the Old Testament idea was much more what may be called the common-sense idea, that strength is strength, that cunning is cunning, that worldly success is worldly success, and that Jehovah uses these things for His own ultimate purpose, just as He uses natural forces or physical elements. He uses the strength of a hero as He uses that of a Mammoth—without any particular respect for the Mammoth. I cannot comprehend how it is that so many simple-minded sceptics have read such stories as the fraud of Jacob and supposed that the man who wrote it (whoever he was) did not know that Jacob was a sneak just as well as we do. The primeval human sense of honour does not change so much as that. But these simple-minded sceptics are, like the majority of modern sceptics, Christians. They fancy that the patriarchs must be meant for patterns; they fancy that Jacob was being set up as some kind of saint; and in that case I do not wonder that they are a little startled. That is not the atmosphere of the Old Testament at all. The heroes of the Old Testament are not the sons of God, but the slaves of God, gigantic and terrible slaves, like the genii, who were the slaves of Aladdin.

The central idea of the great part of the Old Testament may be called the idea of the loneliness of God. God is not only the chief character of the Old Testament; God is properly the only character in the Old Testament. Compared with His clearness of purpose all the other wills are heavy and automatic, like those of animals; compared with His actuality all the sons of flesh are shadows. Again and again the note is struck, 'With whom hath he taken counsel?' 'I have trodden the wine press alone, and of the peoples there was no man with me.' All the patriarchs and prophets are merely His tools or weapons; for the Lord is a man of war. He uses Joshua like an axe or Moses like a measuring-rod. For Him Samson is only a sword and Isaiah a trumpet. The saints of Christianity are supposed to be like God, to be, as it were, little statuettes of

Him. The Old Testament hero is no more supposed to be of the same nature as God than a saw or a hammer is supposed to be of the same shape as the carpenter. This is the main key and characteristic of the Hebrew scriptures as a whole. There are, indeed, in those scriptures innumerable instances of the sort of rugged humour, keen emotion, and powerful individuality which is never wanting in great primitive prose and poetry. Nevertheless the main characteristic remains; the sense not merely that God is stronger than man, not merely that God is more secret than man, but that He means more, that He knows better what He is doing, that compared with Him we have something of the vagueness, the unreason, and the vagrancy of the beasts that perish. 'It is He that sitteth above the earth, and the inhabitants thereof are as grasshoppers.' We might almost put it thus. The book is so intent upon asserting the personality of God that it almost asserts the impersonality of man. Unless this gigantic cosmic brain has conceived a thing, that thing is insecure and void; man has not enough tenacity to ensure its continuance. 'Except the Lord build the house their labour is but lost that build it. Except the Lord keep the city the watchman watcheth but in vain.'

Everywhere else, then, the Old Testament

THE BOOK OF JOB

positively rejoices in the obliteration of man in comparison with the divine purpose. The Book of Job stands definitely alone because the Book of Job definitely asks, 'But what is the purpose of God?' Is it worth the sacrifice even of our miserable humanity? Of course it is easy enough to wipe out our own paltry wills for the sake of a will that is grander and kinder. But is it grander and kinder? Let God use His tools; let God break His tools. But what is He doing and what are they being broken for? It is because of this question that we have to attack as a philosophical riddle the riddle of the Book of Job.

The present importance of the Book of Job cannot be expressed adequately even by saying that it is the most interesting of ancient books. We may almost say of the Book of Job that it is the most interesting of modern books. In truth, of course, neither of the two phrases covers the matter, because fundamental human religion and fundamental human irreligion are both at once old and new; philosophy is either eternal or it is not philosophy. The modern habit of saying, 'This is my opinion, but I may be wrong,' is entirely irrational. If I say that it may be wrong I say that it is not my opinion. The modern habit of saying, 'Every man has a different philosophy; this is my philosophy and it suits me': the habit of saying this is mere weak-mindedness.

A cosmic philosophy is not constructed to fit a man; a cosmic philosophy is constructed to fit a cosmos. A man can no more possess a private religion than he can possess a private sun and moon.

The first of the intellectual beauties of the Book of Job is that it is all concerned with this desire to know the actuality; the desire to know what is, and not merely what seems. If moderns were writing the book we should probably find that Job and his comforters got on quite well together by the simple operation of referring their differences to what is called the temperament, saying that the comforters were by nature 'optimists' and Job by nature a 'pessimist'. And they would be quite comfortable, as people can often be, for some time at least, by agreeing to say what is obviously untrue. For if the word 'pessimist' means anything at all, then emphatically Job is not a pessimist. His case alone is sufficient to refute the modern absurdity of referring everything to physical temperament. Job does not in any sense look at life in a gloomy way. If wishing to be happy and being quite ready to be happy constitute an optimist, Job is an optimist; he is an outraged and insulted optimist. He wishes the universe to justify itself, not because he wishes it to be caught out, but because he really wishes it to be justified. He demands an explanation from God, but he does not do it at all in the spirit in which Hampden might demand an explanation from Charles I. He does it in the spirit in which a wife might demand an explanation from her husband whom she really respected. He remonstrates with his Maker because he is proud of his Maker. He even speaks of the Almighty as his enemy, but he never doubts, at the back of his mind, that his enemy has some kind of a case which he does not understand. In a fine and famous blasphemy he says, 'Oh, that mine adversary had written a book!' It never really occurs to him that it could possibly be a bad book. He is anxious to be convinced, that is, he thinks that God could convince him. In short, we may say again that if the word optimist means anything (which I doubt) Job is an optimist. He shakes the pillars of the world and strikes insanely at the heavens; he lashes the stars, but it is not to silence them; it is to make them speak.

In the same way we may speak of the official optimists, the Comforters of Job. Again, if the word pessimist means anything (which I doubt) the comforters of Job may be called pessimists rather than optimists. All that they really believe is not that God is good but that God is so strong that it is much more judicious to call Him good. It would be the exaggeration of censure to call them evolutionists; but they have something of the vital error of the evolutionary optimist. They will keep on saying that everything in the universe fits into everything else: as if there were anything comforting about a number of nasty things all fitting into each other. We shall see later how God in the great climax of the poem turns this particular argument altogether upside down.

When, at the end of the poem, God enters (somewhat abruptly), is struck the sudden and splendid note which makes the thing as great as it is. All the human beings through the story, and Job especially, have been asking questions of God. A more trivial poet would have made God enter in some sense or other in order to answer the questions. By a touch truly to be called inspired, when God enters, it is to ask a number more questions on His own account. In this drama of scepticism God Himself takes up the rôle of sceptic. He does what all the great voices defending religion have always done. He does, for instance, what Socrates did. He turns rationalism against itself. He seems to say that if it comes to asking questions, He can ask some questions which will fling down and flatten out all conceivable human questioners. The poet by an exquisite intuition has made God ironically accept a kind of controversial equality with His accusers. He is willing to regard it as if it were a fair intellectual duel: 'Gird up now thy loins like a man; for I will demand of thee, and answer thou me.' The everlasting adopts an enormous and sardonic humility. He is quite willing to be prosecuted. He only asks for the right which every prosecuted person possesses; He asks to be allowed to cross-examine the witness for the prosecution. And He carries yet further the correctness of the legal parallel. For the first question, essentially speaking, which He asks of Job is the question that any criminal accused by Job would be most entitled to ask. He asks Job who he is. And Job, being a man of candid intellect, takes a little time to consider, and comes to the conclusion that he does not know.

This is the first great fact to notice about the speech of God, which is the culmination of the inquiry. It represents all human sceptics routed by a higher scepticism. It is this method, used sometimes by supreme and sometimes by mediocre minds, that has ever since been the logical weapon of the true mystic. Socrates, as I have said, used it when he showed that if you only allowed him enough sophistry he could destroy all the sophists. Jesus Christ used it when He reminded the Sadducees, who could not imagine the nature of marriage in heaven, that if it came to that they had not really imagined the nature of marriage at all. In the break up of Christian theology in the eighteenth century, Butler used it, when he pointed out that rationalistic arguments could be used as much against vague religion as against doctrinal religion, as much against rationalist ethics as against Christian ethics. It is the root and reason of the fact that men who have religious faith have also philosophic doubt, like Cardinal Newman, Mr. Balfour, or Mr. Mallock. These are the small streams of the delta; the Book of Job is the first great cataract that creates the river. In dealing with the arrogant asserter of doubt, it is not the right method to tell him to stop doubting. It is rather the right method to tell him to go on doubting, to doubt a little more, to doubt every day newer and wilder things in the universe, until at last, by some strange enlightenment, he may begin to doubt himself.

This, I say, is the first fact touching the speech; the fine inspiration by which God comes in at the end, not to answer riddles, but to propound them. The other great fact which, taken together with this one, makes the whole work religious instead of merely philosophical, is that other great surprise which makes Job suddenly satisfied with the mere presentation of something impenetrable. Verbally speaking the enigmas of Jehovah seem darker and more desolate than the enigmas of Job; yet Job was comfortless before the speech of Jehovah and is comforted after it.

THE BOOK OF JOB

He has been told nothing, but he feels the terrible and tingling atmosphere of something which is too good to be told. The refusal of God to explain His design is itself a burning hint of His design. The riddles of God are more satisfying than the solutions of man.

Thirdly, of course, it is one of the splendid strokes that God rebukes alike the man who accused, and the men who defended Him; that He knocks down pessimists and optimists with the same hammer. And it is in connection with the mechanical and supercilious comforters of Job that there occurs the still deeper and finer inversion of which I have spoken. The mechanical optimist endeavours to justify the universe avowedly upon the ground that it is a rational and consecutive pattern. He points out that the fine thing about the world is that it can all be explained. That is one point, if I may put it so, on which God, in return, is explicit to the point of violence. God says, in effect, that if there is one fine thing about the world, as far as men are concerned, it is that it cannot be explained. He insists on the inexplicableness of everything; 'Hath the rain a father? . . . Out of whose womb came the ice?' He goes farther, and insists on the positive and palpable unreason of things: 'Hast thou sent the rain upon the desert where no man is, and upon the wilderness wherein there is no man?' God will make man see things, if it is only against the black background of nonentity. God will make Job see a startling universe if He can only do it by making Job see an idiotic universe. To startle man God becomes for an instant a blasphemer; one might almost say that God becomes for an instant an atheist. He unrolls before Job a long panorama of created things, the horse, the eagle, the raven, the wild ass, the peacock, the ostrich, the crocodile. He so describes each of them that it sounds like a monster walking in the sun. The whole is a sort of psalm or rhapsody of the sense of wonder. The maker of all things is astonished at the things He has Himself made.

This we may call the third point. Job puts forward a note of interrogation; God answers with a note of exclamation. Instead of proving to Job that it is an explicable world, He insists that is a much stranger world than Job ever thought it was. Lastly, the poet has achieved in this speech, with that unconscious artistic accuracy found in so many of the simpler epics, another and much more delicate thing. Without once relaxing the rigid impenetrability of Jehovah in His deliberate declaration, he has contrived to let fall here and there in the metaphors, in the parenthetical imagery, sudden and splendid suggestions that the secret of God is a bright and not a sad one—semi-accidental suggestions, like light seen for an instant through the cracks of a closed door. It would be difficult to praise too highly, in a purely poetical sense, the instinctive exactitude and ease with which these more optimistic insinuations are let fall in other connections, as if the Almighty Himself were scarcely aware that He was letting them out. For instance, there is that famous passage where Jehovah with devastating sarcasm, asks Job where he was when the foundations of the world were laid, and then (as if merely fixing a date) mentions the time when the sons of God shouted for joy. One cannot help feeling, even upon this meagre information, that they must have had something to shout about. Or again, when God is speaking of snow and hail in the mere catalogue of the physical cosmos, He speaks of them as a treasury that He has laid up against the day of battle—a hint of some huge Armageddon in which evil shall be at last overthrown.

Nothing could be better, artistically speaking, than this optimism breaking through agnosticism like fiery gold round the edges of a black cloud. Those who look superficially at the barbaric origin of the epic may think it fanciful to read so much artistic significance into its casual similes or accidental phrases. But no one who is well acquainted with great examples of semi-barbaric poetry, as in the Song of Roland or the old ballads, will fall into this mistake. No one who knows what primitive poetry is, can fail to realize that while its conscious form is simple some of its finer effects are subtle. The Iliad contrives to express the idea that Hector and Sarpedon have a certain tone or tint of sad and chivalrous resignation, not bitter enough to be called pessimism and not jovial enough to be called optimism; Homer could never have said this in elaborate words. But somehow he contrives to say it in simple words. The Song of Roland contrives to express the idea that Christianity imposes upon its heroes a paradox: a paradox of great humility in the matter of their sins combined with great ferocity in the matter of their ideas. Of course the Song of Roland could not say this; but it conveys this. In the same way the Book of Job must be credited with many subtle effects which were in the author's soul without being, perhaps, in the author's mind. And of these by far the most important remains even yet to be stated. I do not know, and I doubt whether even scholars know, if the Book of Job had a great effect or had any effect upon the after development of Jewish thought. But if it did have any effect it may have saved them from an enormous collapse and decay. Here in this Book the question is really asked whether God invariably punishes vice with terrestrial punishment and rewards virtue with terrestrial prosperity. If the Jews had answered that question wrong they might have lost all their after influence in human history. They might have sunk even down to the level of modern well educated society. For when once people have begun to believe that prosperity is the reward of virtue their next calamity is obvious. If prosperity is regarded as the reward of virtue it will be regarded as the symptom of virtue. Men will leave off the heavy task of making good men successful. They will adopt the easier task of making our successful men good. This, which has happened throughout modern commerce and journalism, is the ultimate Nemesis of the wicked optimism of the comforters of Job. If the Jews could be saved from it, the Book of Job saved them. The Book of Job is chiefly remarkable, as I have insisted throughout, for the fact that it does not end in a way that is conventionally satisfactory. Job is not told that his misfortunes were due to his sins or a part of any plan for his improvement. But in the prologue we see Job tormented not because he was the worst of men, but because he was the best. It is the lesson of the whole work that man is most comforted by paradoxes; and it is by all human testimony the most reassuring. I need not suggest what a high and strange history awaited this paradox of the best man in the worst fortune. I need not say that in the freest and most philosophical sense there is one Old Testament figure who is truly a type; or say what is pre-figured in the wounds of Job.

THE MAN IN THE FIELD[1]

THE opinions which are general and established among the wealthier classes of modern England are marked, here and there, by curious unconscious inconsistencies, even by unconscious hypocrisies. Two thoughts are kept separate in the mind, as it were, though it needs but a touch for them to come together with a click. Thus, for instance, the upper classes flirt with the idea of Catholicism; but they join with Orangemen in Ireland to crush the fact of Catholicism. Thus, again, they glorify national defence even at its fiercest: but in their legend of the 'atrocities' of the French Revolution, they always miss the fact that the fierceness was one of national defence. They think that half an idea is better than no logic—a dangerous error. But, moreover, they think that two halves of two inconsistent ideas make up one idea between them. This is not the case.

But among these inconsistencies of fashionable

[1] *The Cottage Homes of England*, by W. W. Crotch. The Industrial Publishing Co., 1908.

thought one stands up separate and supreme. It will almost universally be found that the average prosperous lady or gentleman holds the fashionable view of Imperialism, but also a certain fashionable pessimism about the chances of putting the English people on the land. In short, the fashionable view is, first, that the Englishman is a good colonist, and second, that it is no good to ask him to colonize his own country. We cannot believe that our best workmen will be successful on the fields and in the villages of their fathers: but we are quite convinced (for some reason) that our worst workmen will be successful in regions as alien as the mountains in the moon. We have made an empire out of our refuse; but we cannot make a nation, even, out of our best material. Such is the vague and half-conscious contradiction that undoubtedly possesses the minds of great masses of the not unkindly rich. Touching the remote empire they feel a vague but vast humanitarian hope; touching the chances of small holdings or rural re-construction in the heart of the Empire, they feel a doubt and a disinclination that is not untouched with despair. Their creed contains two great articles: first, that the common Englishman can get on anywhere, and second, that the common Englishman cannot get on in England.

About this inconsistency there must be some-

THE MAN IN THE FIELD 55

thing irrational and dangerous, something unexplored. Either we are leaning far too heavily on a rotten staff of national character in all our external policies and foreign relations; or else we must be grossly and wickedly neglecting a tool that might redeem our race. This is one of the few problems (far fewer than most modern people suppose) which really cannot be settled by theory, but only by investigation. It is necessary to collect and classify the facts of our rural civilization (or barbarism) before we can be certain of anything in the matter. And we desire primarily to know two things: first, whether the condition of our peasantry is indeed below the normal sanity of mankind; secondly, if it is, whether it is due (as so many of the rich dimly believe) to something weak or hopeless in the English poor, except when they go to colonies (where they are mysteriously changed into Empire-builders), or whether it is rahter due to something quite exceptionally chaotic or unjust about the conditions under which they live. Did we, at some time or other, go very wrong, or are we, for some extraordinary reason, incapable of going right?

It is to answer these two questions, in the main, that Mr. Crotch's book exists. Touching the first question, he deals with it sufficiently trenchantly and clearly in the first few pages, and it must be difficult for any one to remain in much doubt about the answer. Our peasantry has reached a condition, not only of poverty, but often of an ignominy not human. It cannot be more strongly or justly expressed than by simply saying that our peasantry has fallen far below the lineage and dignity of the great name of peasant. That is with us not only a branch, but a withered branch, which is, in nearly all other Christian countries, the root of the tree. It is not so much merely that the peasant is poor; it is that he is not a peasant: he is not even a fixed and calculable type. A common phrase used in every newspaper and book to-day, is a curious symbol of the absence of the peasant; of this great gap in our social picture. Nowadays when we wish to speak of democracy or of the average citizen, we always talk of the 'man in the street'. Real democracies are conscious of the man in the field.

This unimportance in the rural poor is due to something irrational and ramshackle in the framework of their life; they do not feel like low squat pillars of the State, people supporting something, as most peasants do. They feel more like a fugitive and accidental riff-raff, like gypsies or migratory Jews. They are the thistle-down and not the grass. The strong English sense of humour, the perverse English good temper, is indeed not wholly destroyed in the villages. It is not wholly destroyed at the hulks. But no conditions perhaps

THE MAN IN THE FIELD

ever existed which in their absence of security, clear citizenship, religion, or national tradition were so calculated to make a man lose everything, as those which fester behind those flower-clad walls, which Mr. Crotch so vividly describes. He very truly says that the picturesqueness of those rose-covered cottages should not colour our conception too much. The roses are all outside such places; the thorns are within.

Touching the second question, Mr. Crotch answers substantially and positively that this disease of the countryside is not the decay of a people, but the paralysis of a system of government. He points out that the evil is not due to any primal and physical development (such, for instance, as over-population) but to the extraordinary existing arrangements for such people as there are. By a horrible paradox, there is overcrowding even when there are not enough people. Mr. Crotch also goes through the main events of the history of the problem; and propounds, in no uncertain terms, his own views of the mistakes of the past and the best remedies to be employed in the future. But of these, of course, he can speak best for himself.

What is essential to emphasize in any preliminary note is the urgency of the matter. The state of things is growing worse every moment; for all human institutions slide downwards like a landslide, unless they are perpetually forced upwards by criticism and reform. It is vain indeed to speak of conservatism in this world, except as a convenient party label. Unless we are always changing things for the better, they are always changing themselves for the worse. This should be left at the last in the mind of any historic Tory or romantic Englishman who cannot help feeling that public powers or new proposals are breaking up the old rural life of England. Time and sin are already breaking up the old rural life of England; they have already broken it up. All that was good in feudalism is gone; the good humour, the common sports, the apportioned duties, the fraternity that could live without equality. All that is bad in feudalism not only remains but grows, the caprice, the sudden cruelty, the offence to human dignity in the existence of slave and lord. The English squire, the ruler of England, has made the one great mistake of supposing that if you leave a thing alone it goes on as before. If you leave a thing alone it goes to the devil. He rode from the rose-covered cottage, swearing that no one should ever touch its blooming beauty and domesticity. And when he returned in the evening the place was full of darkness and all uncleanness, and worms.

A LETTER TO A CHILD[1]

MY DEAR GOD-DAUGHTER,—
Your mother who wrote these little nursery poems, wrote them for her own two little girls; and it is exactly for that reason that they may really be worth spreading among all the girls and boys in the world. It is generally a good rule that you never understand this great earth until you own a little bit of it; and you do not really know anything about any order of things from cats to angels until you have one of your own. But then, if you are a good child, you probably have a cat, and you certainly have an angel. I myself have quite recently bought a dog; and ever since then I have looked at all the dogs in all the streets and parlours, dogs that I would never have dreamed of looking at before. I did it partly because the dogs were very nice, and also partly, of course, because they were not so nice as mine. Just in the same way your mother wrote these songs partly because she loves

[1] *Meadows of Play*, by Margaret Arndt. Messrs. Elkin Mathews and Marrott, Ltd., 1909.

all the children in the world, and partly because she loves you most of all of them.

You know, of course, that your mother came from my country to yours before you were born. She came from England, where the soldiers and the pillar-boxes are both red; to Germany, where the soldiers and the pillar-boxes are both blue. There are other differences, perhaps, but this is the one that strikes the eye first. And indeed, my dear God-daughter, there are many people in the world who will try to teach you that those sort of differences are everything, and that two great nations are only to be known by how their pillar-boxes are painted or their soldiers' coats buttoned, and who will try and make them quarrel upon lesser counts than these. Some Englishmen will tell you that Germans are just going to blow up England with gun-powder; and some Germans will tell you that Englishmen are just going to do the same thing with gas or dynamite, or something else that is unpleasant. Do not believe them; they are trying to make mischief out of small things, such as the pillar-boxes being red or blue. I want you to remember what is really great in your great country, and perhaps a little also what is great in mine. As for England, you must judge by your mother, and then you will not do us any wrong. But as for Germany, I would like you to remember your

A LETTER TO A CHILD

childhood, and to remember it all your life, whatever happens to Germany or England or all Christian lands. It is a good country for children, Barbara; there is no country that has so much understood that children live in Elf-land; that men and women before they grow up, have to be elves for a little while. Do you remember the little Heinzelmännchen with red caps that you and I used to draw for each other? Your mother found *them* at least in the German forests, though she knows a great deal about the fairies of England too. Even we in England understand that everything that is very good for children comes from Germany. Most of our toys come from Germany, for instance. And when we want a word for the jolly old gentleman who undoubtedly does come down the chimney on Christmas Eve (we must accept him as a fact, whatever his name is), we call him as you do, Santa Claus. We have a man of our own, called Father Christmas. I acted him once at a children's party. But he is much too fat to get down the chimney.

And now, Barbara, there is nothing to talk about except the songs themselves; and what is the good of talking about songs when one ought to be singing them? A great many of these little poems ought to have tunes to them. Perhaps (as you were born in Germany) you will become a monstrously great musician and set them yourself to music of the most excruciatingly subtle sort. If you don't, never mind. There is one of them that I am very fond of, which begins by saying,

> 'Birthday Baby, one year old,
> Would you like a throne of gold?'

I think that it is so nice and sudden. You are not to suppose from this that your mother actually had a throne on the premises; your mother is a poet, and poets seldom have such things. But it is quite true that when little things like you and me are one year old we are so nice that people would give us anything. The great question is, Barbara, can we keep as nice as that? I have my doubts; but we might try. And what fun it would be if we could really keep it up; and when you are dying at ninety-seven and I at a hundred and twenty-seven there was still a golden throne going somewhere. I do not know, dear Barbara, but I am sure your mother knows all about it.

Your helpless God-father,
GILBERT CHESTERTON

DR. JOHNSON [1]

SAMUEL JOHNSON, afterwards so loyal a eulogist of London, only came up to it when he had already experimented in life in various parts of the country. He was born at Lichfield in 1709; his father was a bookseller, and a worthy, if somewhat sombre, type of that old thinking middle-class of England (now so nearly extinct) of which his celebrated son will always be the great historic incarnation. He went to Oxford, to Pembroke College, where venerable tales are told of his independence and eccentricity: he became a master in a school at Market Bosworth, and subsequently the assistant of a bookseller in Birmingham. In his twenty-fifth year occurred the curious and brief episode of his marriage; he married a widow named Porter; she was considerably older than himself, and died very soon after the union. He spoke of her very rarely in after life but then always with marked tenderness.

[1] Samuel Johnson: *Extracts from his Writings*, edited by Alice Meynell and G. K. Chesterton. Messrs. Herbert and Daniel, 1911.

Failing in a second attempt at the trade of schoolmaster, he came to London with David Garrick, his friend and pupil; and began reporting parliamentary debates for *The Gentleman's Magazine*. It was of this task that he sardonically said that he took care that the Whig dogs should not have the best of it. But this remark, like numerous other remarks of Johnson's, has been taken absurdly seriously; and critics have seen a trait of unscrupulous Toryism in what was the very natural and passing jest of a Fleet Street journalist. His poem of *London* had been published in 1738; and his next important work was the celebrated *Vanity of Human Wishes*, published in 1749. It is an impressive if severe meditation in verse, treated with Pope's poetic rationalism but the very opposite of Pope's optimism; some passages, such as that on Charles of Sweden, are still sufficiently attractive to be hackneyed. It is certainly much greater as a poem than his *Irene* (produced in the same year) as a tragedy. Since about 1747 he had been occupied with the Dictionary, which was to be published by subscription. Through a mixture of lethargy and caution he delayed over it, as some thought, unduly, and it was in reply to something like a taunt that he hastily finished and produced it in 1755. It was on the occasion of this publication that the great Lord Chesterfield, who had neglected and repulsed Johnson in his

DR. JOHNSON

poorer days, condescended to that public compliment which was publicly flung back in his face in the famous letter about patrons and patronage. The intervals of his career had been filled up with such things as the *Rambler* and the *Idler*, works on the model of Addison's *Spectator*, but lacking that particular type of lightness which had made Addison's experiment so successful. His two last important books, and perhaps, upon the whole, his two best, were the philosophic romance *Rasselas, Prince of Abyssinia*, in 1759, and the full collection of the *Lives of the Poets*, published in 1777. *Rasselas* is an ironic tale of the disillusionments of a youth among the pompous dignities and philosophies of this world, somewhat to the same tune as the *Vanity of Human Wishes*. The *Lives of the Poets*, with their excellent thumb-nail sketches and rule-of-thumb criticisms, come nearer than anything else he wrote to the almost rollicking sagacity of his conversation. For all the rest of Johnson's life, and that the larger part, is conversation. All the rest is the history of those great friendships with Boswell, with Burke, with Reynolds, with the Thrales, which fill the most inexhaustible of human books; those companionships which Boswell was justified in calling the nights and feasts of the gods.

It is a truism, but none the less a truth for all that, that Samuel Johnson is more vivid to us in a book written by another man than in any of the books that he wrote himself. Few critics, however, have passed from this obvious fact to its yet more obvious explanation. In Johnson's books we have Johnson all alone, and Johnson had a great dislike of being all alone. He had this splendid and satisfying trait of the sane man; that he knew the one or two points on which he was mad. He did not wish his own soul to fill the whole sky; he knew that soul had its accidents and morbidities; and he liked to have it corrected by a varied companionship. Standing by itself in the wilderness, his soul was reverent, reasonable, rather sad and extremely brave. He did not wish this spirit to pervade all God's universe; but it was perfectly natural that it should pervade all his own books. By itself it amounted to something like tragedy; the religious tragedy of the ancients, not the irreligious tragedy of to-day. In the *Vanity of Human Wishes*, and the disappointments of *Rasselas*, we overhear Johnson in soliloquy. Boswell found the comedy by describing his clash with other characters.

This essential comedy of Johnson's character is one which has never, oddly enough, been put upon the stage. There was in his nature one of the unconscious and even agreeable contradictions loved by the true comedian. It is a contradiction not at all uncommon in men of fertile and forcible

DR. JOHNSON

minds. I mean a strenuous and sincere belief in convention, combined with a huge natural inaptitude for observing it. Somebody might make a really entertaining stage-scene out of the inconsistency, while preserving a perfect unity in the character of Johnson. He would have innocently explained that a delicacy towards females is what chiefly separates us from barbarians, with one foot on a lady's skirt and another through her tambour-frame. He would prove that mutual concessions are the charm of city life, while his huge body blocked the traffic of Fleet Street: and he would earnestly demonstrate the sophistry of affecting to ignore small things, with sweeping gestures that left them in fragments all over the drawing-room floor. Yet his preaching was perfectly sincere and very largely right. It was inconsistent with his practice; but it was not inconsistent with his soul, or with the truth of things.

In passing, it may be said that many sayings about Johnson have been too easily swallowed because they were mere sayings of his contemporaries and intimates. But most of his contemporaries, as was natural, saw him somewhat superficially; and most of his intimates were wits, who would not lose the chance of an epigram. In one instance especially I think they managed to miss the full point of the Johnsonian paradox, the combination of great external carelessness with considerable internal care. I mean in those repeated and varied statements of Boswell and the others that Johnson 'talked for victory'. This only happened, I think, when the talk had already become a fight; and every man fights for victory. There is nothing else to fight for. It is true that towards the end of an argument Johnson would shout rude remarks; but so have a vast number of the men, wise and foolish, who have argued with each other in taverns. The only difference is that Johnson could think of rather memorable remarks to shout. I fancy his friends sometimes blamed him, not because he talked for victory, but because he got it. If the idea is that his eye was first on victory and not on truth, I know no man in human history of whom this would be more untrue. Nothing is more notable in page after page of Boswell's biography than the honest effort of Johnson to get his enormous, perhaps elephantine, brain to work on any problem however small that is presented to it, and to produce a sane and reliable reply. On the maddest stretch of metaphysics or the most trivial trouble of clothes or money, he always begins graciously and even impartially. The mountain is in travail to bring forth the mouse—so long as it is a live mouse.

The legend yet alive connects Samuel Johnson chiefly with his Dictionary; and there is a sense in which the symbol is not unfit. In so far as a

DR. JOHNSON

dictionary is dead and mechanical it is specially inadequate to embody one of the most vital and spirited of human souls. Even in so far as a dictionary is serious it is scarce specially appropriate; for Johnson was not always formally serious; was sometimes highly flippant and sometimes magnificently coarse. Nevertheless, there is a sense in which Johnson was like a dictionary. He took each thing, big or small, as it came. He told the truth, but on miscellaneous matters and in an accidental order. One might even amuse oneself with making another Johnson's Dictionary of his conversation, in the order of A, B and C. *'Abstain*; I can, but not be temperate. *Baby;* if left alone in tower with. *Catholics;* harmlessness of doctrines of,' and so on. No man, I think, ever tried to make all his talk as accurate and not only as varied as a dictionary. But then in his Dictionary there was no one to contradict him. And here we find again the true difference between the Works and the Life.

Johnson, it may be repeated, was a splendidly sane man who knew he was a little mad. He was the exact opposite of the literary man of proverbial satire; the poet of *Punch* and 'the artistic temperament'. He was the very opposite of the man who rejoices with the skylark and quarrels with the dinner; who is an optimist to his publisher, and a pessimist to his wife. Johnson was melancholy by physical and mental trend; and grew sad in hours of mere expansion and idleness. But his unconquerable courage and common sense led him to defy his own temperament in every detail of daily life; so that he was cheerful in his conversation and sad only in his books. Had Johnson been in the place of the minor poet of modern satire, his wife and his cook would have had all his happiness. The skylark would have had to bear all his depression; and would probably have borne it pretty well.

It is for this reason that ever since the great Boswellian revelation (one might almost say apocalypse) every one must feel such works as the *Vanity of Human Wishes* as insufficient or even conceivably monotonous. We are alone with the shades of the great mind; without allowing for the thousand lights of laughter, encouragement and camaraderie which he perpetually permitted to play over them and dispel them; we are in some sense seeing the battle without waiting for the victory. And in this connection, as in many others, we are prone to forget one very practical consideration; that a poet, or a symbolic romancer, will generally tend to describe not so much the mental attitudes which he seriously thinks right, as those which are so temperamentally tied on to him, that he knows he can describe them well. Merely as an artist, he is less troubled about the truth, than about whether he can tell it truly. And it was hard if Johnson could not get something out of some of his black hours.

There is another cause that makes his works, as it were, a little monochrome in comparison with the rattling kaleidoscope of his conversations. I mean the fact, very characteristic of his own century, and very uncharacteristic of our own, that if he had essential intellectual injustices (and he had one or two), he did not set out to have them. With the pen positively in his hand, he felt like a judge, as if he had the judge's wig on his head. It required social collision and provocation to sting him into some of those superb exaggerations, things that were the best he ever said, but things that he never would have written. It was that eighteenth-century idea of a responsible and final justice in the arts. Our own time has run away from it, as it has run away from all the really virile and constructive parts of Rationalism, retaining only a few fragments of its verbalism and its historical ignorance.

For all these reasons it is difficult to keep Johnson's actual literary works in a proper prominence among all the facts and fables about him; just as it might be difficult successfully to exhibit six fine etchings or steel engravings among all the gorgeous landscapes or gaudy portraits of the Royal Academy. But if people infer that the etchings and engravings are not good of their kind, then they are very much mistaken. All these Johnsonian etchings fulfil the best artistic test of etching; they are very thoroughly in black and white. All these steel engravings are really steel engravings; they are graven by a brain of steel. What Macaulay said about Johnson in this respect is both neat and true: unlike most of the things he said about Johnson, which were neat and false. Macaulay not only understood Johnsonian criticism, but he foresaw most modern criticism, when he said that the Doctor's comments always at least meant something. He belonged to an age and school that loved to be elaborately lucid; but one must mean something to be able to explain it six times over. Many a modern critic called delicate, elusive, reticent, subtle, individual, has gained this praise by saying something once which any one could see to be rubbish if he had said it twice.

It is with some such considerations that the modern reader should sit down to enjoy the very enjoyable *Rasselas* or the still more enjoyable *Lives of the Poets*. He must get rid of the lazy modern legend that whenever Johnson decides he dogmatizes, and that whenever he dogmatizes he bullies. He must be quit of the commonplace tradition that when Johnson uses a long word he is using a sort of scholastic incantation more or less

DR. JOHNSON

analogous to a curse. He must put himself into an attitude adequately appreciative of the genuine athletics of the intellect in which these giants indulged. Never mind whether the antithesis seems forced; inquire how many modern leader-writers would have been able to force it. Never mind whether the logic seems to lead a man to the right conclusion; ask how many modern essayists have enough logic to lead them anywhere. Wisdom doubtless is a better thing than wit; but when we read the rambling polysyllables of our modern books and magazines, I think it is much clearer that we have lost the wit than it is that we have found the wisdom.

If we pass from the style to the substance of Johnson's criticisms, we find a further rebuke to our own time. The fallacy in the mere notion of progress or 'evolution' is simply this; that as human history really goes one has only to be old-fashioned long enough to be in the very newest fashion. If there were a lady old enough and vain enough to wear an Empire dress since the marriage of Marie Louise, she would have had the first and nearest adumbration of a hobble skirt. If one ancient polytheist had survived long enough he might have lived to hear an Oxford don say to me at a dinner-party that perhaps we are not living in a Universe, but in a Multiverse. This same law, that by lagging behind the times one can generally get in front of them, has operated to the advantage of Johnson. Johnson happened to grow up in an old tradition in the early eighteenth century, before his friend Garrick and others had made the great Shakespeare boom. He therefore wrote of Shakespeare just as if Shakespeare had been a human being; and has been reviled ever since for his vandalism and lack of imagination. In our own time, however, we have seen Mr. Bernard Shaw clinging to the pedestal of Johnson as Caesar to that of Pompey; and protesting (with an exactly typical combination of impudence and truth) that he, Bernard Shaw, is the old classical critic, and has only been carrying on out of the eighteenth century, the old classical criticism of Shakespeare. It is well to take this thought through our excursions into *The Lives of the Poets*. Every comment is lucid; do not be in haste to call any comment antiquated; you never know when it will be new.

For Johnson is immortal in a more solemn sense than that of the common laurel. He is as immortal as mortality. The world will always return to him, almost as it returns to Aristotle; because he also judged all things with a gigantic and detached good sense. One of the bravest men ever born, he was nowhere more devoid of fear than when he confessed the fear of death. There he is the mighty voice of all flesh; heroic because it is

DR. JOHNSON

timid. In the bald catalogue of biography with which I began, I purposely omitted the deathbed in the old bachelor house in Bolt Court in 1784. That was no part of the sociable and literary Johnson, but of the solitary and immortal one. I will not say that he died alone with God, for each of us will do that; but he did in a doubtful and changing world, what in securer civilizations the saints have done. He detached himself from time as in an ecstasy of impartiality; and saw the ages with an equal eye. He was not merely alone with God; he even shared the loneliness of God, which is love.

THE BOOK OF SNOBS AND THACKERAY[1]

THE Book of Snobs, as every one knows, appeared periodically in *Punch*. Much of its best irony depends on a delightfully pompous scheme of scientific inquiry, as in a standard book for specialists; and the actual style and arrangement are often singularly neat and artistic. Nevertheless it shows the unmistakable signs of periodical journalism, signs that are unmistakable at least to any one who has been a periodical journalist. Sometimes the chapter ends with a rolling and really noble piece of rhetoric, like that description of the dreary palace and dreadful bedstead of the bankrupt Lord Carabas, and the tremulous self-congratulations that we at least are of the middle classes, and are out of the reach of that surprising arrogance and that astounding meanness to which the wretched old victim is obliged to mount and descend. Sometimes, again, the chapter will end with pungency but

[1] *The Book of Snobs*, by W. M. Thackeray. Red Letter Library. Messrs. Blackie & Son, Ltd., 1911.

with precipitation, like a hurried stab in a street quarrel; as where Thackeray briefly tells the public that George IV in his coronation robes is on view at the waxworks, price one shilling, children and flunkeys sixpence. 'Go—and pay sixpence.' Sometimes, again, the chapter will end quite suddenly, on some small detail; the journalist has been forced to say anything and end anyhow. Thus *The Book of Snobs* is another example of that strange paradox in the patched plays and borrowed plots of Shakespeare. The thing which is a permanent pleasure for the reader is exactly the thing which (in all probability) was a very brief annoyance to the writer. We cannot really judge this book except as ephemeral journalism; and yet it proves to us how eternal journalism can be.

Punch has good reason to be proud of this as of many other classics, such as 'The Song of the Shirt', and the great pencil strokes of Keene that are embedded in its volumes. And yet the mere statement that the matter appeared in *Punch* may, without further comment, convey a curiously wrong impression to the modern reader. That genial injustice which is the chief English trait (and which explains at once our success with niggers and our failure with Irishmen), is nowhere more marked than in a hearty loyalty to names long after the things for which the names stand have altered or disappeared. Every man knows a cousin or an aunt who still goes to Fisher's Fish Shop or Bootle's Boot Shop, because they belong to old and trustworthy tradesmen; and without the slightest concern for the fact that Bootle has been dead a hundred years, and that Fisher's shop is now a branch of a Trust, and managed by a young American. Everybody notices how boys are sent to the old schools, though under entirely new schoolmasters. Everybody notices how the tea merchant in Brompton reads *The Times* through all the wild revolutions that capture and transform the office of that newspaper. And this obstinate faith in a title and oblivion of a thing may make many people forget how different is the modern *Punch* from the *Punch* to which Thackeray contributed. There are indeed passages and elements in the modern *Punch* which might lead an enemy to call it, not a Book of Snobs, but rather a book by snobs. But apart from fitful lapses into really base class feeling or jingoism, no one who enjoys the modern *Punch* as much as it deserves will deny that it is on the whole a conservative organ, more an expression of the contentment of certain classes in the state. It is therefore all the more difficult for any modern readers to realize that *Punch* was, in the day of Thackeray's great contribution, something very like a revolutionary paper.

This tone in the old *Punch* and its period is not

BOOK OF SNOBS AND THACKERAY

easy to state, and could easily be misstated. Certainly it was never revolutionary as a French or Italian paper can be revolutionary. English Radicalism was an attitude rather than a creed: if it had been a creed it might have won. Perhaps it can best be defined by a comparison with the best sort of modern English humour, much of which is even superior to the old, as far as subtlety and artistic precision are concerned. Many men of real genius to-day are making fun of common life. They make fun of it shrewdly, like Mr. Barry Pain; or humanely, like Mr. Pett Ridge; or sympathetically as to certain types, like Mr. Zangwill; or in a rollicking and almost brotherly style, like Mr. Jacobs. But still it is common life they are making fun of. The man who goes for a pot of beer, the woman who hangs out the washing, these are the definitely funny figures of this earth. Now this humour did also exist in Dickens when he wrote about pickpockets, or Thackeray when he wrote about footmen. But what there was also in the early Victorians, and what there is not in the modern satirists, was the firm, fresh, and unaffected conviction that the great ones of this earth are comic also. In the atmosphere of the early *Punches*, an emperor, an alderman, a bishop, a beadle, are really felt instinctively as grotesques. Thackeray is saying something entirely native and sincere when he says, in this book, that an officer in full uniform is to him 'as great and foolish a monster' as a King of the Cannibal Islands with a top hat and a ring in his nose. Those people did not think of a bishop as a sublime figure in cope and mitre, but quite honestly as a laughable figure in gaiters and an apron. They did not think of a baronet as a baron, even a little baron; they thought of him as a vulgar, trivial creature, with a Bloody Hand and brains to match. I am not discussing here the good and evil of this lost atmosphere; there was very much of both. While we have certainly gained in an imaginative appreciation of tradition, we have as certainly fallen under a much meaner and more emasculate submission to fashion. It is enough to insist here that for Thackeray and his friends snobbishness or social ambition was an enormous idolatry; and they held that the idols ought to be broken, not merely because they were heathen or wicked, but because they were (in Thackeray's eyes) ugly, barbarous and comic.

So far *The Book of Snobs* is at one with its age, or at least with its school or party. It startles us now to think of *Punch* printing a passage which, practically in so many words, calls the head of the Royal Family a Snob. It would surprise us now to find even such a passage as that in which Thackeray calls, with real passion, for somebody to organize equality, and promises that his staff shall swallow all the gold sticks of precedence. But such Jacobin sentiments would have seemed quite common in that time and circle; in the kindly irrelevance of Charles Dickens or the cruel relevancy of Douglas Jerrold: Thackeray's passages might have seemed the mildest in the whole mass. Was there, then, any character quite peculiar to Thackeray in his denunciation of the form of idolatry called gentility? Yes, there was; and this special quality will more than anything else make Thackeray immortal. For it has the paradox of all things perfectly done in letters; it is unique and yet it is universal.

We talk of Thackeray as a satirist; but there is a real sense in which the other anti-snobs of his time were more purely satiric than he. There is a real sense in which Dickens was merciless. That is to say, Dickens was merciless to everybody to whom he was not indulgent. Micawber and Uriah Heep might both be called swindlers or amusing rogues, according to taste; but there is no doubt that Dickens was indulgent to the one and merciless to the other. But the one supreme and even sacred quality in Thackeray's work is that he felt the weakness of all flesh. Whenever he sneers it is at his own potential self, when he rebukes, he knows it is self-rebuke; when he indulges, he knows it is self-indulgence. This makes him less effective for a fierce war against exceptional and definable abuses; but it secures his special value in the ethics of his age. When Dickens makes game of Major Bagstock, we feel that the game (however desirable) is a very long way off. But when Thackeray makes game of Major Ponto, we all feel that the vain, worried, worldly little man is very close to us; it is not impossible that he is even inside us. Here, then, was his special contribution to that chaos of morality which the nineteenth century muddled through: he stood for the remains of Christian humility, as Dickens stood for the remains of Christian charity. Dickens, or Douglas Jerrold, or many others might have planned a Book of Snobs; it was Thackeray and Thackeray alone, who wrote the great sub-title, 'By One of Themselves'. Though he was in motley, he was also in sackcloth. If he failed (unfortunately) to call us to a day of national revolution, he called us at least to a day of national humiliation and penance, and his testimony remains, even with an increasing value, in a civilization which cannot live without combined humility and audacity, and which must find that paradox or perish.

AESOP [1]

AESOP embodies an epigram not uncommon in human history; his fame is all the more deserved because he never deserved it. The firm foundation of common sense, the shrewd shots at uncommon sense, that characterize all the Fables, belong not to him but to humanity. In the earliest human history whatever is authentic is universal; and whatever is universal is anonymous. In such cases there is always some central man who had first the trouble of collecting them, and afterwards the fame of creating them. He had the fame; and on the whole, he earned the fame. There must have been something great and human, something of the human future and the human past, in such a man: even if he only used it to rob the past or deceive the future. The story of Arthur may have been really connected with the most fighting Christianity of falling Rome or with the most heathen traditions hidden in the hills of Wales.

[1] *Aesop's Fables*, a new translation by V. S. Vernon Jones. Messrs. Wm. Heinemann, Ltd., 1912.

But the word 'Mappe' or 'Malory' will always mean King Arthur; even though we find older and better origins than the Mabinogion; or write later and worse versions than the *Idylls of the King*. The nursery fairy tales may have come out of Asia, with the Indo-European race, now fortunately extinct; they may have been invented by some fine French lady or gentleman like Perrault: they may possibly even be what they profess to be. But we shall always call the best selection of such tales Grimm's Tales; simply because it is the best collection.

The historical Aesop, in so far as he was historical, would seem to have been a Phrygian slave, or at least one not to be specially and symbolically adorned with the Phrygian cap of liberty. He lived, if he did live, about the sixth century before Christ, in the time of that Crœsus whose story we love and suspect like everything else in Herodotus. They are also stories of deformity of feature and a ready ribaldry of tongue; stories which (as the celebrated Cardinal said) explain, though they do not excuse, his having been hurled over a high precipice at Delphi. It is for those who read the fables to judge whether he was really thrown over the cliff for being ugly and offensive, or rather for being highly moral and correct. But there is no kind of doubt that the general legend of him may justly rank him with a race too easily forgotten in our modern comparisons; the race of the great philosophic slaves. Aesop may have been a fiction like Uncle Remus: he was also like Uncle Remus, in fact. It is a fact that the slaves in the old world could be worshipped like Aesop or loved like Uncle Remus. It is odd to note that both the great slaves told their best stories about beasts and birds.

But whatever be fairly due to Aesop, the human tradition called Fables is not due to him. This had gone on long before any sarcastic freedman from Phrygia had or had not been flung off a precipice; this has remained long after. It is to our advantage, indeed, to realize the distinction; because it makes Aesop more obviously effective than any other fabulist. *Grimm's Tales*, glorious as they are, were collected by two German students. And if we find it hard to be certain of a German student, at least we know more about him than we know about a Phrygian slave. The truth is, of course, that Aesop's Fables are not Aesop's fables any more than *Grimm's Fairy Tales* were ever Grimm's tales. But the fable and the fairy tale are things utterly distinct. There are many elements of difference. But the plainest is plain enough. There can be no good fable with human beings in it. There can be no good fairy tale without them.

Aesop or Babrius (or whatever his name was)

understood that, for a fable, all the persons must be impersonal. They must be like abstractions in algebra, or like pieces in chess. The lion must always be stronger than the wolf, just as four is always double of two. The fox in a fable must move crooked, as the knight in chess must move crooked. The sheep in a fable must march on, as the pawn in chess must march on. The fable must not allow for the crooked captains of the pawn; it must not allow for what Balzac called 'the revolt of a sheep'. The fairy tale, on the other hand, absolutely revolves on the pivot of human personality. If no hero were there to fight the dragons, we should not even know that they were dragons. If no adventurers were cast on the undiscovered island—it would remain undiscovered. If the miller's third son does not find the enchanted garden where the seven princesses stand white and frozen—why, then, they will remain white and frozen and enchanted. If there is no personal prince to find the Sleeping Beauty she will simply sleep. Fables repose upon quite the opposite idea; that everything is itself, and will in any case speak for itself. The wolf will be always wolfish; the fox will be always foxy. Something of the same sort may have been meant by the animal worship, in which Egyptian and Indian and many other great peoples have been combined. Men do not, I think, love beetles or cats or crocodiles with a wholly personal love; they salute them as expressions of that abstract and anonymous energy in nature which to any one is awful, and to an atheist might be frightful. So in all the fables that are or are not Aesop's all the acquired forces drive like inanimate forces, like great rivers or growing trees. It is the limit and the loss of all such things that they cannot be anything but themselves; it is their tragedy that they could not lose their souls.

This is the immortal justification of the Fable: that we could not teach the plainest truths so simply without turning men into chessmen. We cannot talk of such simple things without using animals that do not talk at all. Suppose, for a moment, that you turn the wolf into a wolfish baron, or the fox into a foxy diplomatist. You will at once remember that even barons are human, you will be unable to forget that even diplomatists are men. You will always be looking for that accidental good-humour that should go with the brutality of a brutal man; for that allowance for all delicate things, including virtue, that should exist in any good diplomatist. Once put a thing on two legs instead of four and pluck it of feathers and you cannot help asking for a human being, either heroic, as in the fairy tales, or unheroic, as in the modern novels.

But by using animals in this austere and arbitrary style as they are used on the shields of heraldry or the hieroglyphics of the ancients, men have really succeeded in handing down those tremendous truths that are called truisms. If the chivalric lion be red and rampant, it is rigidly red and rampant; if the sacred ibis stands anywhere on one leg, it stands on one leg for ever. In this language, like a large animal alphabet, are written some of the first philosophic certainties of men. As the child learns A for Ass or B for Bull or C for Cow, so man has learnt here to connect the simpler and stronger creatures with the simpler and stronger truths. That a flowing stream cannot befoul its own fountain, and that any one who says it does is a tyrant and a liar; that a mouse is too weak to fight a lion but too strong for the cords that can hold a lion; that a fox who gets most out of a flat dish may easily get least out of a deep dish; that the crow whom the gods forbid to sing, the gods nevertheless provide with cheese; that when the goat insults from the mountain-top it is not the goat that insults, but the mountain: all these are deep truths deeply graven on the rocks wherever men have passed. It matters nothing how old they are, or how new; they are the alphabet of humanity, which like so many forms of primitive picture-writing employs any living symbol in preference to man. These ancient and universal tales are all of animals; as the latest discoveries in the oldest caverns are all of animals. Man, in his simpler state, always felt that he himself was something too mysterious to be drawn. But the legend he carved under those cruder symbols was everywhere the same; and whether fables began with Aesop or began with Adam, whether they were German and medieval as Reynard the Fox, or as French and Renaissance as La Fontaine, the upshot is everywhere essentially the same: that superiority is always insolent, because it is always accidental; that pride goes before a fall; and that there is such a thing as being too clever by half. You will not find any other legend but this written upon the rocks by any hand of man. There is every type and time of fable: but there is only one moral to the fable, because there is only one moral to everything.

DICKENS AS SANTA CLAUS[1]

THERE are elements about the position of Dickens in English literature which tend to make him not only heroic, but almost legendary. There is a unique appeal to the comparatively poor, who deal with stories and not story-tellers, just as children do: Pickwick is more real to them than Dickens. There is the curious mixture in his characters of what some describe as unnatural, with what all would recognize as vivid, he is the realist of unrealities. There is, chiefly, the fact that so many of his finest outbursts were concerned with special festivities, notably the Christian festival of Yule. It is no wonder that, instead of being regarded as a mere literary gentleman, like Thackeray, or a mere literary cad like Disraeli, he has come to be regarded vaguely as something more than a gentleman and more even than a man: as an erratic household god like Santa Claus.

But there is yet another reason for this legen-

[1] *A Christmas Carol and Other Tales*, by Charles Dickens. The Waverley Book Company, Ltd., 1913.

dary atmosphere clinging round one of the latest of our great authors. There has sprung up within the last century a very vile habit of talking about the Hour and the Man. It is a superstition, and not even a noble one. No real man appears exactly at the hour, except the little wooden man on the old clocks. Heroes seldom turn up exactly at heroic moments: for punctuality is not one of the virtues of heroes. The great prophets (and prigs) turn up too early; the great magnanimous poets turn up too late. Moreover, to talk of 'the man' is to fling all other men among the beasts of the field. Goliath, who was a Philistine like myself, said, 'Give me a man that we may fight together'. If he had said 'Give me the man', I should have known that he was not a jolly and gigantic Philistine, but a dwarfish and depressed decadent. You or I, being human, ought to take the giant's challenge as addressed to all of us. You ought not to wait for the Man —nor for the Hour. You ought to take the nearest home, which is the next; and the nearest man, which is you.

As a matter of fact most of the millions of sane men and women who have lived and died on this planet have adopted this simple notion of self-respect; they have worked for whatever they thought worth working for and fought for whatever they thought worth fighting for; and they have generally perpetuated *that*, though not themselves. Such a thing as the feast of Christmas in northern Europe has been kept up, as all the old customs are kept up, by a dull democratic tenacity. It has continued and continues through the madness of Calvinism, the grossness of Industrialism and the deepening darkness of Social Reform. Most of these essential things have not been saved by great men, but rather in spite of great men. All the real unforgotten things we owe to the forgotten people.

In all history I can only think of one case in which one might truly say that the Man appeared at the Hour. Napoleon, even, is not really a satisfying example; for the best part of his victories were not due either to the man or to the hour, but to the curious circumstance that Frenchmen fight extremely well. The one real case is that of Dickens and the *Christmas Carol*. The nineteenth-century Christmas and Charles Dickens were really the hour and the man. He was the hero in a hundred ways; but chiefly in this very heroic quality: that he very nearly came too late. He came just in time to save the embers of the Yule Log from being trampled out. It even cost him some trouble to kindle our newer Christian torches in so fading a glow: that is the explanation of the real intensity, almost amounting to irritation, which vibrates through this famous

DICKENS AS SANTA CLAUS

parable and which breaks out like artillery in the more militant parable of *The Chimes*.

For Scrooge, though not perhaps a very real character in fiction, was a very real character in history. There really was a time when the determining mind of England (which was the mind of the more ambitious middle class) came within an ace of admitting the philosophy of Scrooge, with all its frost-bitten efficiency and ungainly bustle. People did say 'let them die and decrease the surplus population.' Many of the followers of Malthus said so openly; and, what is more important, were not kicked for saying it. Now that Malthus has intellectually disappeared (as diabolists always do when they have done all the harm they can); now that their successors, the sociologists of to-day, are much more frightened of the population drying up than of it developing extravagantly, it is really difficult for us to imagine how iron and enormous this economic argument appeared to our grandfathers. People did go about talking of 'the fool who says "A Merry Christmas" '; similar phrases can be found in grave and influential works of Dickens's day. Macaulay, though personally a man munificently charitable, defends faintly, and as if with a dazed respect, the suggestion of Malthusians that charity to the poor should be restricted, or should cease. This horrible frame of mind was, of course, the product of many peculiar causes: chiefly of the fact that the old European religion, struck at so long before, had by this time almost bled to death. It was partly due, again, to that genuine and not unjust fascination that is always exercised on men's minds by a system that is very complete and clear. The old individualistic theory of buying and selling seemed almost unanswerable by arguments, until it began to be answered by facts. It was partly the quite unique commercial success of England: it was partly, again, a real terror of the revolt of the hungry masses, which made men otherwise humane tend to watch them like wolves. For one of the things we never ought to forget, but always do forget, is this: that our grandfathers lived in perpetual expectation of the revolution; the revolution which (alas!) never happened.

In this connection Dickens's *Christmas Carol* is marked by a curious artistic convention as fiction. Scrooge, in this little romance, is a fantastic and old-fashioned miser like Dancer; a type which has existed in all ages, but which exists more openly perhaps in a simpler and ruder age. But the opinions of Scrooge were not merely the opinions of the old men, but of many of the young men of that epoch; of men in good coats and go-ahead businesses, who obtained official positions and wrote in first-class reviews. In real life, old

DICKENS AS SANTA CLAUS

Scrooge would have been quite as likely to be the defender of Christmas and his brisk young nephew its contemptuous enemy. Dickens had discovered this by the time he came to write about Gradgrind and Bounderby and Charlie Hexham.

But the case is even stronger. A real Dickensian, akin to the soul of Dickens, cannot, of course, conceive him otherwise than as the champion of that cheerful and tender-hearted morality which is expressed in the mysteries and mummeries of the Christmas season. But looked at in a more sweeping and superficial way, as his own contemporaries would have looked at it (especially at this early stage of his career) there might well appear something hairbreadth and even accidental about his partisanship. It would seem but touch and go, and he might have made fun of the formalities of Christmas as of the formalities of Chancery, have painted the house-party of the Wardles as scornfully as the house-party of the Dedlocks, and put the praise of Yule not into the mouth of Mrs. Cratchit, but of Mrs. Skewton, as a gushing illusion about 'the good old times'. This is the final fact emphasizing the dramatic importance of this book in history. Even when the champion arrived, those who knew him generally might well have hesitated on which side he would strike. But the champion did not hesitate.

HILAIRE BELLOC [1]

WHEN I first met Belloc he remarked to the friend who introduced us that he was in low spirits. His low spirits were and are much more uproarious and enlivening than anybody else's high spirits. He talked into the night, and left behind in it a glowing track of good things. When I have said that I mean things that are good, and certainly not merely *bons mots,* I have said all that can be said in the most serious aspect about the man who has made the greatest fight for good things of all the men of my time.

We met between a little Soho paper shop and a little Soho restaurant; his arms and pockets were stuffed with French Nationalist and French Atheist newspapers. He wore a straw hat shading his eyes, which are like a sailor's, and emphasizing his Napoleonic chin. He was talking about King John, who, he positively assured me, was *not* (as was often asserted) the best king that

[1] *Hilaire Belloc: The Man and his Work,* by C. C. Mandell and E. Shanks. Messrs. Methuen & Co., Ltd., 1916.

ever reigned in England. Still, there were allowances to be made for him; I mean King John, not Belloc. 'He had been Regent,' said Belloc with forbearance, 'and in all the Middle Ages there is no example of a successful Regent.' I, for one, had not come provided with any successful Regents with whom to counter this generalization; and when I came to think of it, it was quite true. I have noticed the same thing about many other sweeping remarks coming from the same source.

The little restaurant to which we went had already become a haunt for three or four of us who held strong but unfashionable views about the South African War, which was then in its earliest prestige. Most of us were writing on the *Speaker*, edited by Mr. J. L. Hammond with an independence of idealism to which I shall always think that we owe much of the cleaner political criticism of to-day; and Belloc himself was writing in it studies of what proved to be the most baffling irony. To understand how his Latin mastery, especially of historic and foreign things, made him a leader, it is necessary to appreciate something of the peculiar position of that isolated group of 'Pro-Boers'. We were a minority in a minority. Those who honestly disapproved of the Transvaal adventure were few in England; but even of these few a great number, probably the majority, opposed it for reasons not only different but almost contrary to ours. Many were Pacifists, most were Cobdenites; the wisest were healthy but hazy Liberals who rightly felt the tradition of Gladstone to be a safer thing than the opportunism of the Liberal Imperialist. But we might, in one very real sense, be more strictly described as Pro-Boers.

That is, we were much more insistent that the Boers were right in fighting than that the English were wrong in fighting. We disliked cosmopolitan peace almost as much as cosmopolitan war; and it was hard to say whether we more despised those who praised war for the gain of money, or those who blamed war for the loss of it. Not a few men then young were already predisposed to this attitude; Mr. F. Y. Eccles, a French scholar and critic of an authority perhaps too fine for fame, was in possession of the whole classical case against such piratical Prussianism; Mr. Hammond himself, with a careful magnanimity, always attacked Imperialism as a false religion and not merely as a conscious fraud; and I myself had my own hobby of the romance of small things, including small commonwealths. But to all these Belloc entered like a man armed, and as with a clang of iron. He brought with him news from the fronts of history; that French arts could again be rescued by French arms;

that cynical Imperialism not only should be fought, but could be fought and was being fought; that the street fighting which was for me a fairy tale of the future was for him a fact of the past. There were many other uses of his genius, but I am speaking of this first effect of it upon our instinctive and sometimes groping ideals. What he brought into our dream was this Roman appetite for reality and for reason in action, and when he came into the door there entered with him the smell of danger.

There was in him another element of importance which clarified itself in this crisis. It was no small part of the irony in the man that different things strove against each other in him; and these not merely in the common human sense of good against evil, but one good thing against another. The unique attitude of the little group was summed up in him supremely in this: that he did and does humanly and heartily love England, not as a duty but as a pleasure and almost an indulgence; but that he hated as heartily what England seemed trying to become. Out of this appeared in his poetry a sort of fierce doubt or double-mindedness which cannot exist in vague and homogeneous Englishmen; something that occasionally amounted to a mixture of loving and loathing. It is marked, for instance, in the fine break in the middle of the happy song of *camaraderie* called *To the Balliol Men Still in South Africa.*

> 'I have said it before, and I say it again,
> There was treason done and a false word spoken,
> And England under the dregs of men,
> And bribes about and a treaty broken.'

It is supremely characteristic of the time that a weighty and respectable weekly gravely offered to publish the poem if that central verse was omitted. This conflict of emotions has an even higher embodiment in that grand and mysterious poem called *The Leader,* in which the ghost of the nobler militarism passes by to rebuke the baser—

> 'And where had been the rout obscene
> Was an army straight with pride,
> A hundred thousand marching men,
> Of squadrons twenty score,
> And after them all the guns, the guns,
> But She went on before.'

Since that small riot of ours he may be said without exaggeration to have worked three revolutions: the first in all that was represented by the *Eye-Witness,* now the *New Witness,* the repudiation of both Parliamentary parties for common and detailed corrupt practices; second, the alarum against the huge and silent approach of the Servile State, using Socialists and Anti-Socialists alike as its tools; and third, his recent campaign of public education in military affairs. In all these he played the part which he had played for our little party of patriotic Pro-Boers. He was a man of action in abstract things. There was supporting his audacity a great sobriety. It is in this sobriety, and perhaps in this only, that he is essentially French; that he belongs to the most individually prudent and the most collectively reckless of peoples. There is indeed a part of him that is romantic and, in the literal sense, erratic; but that is the English part. But the French people take care of the pence that the pounds may be careless of themselves. And Belloc is almost materialist in his details, that he may be what most Englishmen would call mystical, not to say monstrous, in his aim. In this he is quite in the tradition of the only country of quite successful revolutions. Precisely because France wishes to do wild things, the things must not be too wild. A wild Englishman like Blake or Shelley is content with dreaming them. How Latin is this combination between intellectual economy and energy can be seen by comparing Belloc with his great forerunner Cobbett, who made war on the same Whiggish wealth and secrecy and in defence of the same human dignity and domesticity. But Cobbett, being solely English, was extravagant in his language even about serious public things, and was wildly romantic even when he was merely right. But with

Belloc the style is often restrained; it is the substance that is violent. There is many a paragraph of accusation he has written which might almost be called dull but for the dynamite of its meaning.

It is probable that I have dealt too much with this phase of him, for it is the one in which he appears to me as something different, and therefore dramatic. I have not spoken of those glorious and fantastic guide-books which are, as it were, the textbooks of a whole science of Erratics. In these he is borne beyond the world with those poets whom Keats conceived as supping at a celestial 'Mermaid'. But the 'Mermaid' was English—so was Keats. And though Hilaire Belloc may have a French name, I think that Peter Wanderwide is an Englishman.

I have said nothing of the most real thing about Belloc, the religion, because it is above this purpose, and nothing of the later attacks on him by the chief Newspaper Trust, because they are much below it. There are, of course, many other reasons for passing such matters over here, including the argument of space; but there is also a small reason of my own, which if not exactly a secret is at least a very natural ground of silence. It is that I entertain a very intimate confidence that in a very little time humanity will be saying, 'Who was this So-and-So with whom Belloc seems to have debated?'

WILLIAM COBBETT [1]

WILLIAM COBBETT is the noblest English example of the noble calling of the agitator. The term has come to have a bad sense by a continual reference to cases, some of them true but more of them mythical, in which it has been connected with artificial programmes and with private aims. The truer element refers to a few quacks who have flourished nostrums which were merely novelties. The false is part of a snobbish fairy tale, by which a demagogue was needed to tell a starving man that hunger hurt him, and another to explain to some prostrate person that a policeman had knocked him down. But Cobbett had two clear grounds of defence against the charge of cheap tub-thumping, in those days when he sent a fiery cross through South England, which is perhaps the next thing to setting the Thames on fire. His first defence is that his type of demagogy had all the dangers of isolation. He was far too popular to be fashionable. He spoke for those innumerable who are also inarticulate; and those

[1] *Cottage Economy*, by William Cobbett. Douglas Pepler, 1916; Messrs. Peter Davies, Ltd., 1926.

he sought to help were impotent to help him. He was not paid by the poor to champion their cause: for it is a singular fact, undiscovered by most of our doctors of sociology, that wealth is to be obtained from the wealthy.

The second fact that cleared Cobbett of the charge of quackery was that his nostrums were not novelties, but very much the reverse. To use the language of a religious world which he furiously detested, he was a revivalist. Despite the other connections of the phrase, the real agitator has to be a revivalist: he has to appeal to what remains of a memory, or at least of a legend. What Cobbett attempted to revive was something which almost all political schools in his time especially despised, that is especially misunderstood: it was really medieval England. For the more immediate purpose of politics, it was rural England. But it was not a Byronic repose in a rural barbarism; it was a quite businesslike belief in the possibility, or rather the necessity, of a rural civilization. He believed that agricultural labour could pay; he even entertained the Quixotic fancy that it might pay the agricultural labourer. But that this might come about, he felt it as primarily necessary that the labourer should not be a serf, and even as little as possible a mere tenant. For the purposes of the present introduction, the most important fact is that he saw the cottager as master of his cottage; and had the historical instinct to grasp the great virtues that go with such a small estate. Through all his days he thirsted after freedom. And he understood something that can only accompany freedom—property; and something that can only come with property—thrift.

What distinguishes Cobbett from most rural idealists, such as Ruskin, is that he was a realist as well. Like Ruskin, and long before Ruskin, he denounced the eating up of England by factories and industrial towns. He must have the more credit because he had not, like Ruskin, the advantage of living when the terrible transformation was almost complete; when it was well within sight of its present congestion and collapse. He defied industrialism when it was, if not exactly young and beautiful, at least young and hopeful. But what distinguishes him, as I say, is the practical upshot of his Arcadianism. This can be seen if we compare him with Ruskin even upon Ruskin's own most sacred ground. With no æsthetic culture and nothing of what men would now call a mystical temper, he nevertheless, by his own independent imagination, realized as fully as Ruskin did the overpowering historic importance of the old churches of England. But even here he shows that note of practicality which is also the note of hope. While Ruskin considered how many carvings could be found in a church, Cobbett always considered how many people could be seated in it. An unamiable critic might say that Ruskin knew everything about the building of a church except what it was built for. This would be exaggerative; but it is really relevant to note that Cobbett, in that utterly un-Christian epoch, did understand what it was built for; for it is the same pointed and fruitful attitude that he occupies towards other things, especially towards that thrift of the cottager which is the matter of this book. Ruskin could be trusted to tell his pupils how they should labour with paint or pencil to reproduce every vein and tint upon a cabbage leaf. But few would have trusted Ruskin with the cooking of the cabbage.

Cottage Economy is a book which belongs entirely to this practical and even materialistic side of Cobbett's campaign. Its value, though of the most valid kind, is not of the sort for which it is possible to plead in pen and ink. A cookery book can scarcely be a basis of controversy, though it may be of combat; and the proof of the pudding is in the eating. This is merely the commissariat of his revolutionary army; and, like a good general, he paid a great deal of attention to it. But scattered even through these pages, as through all the pages he wrote upon any subject, there are numerous lively passages which give us glimpses of his philosophy. It can hardly be missed in the case of those two grand survivals of a more Christian England, bacon and beer; but it is quite equally apparent in the study of so small a matter as mustard. I do not profess to know by what process Cobbett discovered that the mustard bought in shops is adulterated, or even relatively poisonous. But it is a perfectly sound criticism on the anonymous tyrannies of trade that we have no possible means of knowing that it is not. The mustard seed that Cobbett advised the cottager to grow in his cottage garden is in this matter as symbolical as the similar seed in the parable. Such seed if sown by the genuine English peasant may yet in truth grow into a great tree; and if we had faith as a grain of mustard seed we could indeed cast all our mountains of oppression into the sea. For a hundred years after Cobbett's forlorn hope we are confronted again by Cobbett's question. We must go back to freedom or forward to slavery. The free man of England, where he still exists, will doubtless find it a colossal enterprise to unwind the coil of three centuries. It is very right that he should consider the danger and pain and heart-rending complication involved in unwinding that coil. But it is also proper that he should consider the alternative; and the alternative is being strangled.

ERIN GO BRAGH! [1]

IT would be difficult to murder a man in a fit of absence of mind; still more difficult to bury him in the garden in the same abstracted and automatic mood. And if the dead man got up out of the grave and walked into the house a week afterwards, the absent-minded murderer might well feel constrained to collect some of his wandering thoughts, and take some notice of the event. But communal action, though real and responsible enough, is never quite so vivid as personal action. And very many respectable English people are quite unconscious that this has been the exact history of their own relations with the Irish people The Englishman has never realized the enormity and simplicity of his own story and its sequel. It was like something done in a dream; because when he did it he was thinking of something else, or trying to think of something else. That the slayer should try to forget the body he has buried may appear natural;

[1] *The Soul of Ireland*, by W. J. Lockington, S.J. Messrs. Harding & More, 1919.

ERIN GO BRAGH!

that he should fail to know it again, when it came walking down the street, will appear more singular. A cynic might say that England need not be concerned about having killed Ireland; but might well feel some concern about having failed to kill her. But cynics are seldom subtle enough to be realists; and the truer way of stating it is that the whole atmosphere of modern Europe, and especially of modern England, has been unfavourable to the telling of a plain tale. Euphemisms and excuses are so elaborate that it is hard for a man to find out what has really happened, even what has happened to him. It is hard for him to say in plain words what has been done, even when he has done it himself.

The resurrection of Ireland, of which Father Lockington writes here with so much spirit and eloquence, is really a historical event that has the appearance of a miracle. That is, it is one of a class of undisputed facts, not actually in form supernatural, but so unique as almost to force anyone, however rationalistic, to an explanation at least transcendental. If the Christian faith is not meant in some fashion to revive and be reunited in Europe, I for one can make no mortal sense of what has happened in Ireland. If the Catholic creeds are not to survive, I cannot imagine why Ireland has survived. Many Englishmen do not see the point; simply because many

Englishmen are in this matter quite ignorant; especially well-educated Englishmen. They do not happen to know how utterly Ireland was crushed; with what finality and fundamental oblivion the nation was once numbered with the dead. A man in the middle of the Age of Reason, the enlightened and humanitarian eighteenth century, would have been more astounded by the present prosperity of the Catholic peasantry than by a revival of the commerce of Carthage. It would have been to him, I will not say like the return of King James, but like the return of King Arthur. It would have been incredible. He would as soon have expected to hear that Atlantis was really re-arisen from the sea, trading and making treaties with America, as to hear that this other island in the Atlantic was increasing in agricultural wealth while retaining its ancient superstitions. The transfiguration happens to have been spread over two or three generations, so that the shock of it is broken; the individuals who saw the death are not those who see the rising from the dead. But to anyone who has learned just enough of history to know that it consists of human beings, to anyone with enough imaginative patience to follow a story clearly from start to finish, the story has been as simple and astonishing as the plain parable of the corpse in the garden with which I began this brief note. A working way of putting it is to say that sixty years ago English newspapers talked hopefully of there being *no* Irish Catholics in a few years; and there are now more than six millions in the United States alone. In a word, the one real crime that England ever attempted has most fortunately failed; and not only England but also Europe has now to deal with a certain recognizable religious civilization, which men may like or dislike, fear or favour, but which is as solid a fact as France. Even those who cannot share Father Lockington's natural enthusiasm for the theological survival will be wise to note all the facts he can adduce about the social success. Judged from a wholly detached and rationalized standpoint, the reality remains: that the one people in Western Europe which has taken the old form of the Christian religion quite seriously, enduring persecution from without and asceticism from within, has before our very eyes turned a sudden corner and stepped into a place in the sun. We can make what we will of this fact; but it is there.

There are but a few of these historical events which while natural in mode seem to be almost supernatural in meaning. One of them is the mysterious international position of the Jews. Another was the historical mission of Joan of Arc. And there goes with that great name a certain hint of hope and consolation even in the case still at issue: the long and tragic entanglement of England and Ireland. The English were the enemies of Joan of Arc; but it is quite inadequate to say they are no longer her enemies; they are all her quite enthusiastic admirers. They are, if possible, even more enthusiastic than the French. I do not despair of the day when the other senseless misunderstanding shall pass in the same fashion; and a patriotic Englishman shall no more be expected to feel a prejudice in the one case than in the other. I hope to see the day when he will no more dream of denying that anybody is oppressed in Ireland than that anybody was burned at Rouen. He will not treat the former torture as more trivial because it lasted longer; or as more obscure because it affected many more people. He will do what he does with the tragedy of the fifteenth century: he will prefer to prove that he is now generous rather than that he was always just. Horrible as is the history, I know my own people are capable of such generosity; and I should be ashamed to write anywhere on this subject without seeking to arouse it.

CECIL CHESTERTON [1]

THE author of this book, my brother, died in a French military hospital of the effects of exposure in the last fierce fighting that broke the Prussian power over Christendom; fighting for which he had volunteered after being invalided home. Any notes I can jot down about him must necessarily seem jerky and incongruous; for in such a relation memory is a medley of generalization and detail, not to be uttered in words. One thing at least may fitly be said here. Before he died he did at least two things that he desired. One may seem much greater than the other; but he would not have shrunk from naming them together. He saw the end of an empire that was the nightmare of the nations; but I believe it pleased him almost as much that he had been able, often in the intervals of bitter warfare and by the aid of a brilliant memory, to put together these pages on the history, so necessary and so strangely neglected,

[1] *A History of the United States*, by Cecil Chesterton. Messrs. Chatto & Windus, 1918.

of the great democracy which he never patronized, which he not only loved but honoured.

Cecil Edward Chesterton was born on 12th November, 1879; and there is a special if a secondary sense in which we may use the phrase that he was born a fighter. It may seem in some sad fashion a flippancy to say that he argued from his very cradle. It is certainly, in the same sad fashion, a comfort to remember one truth about our relations: that we perpetually argued and that we never quarrelled. In a sense it was the psychological truth, I fancy, that we never quarrelled because we always argued. His lucidity and love of truth kept things so much on the level of logic, that the rest of our relations remained, thank God, in solid sympathy; long before that later time when, in substance, our argument had become an agreement. Nor, I think, was the process valueless; for at least we learnt how to argue in defence of our agreement. But the retrospect is only worth a thought now, because it illustrates a duality which seemed to him, and is, very simple; but to many is baffling in its very simplicity. When I say his weapon was logic, it will be currently confused with formality or even frigidity: a silly superstition always pictures the logician as a pale-faced prig. He was a living proof, a very living proof, that the precise contrary is the case. In fact it is generally the warmer and more sanguine sort of man who has an appetite for abstract definitions and even abstract distinctions. He had all the debating dexterity of a genial and generous man like Charles Fox. He could command that more than legal clarity and closeness which really marked the legal arguments of a genial and generous man like Danton. In his wonderfully courageous public speaking, he rather preferred being a debater to being an orator; in a sense he maintained that no man had a right to be an orator without first being a debater. Eloquence, he said, had its proper place when reason had proved a thing to be right, and it was necessary to give men the courage to do what was right. I think he never needed any man's eloquence to give him that. But the substitution of sentiment for reason, in the proper place for reason, affected him 'as musicians are affected by a false note'. It was the combination of this intellectual integrity with extraordinary warmth and simplicity in the affections that made the point of his personality. The snobs and servile apologists of the *régime* he resisted seem to think they can atone for being hard-hearted by being soft-headed. He reversed, if ever a man did, that relation in the organs. The opposite condition really covers all that can be said of him in this brief study; it is the clue not only to his character but to his career.

If rationalism meant being rational (which it hardly ever does) he might at every stage of his life be called a red-hot rationalist. Thus, for instance, he very early became a Socialist and joined the Fabian Society, on the executive of which he played a prominent part for some years. But he afterwards gave the explanation, very characteristic for those who could understand it, that what he liked about the Fabian sort of Socialism was its hardness. He meant intellectual hardness; the fact that the society avoided sentimentalism, and dealt in affirmations and not mere associations. He meant that upon the Fabian basis a Socialist was bound to believe in Socialism, but not in sandals, free love, bookbinding, and immediate disarmament. But he also added that, while he liked their hardness, he disliked their moderation. In other words, when he discovered, or believed that he discovered, that their intellectual hardness was combined with moral hardness, or rather moral deadness, he felt all the intellectual ice melted by a moral flame. He had, so to speak, a reaction of emotional realism, in which he saw, as suddenly as simple men can see simple truths, the potterers of Social Reform as the plotters of the Servile State. He was himself, above all things, a democrat as well as a Socialist; and in that intellectual sect he began to feel as if he were the only Socialist who was also a democrat. His dogmatic, democratic conviction would alone illustrate the falsity of the contrast between logic and life. The idea of human equality existed with extraordinary clarity in his brain, precisely because it existed with extraordinary simplicity in his character. His popular sympathies, unlike so many popular sentiments, could really survive any intimacy with the populace; they followed the poor not only at public meetings but to public-houses. He was literally the only man I ever knew who was not only never a snob, but apparently never tempted to be a snob. The fact is almost more important than his wonderful lack of fear; for such good causes, when they cannot be lost by fear, are often lost by favour.

Thus he came to suspect that Socialism was merely social reform, and that social reform was merely slavery. But the point still is that though his attitude to it was now one of revolt, it was anything but a mere revulsion of feeling. He did, indeed, fall back on fundamental things, on a fury at the oppression of the poor, on a pity for slaves, and especially for contented slaves. But it is the mark of his type of mind that he did not abandon Socialism without a rational case against it, and a rational system to oppose to it. The theory he substituted for Socialism is that which may for convenience be called Distributivism;

the theory that private property is proper to every private citizen. This is no place for its exposition; but it will be evident that such a conversion brings the convert into touch with much older traditions of human freedom, as expressed in the family or the guild. And it was about the same time that, having for some time held an Anglo-Catholic position, he joined the Roman Catholic Church. It is notable, in connection with the general argument, that while the deeper reasons for such a change do not concern such a sketch as this, he was again characteristically amused and annoyed with the sentimentalists, sympathetic or hostile, who supposed he was attracted by ritual, music, and emotional mysticism. He told such people, somewhat to their bewilderment, that he had been converted because Rome alone could satisfy the reason. In his case, of course, as in Newman's and numberless others, well-meaning people conceived a thousand crooked or complicated explanations, rather than suppose that an obviously honest man believed a thing because he thought it was true. He was soon to give a more dramatic manifestation of his strange taste for truth.

The attack on political corruption, the next and perhaps the most important passage in his life, still illustrates the same point, touching reason and enthusiasm. Precisely because he did know what Socialism is and what it is not, precisely because he had at least learned that from the intellectual hardness of the Fabians, he saw the spot where Fabian Socialism is not hard but soft. Socialism means the assumption by the State of all the means of production, distribution, and exchange. To quote (as he often quoted with a rational relish) the words of Mr. Balfour, that is Socialism and nothing else is Socialism. To such clear thinking, it is at once apparent that trusting a thing to the State must always mean trusting it to the statesmen. He could defend Socialism because he could define Socialism; and he was not helped or hindered by the hazy associations of the sort of Socialists who perpetually defended what they never defined. Such men might have a vague vision of red flags and red ties waving in an everlasting riot above the fall of top-hats and Union Jacks; but he knew that Socialism established meant Socialism official, and conducted by some sort of officials. All the primary forms of private property were to be given to the government; and it occurred to him, as a natural precaution, to give a glance at the government. He gave some attention to the actual types and methods of that governing and official class, into whose power trams and trades and shops and houses were already passing, amid loud Fabian cheers for the progress of

Socialism. He looked at modern parliamentary government: he looked at it rationally and steadily and not without reflection. And the consequence was that he was put in the dock, and very nearly put in the lock-up, for calling it what it is.

In collaboration with Mr. Belloc he had written *The Party System*, in which the plutocratic and corrupt nature of our present polity is set forth. And when Mr. Belloc founded the *Eye-Witness*, as a bold and independent organ of the same sort of criticism, he served as the energetic second in command. He subsequently became editor of the *Eye-Witness*, which was renamed as the *New Witness*. It was during the latter period that the great test case of political corruption occurred; pretty well known in England, and unfortunately much better known in Europe, as the Marconi scandal. To narrate its alternate secrecies and sensations would be impossible here; but one fashionable fallacy about it may be exploded with advantage. An extraordinary notion still exists that the *New Witness* denounced Ministers for gambling on the Stock Exchange. It might be improper for Ministers to gamble; but gambling was certainly not a misdemeanour that would have hardened with any special horror so hearty an Anti-Puritan as the man of whom I write. The Marconi case did not raise the difficult ethics of gambling, but the perfectly plain ethics of secret commissions. The charge against the Ministers was that, while a government contract was being considered, they tried to make money out of a secret tip, given them by the very government contractor with whom their government was supposed to be bargaining. This was what their accuser asserted; but this was not what they attempted to answer by a prosecution. He was prosecuted, not for what he had said of the government, but for some secondary things he had said of the government contractor. The latter, Mr. Godfrey Isaacs, gained a verdict for criminal libel; and the judge inflicted a fine of £100. Readers may have chanced to note the subsequent incidents in the life of Mr. Isaacs, but I am here only concerned with incidents in the life of a more interesting person.

In any suggestion of his personality, indeed, the point does not lie in what was done to him, but rather in what was not done. He was positively assured, upon the very strongest and most converging legal authority, that unless he offered certain excuses he would certainly go to prison for several years. He did not offer those excuses; and I believe it never occurred to him to do so. His freedom from fear of all kinds had about it a sort of solid unconsciousness and even innocence. This homogeneous quality in it has been admirably seized and summed up by Mr. Belloc in a tribute of great truth and power. 'His courage was heroic, native, positive and equal: always at the highest potentiality of courage. He never in his life checked an action or a word from a consideration of personal caution, and that is more than can be said of any other man of his time.' After the more or less nominal fine, however, his moral victory was proved in the one way in which a military victory can ever be proved. It is the successful general who continues his own plan of campaign. Whether a battle be ticketed in the history books as lost or won, the test is which side can continue to strike. He continued to strike, and to strike harder than ever, up to the very moment of that yet greater experience which changed all such military symbols into military facts. A man with instincts unspoiled and in that sense almost untouched, he would have always answered quite naturally to the autochthonous appeal of patriotism; but it is again characteristic of him that he desired, in his own phrase, to 'rationalize patriotism', which he did upon the principles of Rousseau, that contractual theory which, in these pages, he connects with the great name of Jefferson. But things even deeper than patriotism impelled him against Prussianism. His enemy was the barbarian when he enslaves, as something more hellish even than the barbarian when he slays. His was the spiritual instinct by which Prussian order was worse than Prussian anarchy; and nothing was so inhuman as an inhuman humanitarianism. If you had asked him for what he fought and died amid the wasted fields of France and Flanders, he might very probably have answered that it was to save the world from German social reforms.

This note, necessarily so broken and bemused, must reach its useless end. I have said nothing of numberless things that should be remembered at the mention of his name; of his books, which were great pamphlets and may yet be permanent pamphlets; of his journalistic exposures of other evils besides the Marconi, exposures that have made a new political atmosphere in the very election that is stirring around us; of his visit to America, which initiated him into an international friendship which is the foundation of this book. Least of all can I write of him apart from his work; of that loss nothing can be said by those who do not suffer it, and less still by those who do. And his experiences in life and death were so much greater even than my experiences of him, that a double incapacity makes me dumb. A portrait is impossible; as a friend he is too near me, and as a hero too far away.

BERNARD CAPES[1]

TO introduce the last book by the late Bernard Capes is a sad sort of honour in more ways than one; for not only was his death untimely and unexpected, but he had a mind of that fertile type which must always leave behind it, with the finished life, a sense of unfinished labour. From the first his prose had a strong element of poetry which an appreciative reader could feel even more, perhaps, when it refined a frankly modern and even melodramatic theme, like that of this mystery story, than when it gave dignity, as in *Our Lady of Darkness*, to more tragic or more historic things. It may seem a paradox to say that he was insufficiently appreciated because he did popular things well. But it is true to say that he always gave a touch of distinction to a detective story or a tale of adventure; and so gave it where it was not valued, because it was not expected. In a sense, in this department of his work at least, he carried on the

[1] *The Skeleton Key*, by Bernard Capes. Messrs. W. Collins, Sons & Co., Ltd., 1919.

tradition of the artistic conscience of Stevenson; the technical liberality of writing a penny-dreadful so as to make it worth a pound. In his short stories, as in his historical studies, he did indeed permit himself to be poetic in a more direct and serious fashion; but in his touch upon such tales as this the same truth may be traced. It is a good general rule that a poet can be known not only in his poems, but in the very titles of his poems. In the case of many works of Bernard Capes, *The Lake of Wine,* for instance, the title is itself a poem. And that case would alone illustrate what I mean about a certain transforming individual magic, with which he touched the mere melodrama of mere modernity. Numberless novels of crime have been concerned with a lost or stolen jewel, and *The Lake of Wine* was merely the name of a ruby. Yet even the name is original, exactly in the detail that is hardly ever original. Hundreds of such precious stones have been scattered through sensational fiction; and hundreds of them have been called 'The Sun of the Sultan' or 'The Eye of Vishnu' or 'The Star of Bengal'. But even in such a trifle as the choice of a title, an indescribable and individual fancy is felt; a subconscious dream of some sea like a sunset, red as blood, and intoxicant as wine. This is but a small example; but the same element clings, as if unconsciously, to the course of the same story. Many another eighteenth-century hero has ridden on a long road to a lonely house; but Bernard Capes by something fine and personal in the treatment does succeed in suggesting that at least along that particular road, to that particular house, no man had ever ridden before. We might put this truth flippantly, and therefore falsely, by saying he put superior work into inferior works. I should not admit the distinction: for I deny that there is anything inferior in sensationalism, when it can really awaken sensations. But the truer way of stating it would perhaps be this: that to a type of work which generally is, for him or anybody else, a work of invention, he always added at least one touch of imagination.

The detective or mystery tale, in which this last book is an experiment, involves in itself a problem for the artist, as odd as any of the problems it puts to the policeman. A detective story might well be in a special sense a spiritual story, since it is a story in which even the moral sympathies may be in doubt. A police romance is almost the only romance in which the hero may turn out a villain, or the villain to be the hero.

We know that Mr. Osbaldistone's business has not been betrayed by his son Frank, though possibly by his nephew Rashleigh. We are quite sure that Colonel Newcome's company has not been conspired against by his son Clive, though possibly by his nephew Barnes. But there is a stage in a story like *The Moonstone* when we are meant to suspect Franklin Blake the hero, as he is suspected by Rachel Verinder the heroine; there is a stage in Mr. Bentley's *Trent's Last Case* when the figure of Mr. Marlowe is as sinister as the figure of Mr. Manderson. The obvious result of this technical trick is to make it impossible, or at least unfair, to comment, not only on the plot, but even on the characters; since each of the characters should be an unknown quantity. The Italians say that translation is treason; and here at least is a case where criticism is treason. I have too great a love or lust for the *roman policier* to spoil sport in so unsportsmanlike a fashion; but I cannot forbear to comment on the ingenious inspiration by which in this story, one of the characters contrives to remain really an unknown quantity, by a trick of verbal evasion, which he himself defends, half convincingly, as a scruple of verbal veracity. That is the quality of Bernard Capes' romances that remains in my own memory; a quality, as it were, too subtle for its own subject. Men may well go back to find the poems thus embedded in the prose.

MY NAME-VILLAGE [1]

I KNOW not by what right I block up the Roman road of this valuable history of Cambridge, unless it be because I have followed it myself with great pleasure, by private favour of the author, or perhaps because my surname happens to be that of a village in the neighbourhood. I have never been to Cambridge except as an admiring visitor; I have never been to Chesterton at all, either from a sense of unworthiness or from a faint superstitious feeling that I might be fulfilling a prophecy in the countryside. Anyone with a sense of the savour of the old English country rhymes and tales will share my vague alarm that the steeple might crack or the market cross fall down, for a smaller thing than the coincidence of a man named Chesterton going to Chesterton. I have never really studied history at Cambridge, or anywhere else. And if I heartily enjoyed this modern history of Cambridge, I fear it is not because it bears a resem-

[1] *Life in Old Cambridge*, by M. E. Monckton Jones. Messrs. W. Heffer & Sons, Ltd., 1920.

MY NAME-VILLAGE

blance to the Cambridge Modern History. In short, while my qualifications for pronouncing on the point at all are highly dubious, the strong sympathy I do feel for the work is mostly due to its marked difference from most academic digests. What is the matter with these academic attempts at universal history is that they are generally so very much the reverse of universal. They assemble the specialists, so as to cover all subjects except the subject. The result is that we only succeed in having all things studied in a narrow spirit, instead of one thing studied in a universal spirit. That is one reason for liking a thing like a local history; that is a large story about a little thing. I prefer the philosophical results of a man examining a mole-hill, rather than those of a million moles exploring a mountain.

It is to be hoped that the example be followed, touching many other English districts; nor is there any particular reason why it should not be followed touching all of them. It is true that the author of this book happens to have to deal with one of the towns universally recognized as historic and picturesque, containing some of the chief monuments of medieval art, as well as some of the chief chairs of Modern Education. But the particular interest of this pageant of successive periods really belongs less to Cambridge as Cambridge than to Cambridge as a country town. Even the most urban towns are mostly made up of country towns; that is, they have grown by absorbing the surrounding towns and villages. We are tempted in a fanciful fashion to forget that sites at least stand for ever, and cannot be created or destroyed. It is as if we imagined that Brixton had appeared recently as a radiant object in the sky, like the New Jerusalem, or that the very earth on which Manchester stands has been manufactured in the Manchester factories. But, indeed, Manchester itself is the clearest of all cases to the contrary. The Manchester school was credited with being unhistorical, or even anti-historical; but the very name of Manchester is a piece of history, and even of ancient and classical history. There are no new places in England; for there is no such thing as a new place in nature or in abstract logic. Therefore there is no reason why we should not have an epic and almost prehistoric study of West Kensington, or the truth about the romantic story of Clapham. It would be some great story of Rome, of the Church, of the Crusade, of the great guilds like those that made the cathedrals, if any one had the moral courage to do for Clapham what the lady who wrote this book has done for Cambridge.

If I might give one example from this book, out of many, of the sort of thing that is so seriously wanted in a popular history, and is so seldom present in one, I would adduce the wisdom of giving in their regular order the actual terms of the charter which King John gave to the burghers. I do not exaggerate when I say I think them far more important than the charter which King John gave to the barons. The latter is always called the great charter, largely because it was chiefly concerned with great lords; but this is concerned with smaller men, and therefore with larger matters. It consists of fourteen clauses, and as we read it, we feel passing before us and around us all the living movement of the Middle Ages. Besides the essential things, the general presence of a sort of ideal trading, analogous to the theory of a just price, we have a hundred little things of singular historic interest, especially when they have since grown into larger things. We have, for instance, reference to certain privileges only belonging 'to the King's moneyers and servants', the latter being the position of the Jews, and probably involving many privileges for the Jews. We have the curious feature of continual reference to something rather unique and characteristic of our own history; the exceptional rôle and position of the City of London. There is an inevitable reference to ale, which flows as in rivers through all such records, and especially of an occasion when the burghers were sternly confined to drinking only one kind of ale, instead of absorbing all possible kinds of ale in their due succession. Men are often confined to a sort of 'scot-ale' in the tied houses of our own time, but to-day the celebration lasts all the year round. In short the mere citation of this medieval document gives the amateur reader like myself a real glimpse of the medieval democracy. From the stock histories of his youth he could have learned little or nothing about that particular date except the extraordinary goodness of the British Constitution. But to those old Cambridge men King John was only the name of the King who happened to give them the glorious rights of guildsmen. And I very much fear that to them, the modern thing called the British Constitution would only be the thing under which the rights and the guilds were alike gone.

THE HUMOUR OF H. M. BATEMAN [1]

IT is well that a draughtsman with the wild exactitude of Mr. Bateman should enjoy one riot of ridiculing modern society before modern society becomes too ridiculous to be ridiculed. For that is the chief danger at present to this branch of art. It is sometimes said that we have no satirists as great as Rabelais or Swift; but satire of that strength depends on a sanity and even sobriety in real things. The imaginative effect of Rabelais owes much to the old medieval and monastic setting at which he mocked; and Swift's wildest fancies can be seen more clearly against the background of clipped hedges and trim gardens in which Queen Anne took her tea. What could Rabelais have said, if he had stopped for wine and refreshment at a real abbey, and found that it deserved rather to be called Nightmare Abbey than the Abbey of Theleme? Suppose Swift, on walking stiffly up to Queen Anne's tea-party, had found it was the

[1] *A Book of Drawings*, by H. M. Bateman. Messrs. Methuen & Co., Ltd., 1921.

Mad Tea Party? Suppose that Anne, like Alice, was already dining with the March Hare, the Mad Hatter and the Dormouse? That is the disconcerting situation in which a satirist finds himself nowadays. And so there is a tendency, in which the talent of Mr. Bateman is at once original and typical, for English pictorial satire to grow more and more fantastic. Otherwise, it might be outstripped by the facts. There was a Victorian epoch when the caricaturists were supposed to caricature the politicians. Now the politicians are caricaturing their own caricatures. Hence it will probably be found that all our ablest artists, in this manner, will grow more and more frantic and farcical, more and more incredible and crazy. They are trying to keep pace with our statesmen and social philosophers.

For instance, there is a delightful design in this book representing the secret and hideous crime of the gentleman who filled a fountain-pen with the ink in the hotel. It is exceedingly funny. But it is not so funny as it would be if a man in a hotel were allowed to fill forty fountain pens and ten large bottles with ink, but were strictly forbidden ever to dip his pen in the ink, taking only what he needed at the moment for addressing an envelope or signing a cheque. It would be funnier still if the law which allowed him to take a bottleful, but forbade him to take a

HUMOUR OF H. M. BATEMAN

pen-full, were called a law for the saving of ink. Yet that is literally and exactly the condition of the existing law for avoiding excess in wine or whisky. A man is not allowed to buy the moderate amount he wants. But he is allowed to buy an immoderate amount in excess of his wants. He is allowed to bear away a bottle of brandy much bigger than a bottle of ink; but he is not allowed to take a drop hardly bigger than the drop on the point of a pen. Now you cannot satirize a law like that; any more than you could satirize the statement that black is white, or that yes is the same as no. You cannot refute what is entirely irrational, any more than you can answer the question of 'Why is a mouse when it spins?' I can imagine Mr. Bateman giving us a dizzy, delirious and doubtless delightful drawing of a mouse when it spins, but hardly of why it spins. And I can imagine him giving us an equally exuberant exhibition of a stampede of stout struggling policemen to arrest a man sipping a small glass of sherry hardly larger than a liqueur; while processions of placid and smiling persons, clasping colossal bottles of gin and brandy, passed by like a calm and continuous background. But this very thing, which the artist might draw as a lark, the politician has already established as a law. And even Mr. Bateman could not draw the mind of the politician who conceived such a regulation. It is beyond the last visions of Futurism and the Fourth Dimension.

Again, I am enchanted with Mr. Bateman's picture of the War-time Match, and the flaming martyrdom endured by the heroic citizen, in order to observe a special sort of economy. But at least that was in itself a reasonable sort of economy, even if it led in this case to a devotion rather mystical than strictly rational. Matches were rare at the time; they are very important at any time; and any regulations for saving them would be quite defensible regulations. I do not call on the average man to follow the council of perfection, and win the heavenly palm and crown, towards which that flaming finger points him. But I can imagine something that would be much more fantastic even than Mr. Bateman's fantasy. Suppose Mr. Bateman were called upon to draw a man thus engaged in saving a single match, while on every side of him match-boxes piled up to the skies, in toppling towers and pyramids, were being given to the flames wholesale, like so much rubbish or mere fuel. Or suppose, in the same vein which is very much his own, he were to draw a policeman putting a very large finger on the lips of a very little boy lest he should whistle, and disturb the repose of the street; while the street, I need hardly say, would be full of motorbuses, brass-bands, backfiring cars, sirens, foghorns, anti-aircraft artillery, guns going off generally and so on. Well, that wild picture would be a literally and rigidly realistic picture of a real regulation. Living in London, and presumably knowing what the noise of London was like all through the War as much as at any other time, the officials actually did make a regulation that no one should whistle for a taxi-cab; like men anxious lest the grasshopper should indeed become a burden, and his chirp disturb us amid the roaring of lions and the trumpeting of elephants. It was felt, and perhaps is still felt, by the same sensitive and delicately balanced minds, that two thin, shrill notes on a small whistle must no longer be allowed to desecrate the deathly silence of Piccadilly and Ludgate Hill.

This sense that society itself is in the rapids, is already of itself tending to extremes and even extravagancies, has brought a fresher, and in one sense a freer element into our ancient English humour, an element of which Mr. Bateman is very typical. It is a telescopic satire, at once logical and ludicrous, which shoots out to the end of any process, and even in exaggerating it, defines it. The French have always possessed it, for the French have always known where they were going, or at any rate where they wanted to go. And most of our own countrymen, happier in some ways, had not even got so far as knowing where they had got to. But if we all know now, at last, where we are really going to, and where science and statesmanship are leading us; and if it is quite obviously to an enormous lunatic asylum, let us at least, by the grace of God, go there in company with a man who has a sense of humour.

JANE AUSTEN [1]

IN a recent newspaper controversy about the conventional silliness and sameness of all the human generations previous to our own, somebody said that in the world of Jane Austen a lady was expected to faint when she received a proposal. To those who happen to have read any of the works of Jane Austen, the connection of ideas will appear slightly comic. Elizabeth Bennet, for instance, received two proposals from two very confident and even masterful admirers; and she certainly did not faint. It would be nearer the truth to say that they did. But in any case it may be amusing to those who are thus amused, and perhaps even instructive to those who thus need to be instructed, to know that the earliest work of Jane Austen, here published for the first time, might be called a satire on the fable of the fainting lady. 'Beware of fainting fits . . . though at times they may be refreshing and agreeable, yet believe me they will in the end,

---

[1] *Love and Freindship and other early works*, by Jane Austen. Messrs. Chatto & Windus, 1922.

if too often repeated and at improper seasons, prove destructive to your Constitution.' Such were the words of the expiring Sophia to the afflicted Laura; and there are modern critics capable of adducing *them* as a proof that all society was in a swoon in the first decade of the nineteenth century. But in truth it is the whole point of this little skit that the swoon of sensibility is not satirized solely because it was a fiction. Laura and Sophia are made ludicrously unlike life by being made to faint as real ladies do not faint. Those ingenious moderns, who say that the real ladies did faint, are actually being taken in by Laura and Sophia, and believing them against Jane Austen. They are believing, not the people of the period but the most nonsensical novels of the period, which even the people of the period who read them did not believe. They have swallowed all the solemnities of the Mysteries of Udolpho, and never even seen the joke of Northanger Abbey.

For if these *juvenilia* of Jane Austen anticipate especially any of her after-works, they certainly anticipate the satiric side of Northanger Abbey. Of their considerable significance on that side something may be said presently; but it will be well to preface it by a word about the works themselves as items of literary history. Every one knows that the novelist left an unfinished fragment, since published under the name of *The Watsons*, and a finished story called *Lady Susan*, in letters, which she had herself apparently decided not to publish. These preferences are all prejudices, in the sense of matters of unmanageable taste; but I confess I think it a strange historical accident that things so comparatively dull as *Lady Susan* should have been printed already, while things so comparatively lively as *Love and Freindship* should never have been printed until now. It is at least a curiosity of literature that such curiosities of literature should have been almost accidentally concealed. Doubtless it was very rightly felt that we may go much too far in the way of emptying the waste-paper basket of a genius on the head of the public; and that there is a sense in which the waste-paper basket is as sacred as the grave. But without arrogating to myself any more right in the matter than anybody has to his own taste, I hope I may be allowed to say that I for one would have willingly left *Lady Susan* in the waste-paper basket, if I could have pieced together *Love and Freindship* for a private scrap-book; a thing to laugh over again and again as one laughs over the great burlesques of Peacock or Max Beerbohm.

Jane Austen left everything she possessed to her sister Cassandra, including these and other manuscripts; and the second volume of them, containing these, was left by Cassandra to her brother, Admiral Sir Francis Austen. He gave it to his daughter Fanny, who left it in turn to her brother Edward, who was the Rector of Barfrestone in Kent, and the father of Mrs. Sanders, to whose wise decision we owe the publication of these first fancies of her great-aunt; whom it might be misleading here to call her great great-aunt. Every one will judge for himself; but I myself think she has added something intrinsically important to literature and to literary history; and that there are cartloads of printed matter, regularly recognized and printed with the works of all great authors, which are far less characteristic and far less significant than these few nursery jests.

For *Love and Freindship*, with some similar passages in the accompanying fragments, is really a rattling burlesque; something much better than what the ladies of the time called an agreeable rattle. It is one of those things that can be the more readily read with enjoyment through being written with enjoyment; in other words, it is all the better for being juvenile in the sense of being joyful. She is said to have written these things at the age of seventeen, evidently in much the same spirit in which people conduct a family magazine; for the medallions included in the manuscript were the work of her sister Cassandra.

The whole thing is full of the sort of high spirits that are always higher in private than in public; as people laugh louder in the house than in the street. Many of her admirers would not expect, perhaps many of her admirers would not admire the sort of fun to be found in the letter of the young lady 'whose feelings were too strong for her judgment', and who remarks incidentally 'I murdered my father at a very early period of my life, I have since murdered my mother, and I am now going to murder my sister'. Personally I think it admirable; not the conduct, but the confession. But there is much more than hilarity in the humour, even at this stage of its growth. There is almost everywhere a certain neatness in the nonsense. There is not a little of the true Austen irony. 'The noble Youth informed us that his name was Lindsay—for particular reasons, however, I shall conceal it under that of Talbot.' Did anyone really desire that to disappear into the waste-paper basket? 'She was nothing more than a mere good-tempered, civil and obliging young woman; as such we could scarcely dislike her—she was only an object of contempt.' Is not that something like the first faint line in the figure of Fanny Price? When a loud knocking is heard on the door of the Rustic Cot by the Uske, the heroine's father inquires the nature of the noise, and by cautious steps of inference they are enabled to define it as somebody outside striking the door. 'Yes (exclaimed I), I cannot help thinking it must be somebody who knocks for admittance.' 'That is another point (replied he) we must not pretend to determine on what motive the person may knock—tho' that some one *does* rap at the door I am partly convinced.' In the exasperating leisure and lucidity of that reply, is there not the foreshadowing of another and more famous father; and do we not hear for a moment, in the rustic cottage by the Uske, the unmistakable voice of Mr. Bennet?

But there is a larger critical reason for taking pleasure in the gaiety of these various travesties and trifles. Mr. Austen-Leigh seems to have thought them not sufficiently serious for the reputation of his great relative; but greatness is not made up of serious things, in the sense of solemn things. The reason here, however, is as serious as even he or anyone else could desire; for it concerns the fundamental quality of one of the finest talents in letters.

A very real psychological interest, almost amounting to a psychological mystery, attaches to any early work of Jane Austen. And for that one reason, among others, which has hardly been sufficiently emphasized. Great as she was, nobody was likely to maintain that she was a poet. But she was a marked example of what is said of the poet; she was born, not made. As compared with her, indeed, some of the poets really were made. Many men who had the air of setting the world on fire have left at least a reasonable discussion about what set them on fire. Men like Coleridge or Carlyle had certainly kindled their first torches from the flambeaux of equally fantastic German mystics or Platonic speculators; they had gone through furnaces of culture where even less creative people might have been inflamed to creation. Jane Austen was not inflamed or inspired or even moved to be a genius; she simply was a genius. Her fire, what there was of it, began with herself; like the fire of the first man who rubbed two dry sticks together. Some would say that they were very dry sticks which she rubbed together. It is certain that she by her own artistic talent made interesting what thousands of superficially similar people would have made dull. There was nothing in her circumstances, or even in her materials, that seems obviously meant for the making of such an artist. It might seem a very wild use of the wrong word to say that Jane Austen was elemental. It might even seem even a little wanton to insist that she was original. Yet this objection would come from the critic not really considering what is meant by an element or an origin. Perhaps it might be as well expressed in what is really meant by an individual. Her ability is an absolute; it cannot be analysed into influences. She has been compared to Shakespeare; and in this sense she really does recall the joke about the man who said he could write like Shakespeare if he had the mind. In this case we seem to see a thousand spinsters sitting at a thousand tea-tables; and they could all have written *Emma* if they had had the mind.

There is therefore, in considering even her crudest early experiments, the interest of looking at a mind and not at a mirror. She may not be conscious of being herself; but she is not, like so many more cultivated imitators, conscious of being somebody else. The force, at its first and feeblest, is coming from within and not merely from without. This interest, which belongs to her as an individual with a superior instinct for the intelligent criticism of life, is the first of the reasons that justify a study of her juvenile vocation. I will not say of the artistic temperament; for nobody ever had less of the tiresome thing commonly so described than Jane Austen. But while this alone would be a reason for finding out how her work began, it becomes yet more relevant when we have found out how it did begin. This is something more than the discovery of a document; it is the discovery of an inspiration. And that inspiration was the inspiration of Gar-

JANE AUSTEN

gantua and of Pickwick; it was the gigantic inspiration of laughter.

If it seemed odd to call her elemental, it may seem equally odd to call her exuberant. These pages betray her secret; which is that she was naturally exuberant. And her power came, as all power comes, from the control and direction of exuberance. But there is the presence and pressure of that vitality behind her thousand trivialities; she could have been extravagant if she liked. She was the very reverse of a starched or a starved spinster; she could have been a buffoon like the Wife of Bath if she chose. This is what gives an infallible force to her irony. This is what gives a stunning weight to her understatements. At the back of this artist also, counted as passionless, there was passion; but her original passion was a sort of joyous scorn and a fighting spirit against all that she regarded as morbid and lax and poisonously silly. The weapons she forged were so finely finished that we might never have known this, but for these glimpses of the crude furnace from which they came. Finally there are two additional facts involved which I will leave the modern critics and correspondents in newspapers to ponder and explain at their leisure. One is that this realist, in rebuking the romantics, is very much concerned with rebuking them for the very thing for which revolutionary sentiment has so much admired them; as for their glorification of ingratitude to parents and their easy assumption that the old are always wrong. 'No!' says the noble Youth in *Love and Freindship*, 'never shall it be said that I obliged my father!' And the other is that there is not a shadow of indication anywhere that this independent intellect and laughing spirit was other than contented with a narrow domestic routine, in which she wrote a story as domestic as a diary in the intervals of pies and puddings, without so much as looking out of the window to notice the French Revolution.

DICKENS'S 'CHRISTMAS CAROL'[1]

THE popular paradox of 'A Christmas Carol' is very well symbolized in its title. Everybody has heard Christmas carols; and certainly everybody has heard of Christmas. Yet these things are only popular because they are traditional; and the tradition has often been in need of defence, as Dickens here defended it. If a little more success had crowned the Puritan movement of the seventeenth century, or the Utilitarian movement of the nineteenth century, these things would, humanly speaking, have become merely details of the neglected past, a past of history or even of archæology. The very word Christmas would now sound like the word Candlemas. Perhaps the very word carol would sound like the word villanelle. In this sense a Christmas carol was only one historical type of poem, and Christmas one historical type of festival. Dickens might seem a strange champion for so historical and

[1] *A Christmas Carol*, by Charles Dickens. Cecil Palmer, 1922.

poetical a tradition. He wrote no poetry; he knew no history. For the historical book he wrote for children has not half so much right to be called history as Sam Weller's cheerful song beginning 'Bold Turpin vunce' has to be called poetry. He saved Christmas not because it was historic, but because it was human; but his own adventure serves to show how many things equally human had been suffered to become merely historic.

Dickens struck in time, and saved a popular institution while it was still popular. A hundred æsthetes are always ready to revive it as soon as it has become unpopular. The modern intellectuals show great eagerness in reviving an old custom when once it is destroyed. They show particular eagerness in reviving it when they have themselves destroyed it. The educated classes are everlastingly sweeping things away as vulgar errors, and then trying to recall them as cultured eccentricities. The intellectuals of the twentieth century are now crying out for the folk-songs and morris dances which the intellectuals of the nineteenth century condemned as superstition, and the intellectuals of the seventeenth century as sin. It would be an exaggeration perhaps to say that the advanced intelligence is always wrong. But it would be safe to say at least that it is always too late.

But Dickens was not too late. It was precisely because he was a man of the people that he was able to perpetuate the popular hold upon one of the customs that had only begun to slip from the popular grasp. If he had appeared twenty years later, when the new Puritanism of the industrial age had run its course, the popular enjoyments of Christmas might have become refined merely by becoming rare. Art critics might be talking about the exquisite proportions of a plum-pudding as of an Etruscan pot; and cultured persons might be hanging stockings on their bed-posts as gravely as they hung Morris curtains on their walls. But coming when he did, Dickens could appeal to a living tradition and not to a lost art. He was able to save the thing from dying, instead of trying to raise it from the dead.

In this one work of Dickens, therefore, the historical and moral importance is really even greater than the literary importance. In this respect it bears some resemblance to another of his works, which might seem superficially its very contrary. *A Christmas Carol* is perhaps the most genial and fanciful of all his stories. *Hard Times* is perhaps the most grim and realistic, but in both cases the moral beauty is perhaps greater than the artistic beauty; and both stand higher in any study of the man than of the writer. And although one represents the first skirmish in defence of the old tradition, and the second the final pitched battle against the new theories, in both cases the author is fighting for the same cause. He is fighting an old miser named Scrooge, and a new miser named Gradgrind, but it is not only true that the new miser has the old avarice, it is also true that the old miser has the new arguments. Scrooge is a utilitarian and an individualist; that is, he is a miser in theory as well as in practice. He utters all the sophistries by which the age of machinery has tried to turn the virtue of charity into a vice. Indeed this is something of an understatement. Scrooge is not only as modern as Gradgrind but more modern than Gradgrind. He belongs not only to the hard times of the middle of the nineteenth century, but to the harder times of the beginning of the twentieth century; the yet harder times in which we live. Many amiable sociologists will say, as he said, 'Let them die and decrease the surplus population.' The improved proposal is that they should die before they are born.

It is notable also that Dickens gives the right reply; and that with a deadly directness worthy of a much older and more subtle controversionalist. The answer to anyone who talks about the surplus population is to ask him whether he is the surplus population, or if he is not, how he knows he is not. That is the answer which the Spirit of Christmas gives to Scrooge; and there is more than one fine element of irony involved in it. There is this very mordant moral truth, among others; that Scrooge is exactly the sort of man who would really talk of the superfluous poor as of something dim and distant; and yet he is also exactly the kind of man whom others might regard as sufficiently dim, not to say dingy, to be himself superfluous. There is something of a higher sarcasm, even than that to be read on the surface, in the image of that wretched little rag of a man so confident that the rags and refuse of humanity can be safely swept away and burned; in the miser who himself looks so like a pauper, confidently ordering a massacre of paupers. This is true enough even to more modern life; and we have all met mental defectives in the comfortable classes who are humoured, as with a kind of hobby, by being allowed to go about lecturing on the mental deficiency of poor people. We have all met professors, of stunted figure and the most startling ugliness, who explain that all save the strong and beautiful should be painlessly extinguished in the interests of the race. We have all seen the most sedentary of scholars proving on paper that none should survive save the victors of aggressive war and the physical struggle for life; we have all heard the idle rich explaining why the idle poor deserve to be left to die of hunger. In all this the spirit of Scrooge survives; especially in that central irony of his unconsciousness of the application of his own argument to his own case. But in justice to Scrooge, we must admit that in some respects the later developments of his heathen philosophy have gone beyond him. If Scrooge was an individualist, he had something of the good as well as the evil of individualism. He believed at least in the negative liberty of the Utilitarians. He was ready to live and let live, even if the standard of living was very near to that of dying and letting die. He partook of gruel while his nephew partook of punch; but it never occurred to him that he could forcibly forbid a grown man like his nephew to consume punch, or coerce him into consuming gruel. In that he was far behind the ferocity and tyranny of the social reformers of our own day. If he refused to subscribe to a scheme for giving people Christmas dinners, at least he did not subscribe (as the reformers do) to a scheme for taking away the Christmas dinners they have already got. He had no part in the blasphemy of abolishing in workhouses the Christmas ale that had been the charity of Christian people. Doubtless he would have regarded the charity as folly, but he would also have regarded the forcible reversal of it as theft. He would not have thought it natural to pursue Bob Cratchit to his own home, to spy on him, to steal his turkey, to run away with his punch-bowl, to kidnap his crippled child, and put him in prison as a defective. To do these things he would need to be the more enlightened employee of a more progressive age than that in which *A Christmas Carol* was written. These antics were far beyond the activities of poor Scrooge, whose figure shines by comparison with something of humour and humanity.

UTOPIAS [1]

IN writing a few prefatory words to Father Dudley's apt and spirited criticisms I may be allowed rather to emphasize and expand one or two of his suggestions than to add anything to them. His book is concerned with a highly practical and even topical point in the controversies of the day. It is the question implied in the Utopias of Mr. H. G. Wells and in most of the new religions or new substitutes for religion. Father Dudley reviews all that humanitarianism which is so much connected with hedonism, and questions whether it is very much connected with happiness. Would the world even be happy, if it gave up all that has been counted holy? In this connection I would suggest only one query. The study of one of the Wellsian Utopias, or indeed of any other Utopias, has often been interesting; but did anyone ever find it exhilarating? Does anyone feel those descriptions to glow in his memory like

[1] *Will Men be like Gods?* by O. F. Dudley. Messrs. Longmans, Green & Co., Ltd., 1924.

the real memories of human enjoyment? Does he, as Mr. Tony Weller said, feel his spirits rose; does he feel it half as much in the atmosphere of a tavern with Mr. Tony Weller himself? There is something wanting in these ideals; and here the critic finds it in the very limitation of humanity to human things. It is all the more irreligious because it is a religion; that is, because it is taken seriously. Father Dudley practically identifies the humanitarianism of Wells with the humanity-worship of Comte. In this concentration he finds the key to its failure to produce happiness.

Perhaps the most interesting of the suggestions of Father Dudley, at least so far as I am concerned, is one that concerns the paradox of taking an irreligious humanity as a religion. It is actually much more difficult to worship a humanity that is not worshipping. So much of what is best in our race is bound up with its religious emotions and traditions, that to worship it without those intimations of the best would come very near to worshipping it at its worst. It is not so much that mankind is not enough as that mankind has never felt it enough to be enough. Man is maimed as well as limited by arresting those upward gestures that are so natural to him. Even if mankind could become such a mutual admiration society, men would in fact find each other less admirable. A self-contained and self-centred humanity would chill us in the same way as a self-contained and self-centred human being. For the spiritual hungers of humanity are never merely hungers for humanity. They are never merely aspirations for a completely humanized humanity, even as they exist in humanitarians. The proof of this is not peculiar to theology or even to religion; it is equally apparent in poetry and all imaginative arts. The child in the field, if left entirely to himself, does not merely wish to find the perfect parish ruled over by the perfect parish council. The child in the field wants to find fairyland; and that type of fancy must either be satisfied or thwarted; but it cannot be turned into something totally different. The poet does not merely wish to be with men; though the sanest sort of poet will wish this also on suitable occasions. But even the sanest sort of poet will often wish to be away from men and alone with something else. If he is a philosopher as well as a poet, he will probably want some intelligent identification of that something else; and if he looks for it, he will probably become a theologian as well as a philosopher. But even if he is only a poet, he will be haunted by something which is emphatically not human; and which he could really only rationally explain by calling it superhuman. In other words, it is impossible to turn all the eyes of that mutual admiration society inwards. Any number of their eyes always have been and always will be turned outwards, if only to a vague elemental environment of primeval mysteries and natural magic. To teach people to believe in God may be in its highest sense a hard task even among Christians. But to prevent people from thinking about God will be an impossible task even among agnostics; or perhaps especially among agnostics. It will be particularly impossible among agnostics who are also artists. If it has sometimes been difficult to keep the poet tied to home, it will be ten times more difficult to keep him tied to humanity. Comte, like Plato, will certainly have to expel poets from his Republic.

The other important part of the thesis, to my mind, concerns, not so much this paradox which is false, as another paradox which is true. It is the paradox that it is more possible to love men indirectly than to love them directly. There is such a thing as a passionate enthusiasm or tenderness for the ordinary man. But generally speaking it is rather an extraordinary man who feels it. Or, if this be not necessarily true, it is at least only felt by the ordinary man at extraordinary moments; that is, in extraordinary moods. Now if those moods and moments be sympathetically considered, I fancy it will always be found that they are what may be called mystical moods and moments. I mean that they are experiences in which the external manifestation of mankind seems to mean more than meets the eye; in which a crowd takes on a corporate character like a cloud; or in which a human face has the mask and the secret of a sphinx. Few are fired with a direct individual affection for the five people sitting on the other side of a railway-carriage; let us say a wealthy matron, given to snorting and sneering, a bright little Jew stockbroker, a large and vacant farmer, a pale and weary youth with a limp cigarette and a young woman perpetually powdering her nose. All these are sacred beings of equal value in the sight of God with the souls of Hildebrand and Shakespeare; but a man needs to be a little of a mystic to think so; or even to feel anything like it. In a vacuum of absolute agnosticism, in an utterly dry light of detached objectivity and positive knowledge, it is questionable whether he would feel it at all. If, as it is, he feels it occasionally and vaguely, it is really because he feels the remains of the old religious sentiment occasionally and vaguely. In the right mood he can still see a halo round humanity, because he still half-believes that humanity is half-divine. But that the stockbroker can be positively proved to be half-divine there is no proof. That the halo will in any case shine out

UTOPIAS

of the interior of the fat farmer, by itself, and be visible to anybody anywhere, has never been scientifically demonstrated.

Now just as that vague hope that we call romance or poetry points to a paradise even if it be called elf-land, so this vague charity or sense of sacred human values really points to a higher standard of sacredness. We have to look at men in a certain light in order to love them all; and the most agnostic of us know that it is not exactly identical with the light of common day. But the mystery is immediately explained when we turn towards that light itself; which is the light that lighteth every man that cometh into the world. Ordinary men find it difficult to love ordinary men; at least in an ordinary way. But ordinary men can love the love of ordinary men. They can love the lover of ordinary men, who loves them in an extraordinary way. It may be difficult to get a fat burgess and a fierce and hungry robber to love each other; but it is much easier to get them both to love St. Francis of Assisi for being able to love them both. And what is true of St. Francis is more true of his Divine model; men can admire perfect charity before they practise even imperfect charity; and that is by far the most practical way of getting them to practise it. It is not to leave men merely staring at each other and standing face to face to criticize and grow weary; it is rather to see them standing side by side and looking out together at a third thing; the world's desire and the love-affair of all humanity; which is really a human sun that can shine upon the evil and the good.

GEORGE MACDONALD [1]

CERTAIN magazines have symposiums (I will call them 'symposia' if I am allowed to call the two separate South Kensington collections 'musea') in which persons are asked to name 'Books that have Influenced Me', on the lines of 'Hymns that have Helped Me'. It is not a very realistic process as a rule, for our minds are mostly a vast uncatalogued library; and for a man to be photographed with one of the books in his hand generally means at best that he has chosen at random, and at worst that he is posing for effect. But in a certain rather special sense I for one can really testify to a book that has made a difference to my whole existence, which helped me to see things in a certain way from the start; a vision of things which even so real a revolution as a change of religious allegiance has substantially only crowned and confirmed. Of all the stories I have read, including even all the novels of the same novelist, it remains the

[1] *George MacDonald and His Wife*, by Greville M. MacDonald. Messrs. George Allen & Unwin, Ltd., 1924.

most real, the most realistic, in the exact sense of the phrase the most like life. It is called *The Princess and the Goblin*, and is by George MacDonald, the man who is the subject of this book. When I say it is like life, what I mean is this. It describes a little princess living in a castle in the mountains which is perpetually undermined, so to speak, by subterranean demons who sometimes come up through the cellars. She climbs up the castle stairways to the nursery or the other rooms; but now and again the stairs do not lead to the usual landings, but to a new room she has never seen before, and cannot generally find again. Here a good great-grandmother, who is a sort of fairy godmother, is perpetually spinning and speaking words of understanding and encouragement. When I read it as a child, I felt that the whole thing was happening inside a real human house, not essentially unlike the house I was living in, which also had staircases and rooms and cellars. This is where the fairy-tale differed from many other fairy-tales; above all, this is where the philosophy differed from many other philosophies. I have always felt a certain insufficiency about the ideal of Progress, even of the best sort which is a Pilgrim's Progress. It hardly suggests how near both the best and the worst things are to us from the first; even perhaps especially at the first. And though like every other sane person I value and revere the ordinary fairy-tale of the miller's third son who set out to seek his fortune (a form which MacDonald himself followed in the sequel called *The Princess and Curdie*), the very suggestion of travelling to a far-off fairyland, which is the soul of it, prevents it from achieving this particular purpose of making all the ordinary staircases and doors and windows into magical things.

Dr. Greville MacDonald, in his intensely interesting memoir of his father which follows, has I think mentioned somewhere his sense of the strange symbolism of stairs. Another recurrent image in his romances was a great white horse; the father of the princess had one, and there was another in *The Back of the North Wind*. To this day I can never see a big white horse in the street without a sudden sense of indescribable things. But for the moment I am speaking of what may emphatically be called the presence of household gods—and household goblins. And the picture of life in this parable is not only truer than the image of a journey like that of the Pilgrim's Progress, it is even truer than the mere image of a siege like that of The Holy War. There is something not only imaginative but intimately true about the idea of the goblins being below the house and capable of besieging it from the cellars. When the evil things besieging us do appear, they do not appear outside but inside. Anyhow, that simple image of a house that is our home, that is rightly loved as our home, but of which we hardly know the best or the worst, and must always wait for the one and watch against the other, has always remained in my mind as something singularly solid and unanswerable; and was more corroborated than corrected when I came to give a more definite name to the lady watching over us from the turret, and perhaps to take a more practical view of the goblins under the floor. Since I first read that story some five alternative philosophies of the universe have come to our colleges out of Germany, blowing through the world like the east wind. But for me that castle is still standing in the mountains and the light in its tower is not put out.

All George MacDonald's other stories, interesting and suggestive in their several ways, seem to be illustrations and even disguises of that one. I say disguises, for this is the very important difference between his sort of mystery and mere allegory. The commonplace allegory takes what it regards as the commonplaces or conventions necessary to ordinary men and women, and tries to make them pleasant or picturesque by dressing them up as princesses or goblins or good fairies. But George MacDonald did really believe that people were princesses and goblins and good fairies, and he dressed them up as ordinary men and women. The fairy-tale was the inside of the ordinary story and not the outside. One result of this is that all the inanimate objects that are the stage properties of the story retain that nameless glamour which they have in a literal fairytale. The staircase in *Robert Falconer* is as much of a magic ladder as the staircase in the *Princess and the Goblin*; and when the boys are making the boat and the girl is reciting verses to them, in *Alec Forbes*, and some old gentleman says playfully that it will rise to song like a magic Scandinavian ship, it always seemed to me as if he were describing the reality, apart from the appearance, of the incident. The novels as novels are uneven, but as fairy-tales they are extraordinarily consistent. He never for a moment loses his own inner thread that runs through the patchwork, and it is the thread that the fairy great-grandmother put into the hands of Curdie to guide him out of the mazes of the goblins.

The originality of George MacDonald has also a historical significance, which perhaps can best be estimated by comparing him with his great countryman Carlyle. It is a measure of the very real power and even popularity of Puritanism in Scotland that Carlyle never lost the Puritan mood even when he lost the whole of the

Puritan theology. If an escape from the bias of environment be the test of originality, Carlyle never completely escaped, and George MacDonald did. He evolved out of his own mystical meditations a complete alternative theology leading to a completely contrary mood. And in those mystical meditations he learned secrets far beyond the mere extension of Puritan indignation to ethics and politics. For in the real genius of Carlyle there was a touch of the bully, and wherever there is an element of bullying there is an element of platitude, of reiteration and repeated orders. Carlyle could never have said anything so subtle and simple as MacDonald's saying that God is easy to please and hard to satisfy. Carlyle was too obviously occupied with insisting that God was hard to satisfy; just as some optimists are doubtless too much occupied with insisting that He is easy to please. In other words, MacDonald had made for himself a sort of spiritual environment, a space and transparency of mystical light, which was quite exceptional in his national and denominational environment. He said things that were like the Cavalier mystics, like the Catholic saints, sometimes perhaps like the Platonists or the Swedenborgians, but not in the least like the Calvinists, even as Calvinism remained in a man like Carlyle. And when he comes to be more carefully studied as a mystic, as I think he will be when people discover the possibility of collecting jewels scattered in a rather irregular setting, it will be found, I fancy, that he stands for a rather important turning-point in the history of Christendom, as representing the particular Christian nation of the Scots. As Protestants speak of the morning stars of the Reformation, we may be allowed to note such names here and there as morning stars of the Reunion.

The spiritual colour of Scotland, like the local colour of so many Scottish moors, is a purple that in some lights can look like grey. The national character is in reality intensely romantic and passionate—indeed, excessively and dangerously romantic and passionate. Its emotional torrent has only too often been turned towards revenge, or lust, or cruelty, or witchcraft. There is no drunkenness like Scotch drunkenness; it has in it the ancient shriek and the wild shriliness of the Maenads on the mountains. And of course it is equally true on the good side, as in the great literature of the nation. Stopford Brooke and other critics have truly pointed out that a vivid sense of colour appears in the medieval Scottish poets before it really appears in any English poets. And it is absurd to be talking of the hard and shrewd sobriety of a national type that has made itself best known throughout the modern world by the prosaic literalism of *Treasure Island* and the humdrum realism of *Peter Pan*. Nevertheless, by a queer historical accident this vivid and coloured people have been forced to 'wear their blacks' in a sort of endless funeral on an eternal Sabbath. In most plays and pictures, however, in which they are represented as wearing their blacks, some instinct makes the actor or the artist see that they fit very badly. And so they do.

The passionate and poetical Scots ought obviously, like the passionate and poetical Italians, to have had a religion which competed with the beauty and vividness of the passions, which did not let the devil have all the bright colours, which fought glory with glory and flame with flame. It should have balanced Leonardo with St. Francis; no young and lively person really thinks he can be balanced with John Knox. The consequence was that this power in Scottish letters, especially in the day (or night) of complete Calvinistic orthodoxy, was weakened and wasted in a hundred ways. In Burns it was driven out of its due course like a madness; in Scott it was only tolerated as a memory. Scott could only be a medievalist by becoming what he would call an antiquary, or what we should call an æsthete. He had to pretend his love was dead, that he might be allowed to love her. As Nicodemus came to

Jesus by night, the æsthete only comes to church by moonlight.

Now, among the many men of genius Scotland produced in the nineteenth century, there was only one so original as to go back to this origin. There was only one who really represented what Scottish religion should have been, if it had continued the colour of the Scottish medieval poetry. In his particular type of literary work he did indeed realize the apparent paradox of a St. Francis of Aberdeen, seeing the same sort of halo round every flower and bird. It is not the same thing as any poet's appreciation of the beauty of the flower or bird. A heathen can feel that and remain heathen, or in other words remain sad. It is a certain special sense of significance, which the tradition that most values it calls sacramental. To have got back to it, or forward to it, at one bound of boyhood, out of the black Sabbath of a Calvinist town, was a miracle of imagination.

In noting that he may well have this place in history in the sense of religious and of national history, I make no attempt here to fix his place in literature. He is in any case one of the kind that it is most difficult to fix. He wrote nothing empty; but he wrote much that is rather too full, and of which the appreciation depends rather on a sympathy with the substance than on the first sight of the form. As a matter of fact, the mystics have not often been men of letters in the finished and almost professional sense. A thoughtful man will now find more to think about in Vaughan or Crashaw than in Milton, but he will also find more to criticize; and nobody need deny that in the ordinary sense a casual reader may wish there was less of Blake and more of Keats. But even this allowance must not be exaggerated; and it is in exactly the same sense in which we pity a man who has missed the whole of Keats or Milton, that we can feel compassion for the critic who has not walked in the forest of Phantastes or made the acquaintance of Mr. Cupples in the adventures of Alec Forbes.

DETECTIVE STORIES [1]

I CAN say with all sincerity, nay with all solemn responsibility, that this detective mystery deceived me. And as I have been looking out for a long time for a detective mystery that should be at least deceptive, whatever its other merits or demerits in being detective, I very willingly write a word to serve as a preface to it, though such books ought not to need such prefaces. The detective story is in this way a paradox (if I may use a word that has very painful memories for me) because the true reader and critic not only desires to be gulled, but even desires to be gullible. I wish when reading such a story to become as simple as Dr. Watson; to be in the happy, cheerful, childlike, radiant condition of Dr. Watson and not in the much more dark and disillusioned and satiated and sceptical condition of Sherlock Holmes. I generally am in that childlike condition. But in every case it is my ardent and aspiring ambition to be

[1] *The Wrong Letter*, by Walter S. Masterman. Messrs. Methuen & Co., Ltd., 1925.

stupider than the man who wrote the story. And in the case of this story I actually succeeded.

This desire to be deceived is really peculiar to detective romance. It is in another sense that we say the same thing of other types of romance. It is sometimes said that when we go to the theatre we pay to be deceived. But we are not really deceived; we do not think that the dramatist intends something that he does not intend; we do not think the actor is doing something that he is not doing. We only forget, or half forget, for a moment, in the continuity and consistency of certain events, the fact that they came from a dramatist and an actor. But if we happen to remember it, we do not remember it with surprise. We are not astonished to discover that there is an actor on the stage, as we are (or ought to be) astonished to discover that there is a corpse in the summer-house. We do not feel a momentary incredulity when we are told that the play was written by a playwright, as we do feel (or ought to feel) when we are told that the crime was committed by a curate. We watch a great actor performing Hamlet so well that (if we have luck) we lose for an instant the sense that he is a great actor; we feel for the moment that he is young Hamlet trying to avenge the death of old Hamlet upon Claudius. But we do not, either in forgetting or remembering, feel any shock of fact or the change of fact. We do not feel as we should feel if the play took a new and sudden turn, and we found that Hamlet had killed his own father and that his uncle was a perfectly blameless character. That would be the Detective Drama of Hamlet, Prince of Denmark, and now that so many peculiar experiments are being tried with that tragedy, I respectfully suggest it to the managers of the London Theatres.

If it is the first rule of the writer of mystery stories to conceal the secret from the reader, it is the first duty of the critic to conceal it from the public. I will therefore put my hand upon my mouth; and tortures shall not reveal the precise point in this story at which a person whom I had really regarded as figuring in one legitimate capacity suddenly began to figure in another, which was far from legitimate. I must not breathe a word about what the writer of this dramatic mystery does. I will confine myself strictly to saying what he does not do. And merely out of the things which he does not do, I could construct an enthusiastic eulogy. On the firm foundation of the things he does not do, I could erect an eternal tower of brass. For the things he does not do are the things being done everywhere to-day, to the destruction of true detective fiction and the loss of this legitimate and delightful form of art. He does not introduce into the story a vast but invisible secret society with branches in every part of the world, with ruffians who can be brought in to do anything or underground cellars that can be used to hide anybody. He does not mar the pure and lovely outlines of a classical murder or burglary by wreathing it round and round with the dirty and dingy red tape of international diplomacy; he does not lower our lofty ideals of crime to the level of foreign politics. He does not introduce suddenly at the end somebody's brother from New Zealand, who is exactly like him. He does not trace the crime hurriedly in the last page or two to some totally insignificant character, whom we never suspected because we never remembered. He does not get over the difficulty of choosing between the hero and the villain by falling back on the hero's cabman or the villain's valet. He does not introduce a professional criminal to take the blame of a private crime; a thoroughly unsportsmanlike course of action and another proof of how professionalism is ruining our national sense of sport. He does not introduce about six people in succession to do little bits of the same small murder; one man to bring the dagger and another to point it and another to stick it in properly. He does not say it was all a mistake, and that nobody ever meant to murder anybody at all, to the serious disappointment of all humane and sympathetic readers. He does not make the general mistake of thinking that the more complicated the story is the better. His story is complicated enough, and on many points open to criticism; but the secret of it is found in the centre; and that is the central matter in any work of art.

A STORY FROM THE GOTHIC[1], [2]

A GREAT many years ago I wrote for the *Daily News* an article which was afterwards re-published in a book of essays under the name of *The Architect of Spears*. It attempted to describe a quality in a Gothic church which is militant and like an army on the march; as if the medieval cathedral were the static expression of the medieval crusade. Extending this into an extravaganza, I pictured the whole elaborate building as stirring into life, or rather into lives. For if such a stone church did indeed come to life, it would not come to life like a statue, but rather like a crowd. It would wake as a town wakes when the cock crows and the dogs bark and the windows open, and the wheels begin to rattle on the stones; or as all the motley and complicated life of a royal court began to stir

[1] *Abishag* (translated by Joyce Davis), by Alexandre Arnoux. Messrs. Thornton Butterworth, Ltd., 1925.
[2] A few lines at the very beginning and a few more in the middle have been excised from the original draft of this introduction.

again when the spell was broken in the tale of The Sleeping Beauty. So the Christian church would awaken, not as one thing but as many, its graven birds beating their wings in crypts and nooks like nests, or its gargoyles barking like winged dogs above the street. For this is the character of Christian art as it flourished in the Middle Ages, a character of genial complexity and even contradiction that would in itself contradict the very merits of the finest art of heathen antiquity. Memnon may sing at morning; but it is impossible to imagine him leading a convivial chorus accompanied with a dance of flamingoes and crocodiles. Some of the early statues of Apollo, I believe, represented him for some reason now forgotten as accompanied by a mouse; but we cannot fancy the squeak of the mouse being allowed to mingle with the song of the god. But there is something in the very way in which diverse elements in Gothic art are allowed to cluster almost in confusion, which suggests that if they could speak their voices would mingle in a sort of clamour. In one sense, certainly, in that Christian art, the lion does lie down with the lamb; only the bleating of the lamb might be almost louder than the roaring of the lion.

Nevertheless, the medieval architecture, like the medieval order, really is an order. It had its own discipline, because it had its own direction; but it was like the discipline of a great multitude marching to one goal. It was the spirit of very varied things united by movement; not like the simple lines of a classical thing united in repose. I therefore described it in my little essay as marching along the highway like a sort of militant pilgrimage. I conceived the cathedral as passing over land and sea like a portent; its pillars swaying like the feet of elephants, or its great bells going like the great guns of an advancing train of artillery. I suggested, if I remember right, that it might slumber on the march and wake in strange lands, or find all its restless complexity alone in the circle of great deserts. Finally, I hinted that a fine romance might be written developing the notion in detail, by somebody more capable of a really detailed æsthetic and historical reconstruction than I am. A little while afterwards I received a very charming and entertaining letter from France, I believe from M. Arnoux himself, telling me that the romance had really been written, and corresponded in many curious particulars to my own sketch. There is, of course, no real comparison between the rich and varied development of the novel and the rude and random notion that was outlined in the newspaper article. In the novel certain fantastic figures detach themselves not only from the stone, but even in a sense from the story.

A STORY FROM THE GOTHIC

They develop individualities more like the individual characters of a real or rather a realistic novel. They become the spokesmen of a satire and philosophy that is their own; not always necessarily the author's, let alone mine. King Solomon, or the gay, goatlike child who stands for the spirit of paganism, become voices necessarily distinct and different from the first conception of the chorus of a marching cathedral. But I think the author has contrived with fine skill and felicity to preserve the artistic, we may say the architectural, atmosphere or background, whatever differences there may be about the philosophical background. The satyr is still a Gothic satyr and not a Greek satyr; and Solomon has stepped out of the stone carvings of Notre Dame and not out of those of Nineveh or Thebes. Considered merely as the fanciful loosening of the figures frozen in the grey forest of medieval imagery, the wandering tale is true to the original æsthetic impulse.

It is after a very long interval, I must confess with shame and apologies, that I come back to redeem the promise to write a preface to the English edition of M. Arnoux's story, that I gave in those remote days. Since then a great war has filled the world, and the guns of the barbarians, the enemies of Christendom, have shamefully battered and blasted the medieval masterpieces of architecture and sculpture that were the creation and the crown of France. Since then it may be these things have taken on a new sacredness in the eyes even of those Frenchmen to whom they were not in the highest sense sacred. And since then, I who write these words have passed through a change which is to the individual greater than a great war; a change after which I can never regard these things in quite the light and irresponsible spirit of artistic detachment which was mine when I made those idle suggestions in the great Liberal newspaper or gave that promise to the friendly French gentleman long ago. I have come to believe in a Church that is even more on the march and less subject to mutiny and mutilation; a Church Militant going to the last battle that shall turn it into the Church Triumphant. The architectural procession I should see now is at once less frivolous and less sad than that which trailed after the buoyant monster Rusticula. And though I can enjoy as much as ever the very national irony which ends upon that note about the American millionaire, and the modern method of moving cathedrals, I am not disillusioned about my own movement. I know there is already a great tradition in that great national literature by which men could appreciate the churches even when they could not appreciate the Church. I know that, even through the most sceptical interlude, the great French school of letters did justice to the great French school of architecture. I believe that Hugo's great romance of Notre Dame de Paris would have been more truly of Paris if it had been more truly of Notre Dame. I believe it would have been more philosophical if the author's own philosophy had been nearer to the myriad words of faith that are graven deep into those walls, and less limited to the one word of fatalism that is idly scribbled upon them. I believe that the medieval sketches of Anatole France would be more accurate if they were sketched from inside the cathedral and not outside. But that is no reason for losing our realization of the rich imaginative tradition of the most varied literary creations, by which the literature of the world has recognized the art of the Church; from the blazoned window which Villon offered to his mother like a vision of Paradise to this last literary gargoyle of the walking statues and the wandering bell. We shall value all the more the implication that even the most detached fancy finds its most spirited imagery in the æsthetics of the age of faith; and that all civilized men are now united in that tribute to the craftsmanship and culture of our fathers,

FRIENDS, ROMANS, COUNTRYMEN [1]

AN introduction to a work of reference has in it of necessity something clumsy, inopportune and out of proportion. A man who consults a work of reference is generally a man in a hurry. A man who reads an introduction to a work of reference is always a man of unusual and almost unnatural leisure; indeed, he must be a man whose leisure has developed into devouring tedium; and whose tedium has reached the point of desperation and recklessness. He must have collected and studied stray scraps of newspaper; he must have read carefully everything that is printed on his railway ticket; he must have read Bradshaw and Mrs. Eddy and every last hope of a desperate reader before he falls back on the introduction to a directory or dictionary of proper names; even if it be so important for other reasons as the *Catholic Who's Who*. I cannot remember at the moment that I ever met a man who ever had read the introduction

[1] *The Catholic Who's Who and Year Book*, 1925. Messrs. Burns, Oates & Washbourne, Ltd., 1925.

to any such book as *Who's Who*. Certainly it never occurred to me to read it; and it is only through the desire of others that it occurs to me to write it. If it has to be written, I should have thought there were hundreds of other Catholics, of far older and higher standing and far larger and more detailed information, who could write it very much better in every way. But if I am privileged to write it, I am at least comforted by this reflection: that not many people are likely to read it. This thought gives to the writer a sort of rich mental repose which is mistaken by some for lack of responsibility. Yet though the preface to this compilation be little read, and be very inadequately written, the compilation itself (to which most people may be trusted to go direct) is the most practical and important record in modern England. It is the record of how much of modern England remains or returns to that without which her civilization will perish.

Such a compilation can indeed only very imperfectly represent the main truths of such a position. There is a peculiarity about the position of Catholics, in this country and at this moment, which it is particularly difficult to convey by any such list of names. We are glad to believe, or rather to know, that that list of names is always being extended; that new names are always being added to it. We are even more glad to know that there are multitudes of new names in this category which cannot be included in this book. We are most glad of all of that great principle of our faith, the principle which gives its only meaning to democracy and which even the Bolshevists have only stolen without understanding; the principle that the conversion of an Emperor or a President of the United States is of exactly the same value as the conversion of a tramp under a hedge or a convict under a gibbet. A list of persons of distinction can therefore give even less idea in our case than in most cases of the extent of our reasons for rejoicing. But, over and above this, there is a further point of distinction or differentiation in the present condition of England and of the Catholic Church in England. It refers to a change in the immediate policy of that Church, which is partly the result and partly the cause of a change in the atmosphere of that country. It has a particular effect upon our view of anything like an established list of notable names and prominent men.

It might be stated shortly by saying that the prominent men are now much more prominent. The names that were always notable are now much more noted. This is due to what has been called the Forward Movement; and it is an excellent example of the sort of reality that cannot always be tested by statistics or even statements of fact. In many pages of this book the same names stand in the same position as they stood in any other issue of the publication for years past. But the men do not stand in the same position by any manner of means. They may have received no particular professional promotion, though they have often done so; they may have added no new letters to their names, though they continually do; they may not have occupied any particular office or entered any particular practical field, though they are doing so more and more. But their figures stand out in the public scene as their names would now stand out of the page, even for a non-Catholic reader, if he were turning over these pages. In many of those pages perhaps, so far as printed words are concerned, the change would hardly be perceptible. In the street outside it is perceptible; in the world and the open road it is perceptible, and the world perceives it as an advancing army, the multitude of faces and the march of feet, men going forward when they have seen a sign.

But though this movement cannot be measured by any changes in this edition, the marks of it will probably be found there. There has been a great increase in the number of Catholics interesting themselves in all kinds of political and especially municipal activity. It can certainly be said of our people in Tennyson's phrase, that 'more and more the people throng the chairs and thrones of civil power'. I do not know whether Catholics are to be congratulated more upon being such good citizens or upon so often and so wisely limiting themselves to the true citizenship of the city; and not being entirely distracted from it by the much more unreal and unrepresentative modern citizenship of the state. For it was in these civic areas, with their more direct democratic life, that there grew up those great Catholic institutions that may yet be the solution of our social misery; the Guild and the Jury and the Just Price; and it has been found again and again in history that locality is almost another name for liberty. But that medieval localism was only possible because a common working philosophy and morality allowed small groups to deal with each other; and we shall probably never find out how far such freedom may safely be carried, till we have once more a general test of truth. Over the ship which sailed to found the free Catholic colony of Maryland were written the words: 'Where is the spirit of God, there is Liberty.'

GILBERT AND SULLIVAN [1]

THE best work of the Victorian age, perhaps the most Victorian work of the Victorian age, was its satire upon itself. It would be well if this were remembered more often by those who talk of nothing but its pomposity and conventionality. There was, indeed, a strain in it, not only of pomposity, but of hypocrisy; but like everything English, it was rather subtle. In so far as it existed it should be called rather humbug than hypocrisy, for hypocrisy implies intellectual clarity, and humbug suggests rather that convenient possession, a confused mind. The exclamation that a thing is all damned humbug is of the same sort as the exclamation that it is all damned nonsense. English humbug has had at least the comforting quality of nonsense, and something of that quality belongs even to the nonsense which made fun of the nonsense. And it will be found, I think, in the long run that this Victorian nonsense will prove more

[1] *Gilbert and Sullivan*, by A. H. Godwin. Messrs. J. M Dent & Sons, Ltd., 1926.

valuable than all that was considered the solid Victorian sense.

It is idle to prophesy about tastes and fashion; but to speak of the failure of the practical compromise of our great unwritten Constitution, for instance, is not to prophesy. It is merely to record. All that side of the British pomposity of the time has obviously collapsed in our time. The political balance and repose of the Victorians, the serious satisfaction of their social arrangements, is already a thing of the past; and perhaps this unbalanced absurdity may prove far more permanent in the future. But it is not only true of practical politics, which have become so exceedingly unpractical. It is true even of pure literature, which in one sense can always remain ideal. The Gilbert and Sullivan Operas can still be revived, and revived with complete popular success. I think it very doubtful whether *The Idylls of the King*, if they were published now, would produce the same sort of effect as when they were published then. I doubt whether Longfellow would immediately obtain his large crowd or Browning his small one. It is not a question of the merits of the poetry or even of the truth of the criticism. People who talk thus about the appeal to posterity often seem to forget that posterity may be wrong—especially about the books that it has not read. Browning's work will always be worthy of study, just as Donne's work will always be worthy of study, but it would be rash to infer that it is always studied. Tennyson will always present certain triumphs of diction for those who are acquainted with the English language. But when Anglo-Saxon is talked all over the world, those acquainted with the English language may be comparatively few. There may be a very general neglect of the Victorian achievements, and as this will be merely an effect of time, it may be merely temporary. But as things stand, the Victorian monument which best supports and survives the change of fashion is not the Laureate ode and office any more than the Albert Memorial: it is all that remains of the Savoy Opera.

But anyone who understands what was really to be said for and against the Victorian interlude or compromise will note with interest that the Victorian satirist did lash the age, in the old phrase; and if in a sense he lashed lightly he also lashed with precision; he touched the spot. He was an inquisitor, as waggish as his own Inquisitor in *The Gondoliers*, but he did really persecute the rather hazy heresies of the hour. He did really persecute in the exact sense of pursue; he tracked an untrue or unreasonable idea back to its first principle. Gilbert's gayest songs and most farcical rhymes are full of examples which a philosopher or a logician will value as real ideas or criticisms of ideas. And it was always the criticism really demanded by the half-formed ideas of the Victorians, those half-warmed fish which the Spooners of the age had in their hearts, but not very clearly in their heads. Any number of examples of this sort of thing could be given. For instance, nothing was more subtly false in the Victorians' conception of success than a certain conception of the elect who were above temptation. There was a queer sort of cheery Calvinism in it; a sort of jovial predestination. Certain social types, the good sportsman, the English lady, the frank and fearless English schoolboy (provided, of course, he were a public schoolboy), were regarded, not as heroes who had overcome the baser passions, but as gods who could never have been touched by them. The phraseology of the time testified to the notion again and again. Such people were not innocent of a crime; they were 'incapable' of it. Political corruption (which was increasing by leaps and bounds) was calmly ignored on the assumption of it being simply 'impossible' in what was generally described as 'a man of that position'. Men who really preserved their honour under trials had no reward or recognition of their real merit, if they were of the sort in whom such things were supposed to be inconceivable. Every one who had read the novels and newspapers of that time will recognize this formless impression, but not everybody could have put it into logical form. Yet it is pricked or stabbed with deadly precision in five or six absurd lines of a light refrain in *The Mikado*:

> 'We know him well,
> He cannot tell
> Untrue or groundless tales—
> He always tries
> To utter lies
> And every time he fails.'

It is the same with the heresy that haunted the great Victorian virtue of patriotism. What was the matter with it was that it was a sort of unconscious shuffling of an unselfish into a selfish emotion. It was not so much that a man was proud of England, as that he was proud of being an Englishman, which is quite a different thing. Being proud of your country is only like being proud of your father or your friend; it is not, in the spiritual and evil sense, really pride at all. But being proud of yourself for being a citizen of that country is really using something else as an excuse for being proud of yourself. Now, the logical or illogical point of that process is in the matter of merit, and the satirist really hits it with the exactitude of a subtle theologian. It is a question of how much there is implied some moral superiority such as ought to be founded on the individual will, and it could not be better exposed than in the few words of that old familiar and even rowdy song:

> 'But in spite of all temptations
> To belong to other nations
> He remains an Englishman.'

The rapier of Voltaire could not have run a thing more straight through the heart. Now the work of Gilbert, especially in his operas, but very notably also in his *Bab Ballads*, is full of triumphs of that intellectual and even theoretical sort. There was even something about him personally not altogether unlike the tone of the theologian and inquisitor; his wit was staccato and sometimes harsh, and he was not happy in his own age and atmosphere. It did not provide him with any positive philosophy for which to fight, but that was not his fault. He did fight for what he conceived to be common sense, and he found plenty of things that wanted fighting.

And then the odd thing happened that was like a lucky coincidence in a farce or a magic gift in a fairy-tale. As it stood, his satire was really much too intelligent to be intelligible. It is doubtful whether by itself it would ever have been completely popular. Something came to his aid which is much more popular than the love of satire: the profound and popular love of songs. A genius in another school of art crossed his path and co-operated in his work; giving wings to his words, and sending them soaring into the sky. Perhaps no other musician except Sullivan would have done it in exactly the right way; would have been in exactly the right degree frivolous and exactly the right degree fastidious. A certain fine unreality had to hang over all the fantasies; there was nothing rowdy, there was nothing in the special sense even rousing about such song, as there is in a serious, patriotic, or revolutionary song, or even drinking song. Everything must be seen in a magic mirror, a little more delicately distorted than the mirror of Shalott; there must be no looking out directly upon passing events. The satiric figures were typical but not topical. All that precise degree of levity and distance from reality seemed to be expressed, as nothing else could express it, in the very notes of the music; almost, one might say, in the note of the laughter that followed it. And it may be that in the remote future that laughter will still be heard, when all the voices of that age are silent.

RASSELAS [1]

DR. JOHNSON, in the opinion of Lord Macaulay, was a little too fond of paradox; and certainly many of Macaulay's most positive judgments sound rather like a sort of plangent platitude, compared with the deep and almost mocking mysteries that are sometimes to be found, by those who know how to look for them, in the mere flippancies and jests of Johnson. But Macaulay, to do him justice, did perceive something of the element of paradox in Johnson's personality and position in history. And having once seen a true antithesis, Macaulay could always express it with a brilliant and conclusive clearness. Nothing, in his own way, could be truer or better expressed than the statement that it was the destiny of Samuel Johnson 'to be known in his own time as a classic and in ours as a companion'.

But there were other elements of paradox in his existence which only Macaulay could have

[1] *The History of Rasselas, Prince of Abissinia*, by Dr. Johnson. Messrs. J. M. Dent & Sons, Ltd., 1926.

put in a sufficiently pointed fashion. And one of them was this: that while there is a sort of humorous atmosphere round much of his work that was then counted most serious, or at any rate most solid, a more melancholy atmosphere clings to everything that could be counted more light. His Dictionary has become a sort of joke; and did actually contain several jokes, or things that are only defensible as jokes. But when he wrote a sort of fairy-tale, it became weighted with all the woes and lamentations of the Vanity of Human Wishes. It could not be said of him, as he said of that friend and fellow genius whom he so nobly pitied and understood, that he touched nothing that he did not adorn. That would imply an unvarying lightness of touch that was not likely to be classed among the merits of Johnson, any more than among the merits of Quasind, the strong man of the Red Indians who broke every bow he touched and snapped asunder every arrow. But it can be said of him that he touched nothing that he did not touch with a certain mighty strength of controlled laughter; and that this can be felt even when his work was only hard work, or even hack work. But it is perhaps least present when he was deliberately and consciously at play. Then the sadness that filled his blank hours became more apparent; and in a sense his labour was more jovial than his leisure. The jests that were struck out of him in the serious collisions of controversy or conduct were often gigantic jests and worthy of Rabelais. But when he sat down deliberately to make a jest, or at least to make a toy or trifle, the gravity of his fundamental mood appeared through the very freedom of fancy. In *Rasselas* he wrote one of those fables which were the first examples of what we now call fiction. It was the nearest he ever came to writing a novel. But in the very irresponsibility of a work of the imagination (if we can ever attribute irresponsibility of Johnson) he became conscious of the philosophical background of himself and his time; and even produced a sort of philosophical satire on philosophy.

In form the book may be said to belong to a type and even a fashion. It can in one sense be classified; though any good book is much more easily classified than criticized. The individual quality is always more important than any that it shares with similar works; still, in that sense, there have been similar works. Carlyle said very truly that Johnson was none the less a strongly original man because he believed in tradition and even convention. In one sense he was original enough not to be afraid of imitation. As he had written letters and light essays in the manner of Addison, so he wrote here a long parable rather like those associated with Voltaire. In the sense in which the play of *Irene* resembles the play of *Cato*, the romance of *Rasselas* resembles the romance of *Candide*. They bear all the marks of an age that still believed in final and fixed forms of art, in lucidity of expression and continuity of aim; and in which even the revolutionary literature was also classical literature. Voltaire never forgets that he is writing a certain sort of satire on Optimism; he would never, for instance, have put a fragment of serious Alexandrine poetry in praise of Henri Quatre into the middle of his meandering irony; as Byron afterwards flung the burning fragment of *The Isles of Greece* into the very middle of *Don Juan*. Similarly Johnson never forgets that he is writing a certain type of tale, with certain conventions and certain licences that are really conventions. It is this quality that has produced the false rumour that works like *Rasselas* are merely dull. By Byron's time, some of the Romantics had reached a state of mind in which they thought that a thing must be dull unless it was disjointed. But even in Johnson's time elements were creeping in which were destined to swell the riot of the Romantic change. There was already something of that more or less indirect Eastern influence which was to spread into the vast popularity of the Arabian Nights and which led Byron himself to describe a number of nights that were decidedly Arabian. It was as yet felt half humorously, as in the imaginary Chinaman of Oliver Goldsmith or the visits of Gulliver to the isles of the Far East. There is a touch of the fashionable Arabian tale of the eighteenth century in *Rasselas*, that vague potentate of Abyssinia, though much of the story is concerned rather with the traditions of classical antiquity. Thus Johnson, who so nearly approached to the virtues of the Stoic, was very ready to make fun of stoicism. But this romantic influence was still very faint; and even what there was of it reveals a certain insufficiency, which has much to do with the moral of the tale.

What the eighteenth century lacked was colour. It put down everything in black and white. It could not understand, as the medieval illuminator understood, that things are really plainer in gold and purple than in black and white. It did not understand that there could be a positive pleasure or a positive passion about mystical things. It is an exaggeration to call it entirely irreligious; some of its very greatest men, like Johnson and even Swift, were profoundly religious. But their religion had not enough colour and therefore not enough positive joy. Even when they put up churches to Christ they were like temples to Pallas Athene; even when they wrote translations of the Psalms they sounded like translations of the Georgics. Even Voltaire put up a stone altar to God, but he would never have put up a stained-glass window to anybody. It is perhaps this absence of the pleasures of religion that we feel as the only gap in the mind of that great religious genius, who appears here as a philosopher mocking philosophers. It was partly, though not entirely, the explanation of his personal melancholy; that melancholy which he could dismiss for work but hardly for play. Those who read *Rasselas* now, after the Romantic movement has rolled on us a purple sea of perhaps only too much colour, may find at first something almost colourless in the clarity and dryness of its narration; but though it may be an acquired taste, they will find it is in truth a very fine taste. And the more they read the more they will respect the mind of that austere virility, which not only saw things in black and white, but in light and darkness; and suffering so much of the darkness, remained always the lover of the light.

THE MAN WHO WAS THURSDAY [1]

IT is the more desirable that I should write a few lines to express my thanks to those who have here paid my story the compliment of casting it in another and (quite probably) a better form, because long after I had given to them, and to them alone, such authorization as I am capable of giving, a rather ridiculous rivalry or invasion of their rights in the matter occurred, it would appear, in Eastern Europe. The Bolshevists have done a good many silly things; but the most strangely silly thing that ever I heard of was that they tried to turn this Anti-Anarchist romance into an Anarchist play. Heaven only knows what they really made of it; beyond apparently making it mean the opposite of everything it meant. Probably they thought that being able to see that a policeman is funny means thinking that a policeman is futile. Probably they would say that thinking Don Quixote funny

[1] *The Man Who Was Thursday* (a play in three acts, adapted from the novel by G. K. Chesterton), by Mrs. Cecil Chesterton and Ralph Neale. Messrs. Ernest Benn, Ltd., 1926.

means thinking chivalry futile; in other words, they are barbarians and have not learnt how to laugh. But in this case a certain consequence follows. Making fun of a policeman would always be fun enough for me. Treating this tale as a farce of balloons and escaped elephants would never trouble me; and I would never bore anybody about the meaning of the allegory. But if somebody, even in Moscow or Vienna, starts making it mean something totally different, or flatly contrary, I cannot avoid a word about its real origin or outline. I do not want to take myself seriously; it is Bolshevism, among its other crimes, that is making me a serious person for a moment.

So many people have lately been occupied in turning good novels into bad plays, that the authors of this adaption have conceived the bolder and more hopeful scheme of turning a bad novel into a good play. For though I know very little about *The Man Who Was Thursday*, only a very casual acquaintance is needed to make sure that if it is a novel it is a bad novel. To do it justice, by its own description, it is not a novel but a nightmare. And since that sub-title is perhaps the only true and reliable statement in the book, I may plead it as a sort of excuse for my share in the matter. Nightmares on the stage are not uncommon nowadays; and some of them are regarded as realistic studies, because they are examples of that very deep and bottomless sort of nightmare from which it happens to be difficult to wake up. Nevertheless, a distinction between the dreams of to-day and those of that remoter day, or rather night, is essential to understanding whatever there may be to understand. To do them justice, the new nightmares do generally belong to a night: as day-dreams belong to a day. They are aspects; they are fragmentary and, to do them justice, they are frivolous. It was not so with a certain spirit that brooded for a certain time over the literature of my youth. I can remember the time when pessimism was dogmatic, when it was even orthodox. The people who had read Schopenhauer regarded themselves as having found out everything and found that it was nothing. Their system was a system, and therefore had a character of surrounding the mind. It therefore really resembled a nightmare, in the sense of being imprisoned or even bound hand and foot; of being none the less captive because it was rather in a lunatic asylum than a reasonable hell or place of punishment. There is a great deal in the modern world that I think evil and a great deal more that I think silly; but it does seem to me to have escaped from this mere prison of pessimism. Our civilization may be breaking up; there are not wanting many exhilarating signs of it breaking down. But it is not merely closing in; and therefore it is not a nightmare, like the narrow despair of the nineties. In so far as it is breaking down, it seems to me more of a mental breakdown than a moral breakdown. In so far as it is breaking up, it may let in a certain amount of daylight as well as a great deal of wind. But it is not stifling like positive pessimism and materialism; and it was in the middle of a thick London fog of these things that I sat down and tried to write this story, nearly twenty years ago.

It is in relation to that particular heresy that much of its main suggestion must be understood. Perhaps it is not worth while to try to kill heresies which so rapidly kill themselves—and the cult of suicide committed suicide some time ago. But I should not wish it supposed, as some I think have supposed, that in resisting the heresy of pessimism I implied the equally morbid and diseased insanity of optimism. I was not then considering whether anything is really evil, but whether everything is really evil; and in relation to the latter nightmare it does still seem to me relevant to say that nightmares are not true; and that in them even the faces of friends may appear as the faces of fiends. I tried to turn this notion of resistance to a nightmare into a topsy-turvy tale about a man who fancied himself alone among enemies, and found that each of the enemies was in fact on his own side and in his own solitude. That is the only thing that can be called a meaning in the story; all the rest of it was written for fun; and though it was great fun for me, I do not forget that sobering epigram which tells us that easy writing is dashed hard reading. I think, however, the thing has possibilities as a play; because by the plan of it the changes are, as they should be in drama, only half expected but not wholly unexpected. I have been responsible for many murders in my time, generally in the milder and more vicarious forms of detective stories; and I have noticed a fashionable fallacy that is not irrelevant here. Because murdering or being murdered is generally felt by the individual involved to have something about it dramatic and striking, it is often supposed that any detective story will make a drama. The thing has been done and may be done again, but it is not easy to do. In such a story the secret is too sensational to be dramatic. The revelation comes too suddenly to be understood; and until it is understood all that ought to seem mystifying only seems meaningless. But in this foolish farce, it is at least true that the action proceeds along a certain course that can be followed, and I offer it gravely as an attempt to restore the canons of Aristotle and the classical unities of antiquity.

In other words, a man may watch for the end of the play, when he would put down the book under the impression that he knew the story by having read half of it.

WOMEN IN DICKENS [1]

THERE is, as every one knows or ought to know, a thing called the Dickens Fellowship, a body whose buoyant vitality was once sufficient even to support the incubus of myself as a president; but in a larger and looser but not less real sense there is everywhere and in every way a thing to be called the fellowship of Dickens. The aptness of the term does not depend entirely on the conviviality or camaraderie often described by Dickens when he is most Dickensian. It is something in the nature of the literary methods and literary merits of Dickens, in dealing with this or any other subject. Dickens's characters are not always passing the bowl, but there is a sense in which Dickens's readers are always passing on the book; Mr. Pickwick was not always drinking punch, but several people at once manage to dip together into Pickwick, as they dip together into a punchbowl. The pleasure of his work at its best,

[1] *Some Dickens Women*, by Edwin Charles. Messrs. T. Werner Laurie, Ltd., 1926.

which generally means at its funniest, is of the sort that permits a number of very different people to join in the fun. His work is work to be shared; there are friendships almost founded upon Dickens; and such friends will sit up all night together, each elaborately reciting the passage that the other knows by heart. This quality stands for something which is none the less subtle for being universal; the sort of thing about which it is easy to offer trite explanations and very hard to offer true ones; it is as easy to confuse communion with communism as it is to confuse sentiment with sentimentalism. It is certainly not mere maudlin amiability; on the contrary it is an eminently masculine pleasure, and in that sense an impersonal pleasure. It is essential that the two Dickensians should be thinking about Dickens and not about each other. Yet it does generally found and fortify them unconsciously in a lasting friendship with each other. It is certainly not the mere fact of literary excellence on the one hand or of literary popularity on the other. There is many a book that has been read by ten thousand people that could not be read aloud to ten people. There is many a literary masterpiece that a million men have enjoyed, but every man has enjoyed alone. Whatever be the reason, those who like Dickens like talking about Dickens and like the people who will talk about him.

I find myself associated with Mr. Edwin Charles, not only in this large and informal fellowship of Dickensians, but in many other connexions, some more important and some more trivial. I first had the pleasure of meeting him in his Dickensian capacity, I think, when he wrote an ingenious explanation of the Mystery of Edwin Drood. I represent that aggravating type of Dickensian critic who has no theory at all about Edwin Drood; but who criticizes, generally unfavourably, any theory that anybody attempts to advance. But I remember being very much struck by Mr. Edwin Charles's suggestions for a solution and thinking them far more pregnant and probable than some that were much more widely advertised. It very emphatically needs a Dickensian to finish Dickens's unfinished story. It is useless to attack it as one might attack an abstract problem (illustrated with a diagram) of which the characters are christened only A and B. Dickens was never interested in the adventures of A and B unless the B stood for Bazzard or Bud; and we have always to remember that the A very decidedly stood for Author. We have to consider what Dickens would do as well as what Bazzard would do; and even what Bazzard would do in a Dickens book is quite different from what the same sort of character would do in somebody else's book.

It is useless to fit it together like a jigsaw puzzle, on the plea that you have managed to fit in all the pieces somewhere; the thing must be judged, not only as a puzzle, but also as a pattern; and a pattern has a certain artistic character belonging to a certain artistic mind. That reverence for the novelist, which the novelist's son truly noted in Mr. Charles, was not a weakness, but a strength for the exposition of the novel. It ensured that the story would be carried on, if not by the same mind, to some extent in the same mood. It would not be a case of a man explaining a book in the spirit of winning a bet; the *tour de force* of doing it somehow. The same sympathy and enthusiasm has led Mr. Charles to these studies of some of the feminine characters in Dickens; and being myself the sort of good Dickensian who talks all night, I should be delighted to talk all night about each of his subjects. In many cases I should agree with him; in some cases I should argue with him; but in no cases, supposing appropriate and ideal conditions, should we go home till morning. I regret the omission of any study of Mrs. Wilfer, whom I myself regard as a mighty tower rigidly and royally supporting the whole temple of the Dickens reputation. I disapprove of any disparagement of Miss Bates even for the glorification of Mrs. Nickleby; indeed, I think an interesting essay might be written on the deep difference under the superficial similarity; for the garrulity of Miss Bates was that of a spinster full of adventurous enquiry, while that of Mrs. Nickleby was that of a married woman who had simply got used to talking as a river to flowing. But I am not going to begin any of my arguments with Mr. Edwin Charles at present; at any rate not in public. I am content to salute him as one of the fellowship who keep alive the one really living tradition of a literary personality that exists in our time and which shows no signs of failing. A man may be satisfied with his solution of Drood; but none of us will ever be satisfied with our solution of Dickens; and the mystery is always fresh.

SOME FELLOWS [1]

THIS collection of five papers and one Professorial Lecture recently read before the Royal Society of Literature covers, as is natural, a very wide and varied world of topics; and yet in this case, if only by accident, there is a certain general trend or train of thought. Lord Crewe's clear and compact summary of the whole story of the institution itself serves not only as an introduction, but as a sort of framework, and can be used not only as a gate, but

[1] *Essays by Divers Hands.* Being the Transactions of the Royal Society of Literature of the United Kingdom. New Series. Vol. VI, edited by G. K. Chesterton. The Oxford University Press, 1926.
CONTENTS:—I The Royal Society of Literature: an Outline. By the Most Hon. The Marquess of Crewe, K.G., President, R.S.L.—II Ballads. By Mrs. Margaret L. Woods, F.R.S.L.—III A Franciscan Poet—Jacopone da Todi. By Evelyn Underhill, F.R.S.L.—IV Christina Rossetti. By Walter de la Mare, LL.D., F.R.S.L.—V Swinburne and Baudelaire. By the Hon. Harold Nicolson, C.M.G., F.R.S.L.—VI The Art of the Biographer. By A. C. Benson, Esq., C.V.O., LL.D., F.R.S.L.—VII Address by Mr. Rudyard Kipling.

as a ground-plan. It appears plainly enough in such an outline that this Society passed through certain changes parallel to the changes in the modern national history and not without reference to the most recent names. It was first encouraged by George the Fourth, a man who had the makings of a very fine, because a very free, patron of letters; for in his youth he loved not only literature, but liberty. He was broken by an abrupt degeneration never fully explained, but one which was certainly not entirely his own fault. Unfortunately it would hardly be an exaggeration to say that he died as a man on the day he was crowned as a king. In some ways, therefore, it would be an even better symbol if we could say that this Academy was patronized, not by George the Fourth, but by the Prince Regent. For the Regency had some kinship with the Romantic movement. There was in it something of the glow and glamour and extravagance of the revolutionary epoch—what made the French themselves describe a dandy as an Incredible. Thus we find, in Lord Crewe's account, that the very first phase of the Society was really liberal and literary; and a gleam of that old elemental light shines on it with the name of Coleridge. Then it would appear that the Society, like its founder, rather lost its hold on these larger and more liberal elements; and suffered, not indeed a degeneration, but what we may reasonably call a desiccation, and debated points of pure scholarship rather than of pure literature. Even in this period it doubtless did good service; but it was the sort of service that is done by antiquaries whose favourite reading is of obelisks and hieroglyphic epitaphs. Then it expanded once more, and in our own time has come to include every kind of literary man and some connected with even light forms of literature; including one, at least, innocent of the least influence of obelisks. Anyhow, it has come to include not only living, but very living, persons, of the most varied tastes and talents. The names attached to these lectures would be alone enough to prove that.

Now, taking Lord Crewe's outline as a sort of guide, we have here something like an explanation of the position and an answer to a very common criticism. It has been the custom to accuse an academy of being academic, though it was, in many cases, only an excuse for sneering at the French Academy for being French. It was common to say that such institutions neglect real genius, never encourage anything but official mediocrity, and trim the paradise of poetry into a suburban park, full of notices to keep off the grass. Such a scene does not immediately call up all the visions of Coleridge at the beginning of the story or of Mr. de la Mare at the end of it. But it may correspond to something in the middle; and the realization of what it was throws a certain light upon many of these studies. The intermediary period roughly corresponded to that in which an extreme individualism, based on rather cocksure arguments from commerce and economics, had made the English nation unnaturally suspicious of things like the French Academy. But it must always be remembered that the Early Victorians and Englishmen of the mid-nineteenth century, who felt this contempt for the academic method, had complete confidence in their own method. They were comparing the pedantry and futility of academies with the prosperity and success of the things in which they most believed —competition, publicity, the open market and the struggle for existence. Macaulay wrote a skit on a Royal Society of Literature on the parallel of a Royal Society of Wines, frankly using the commercial argument, that such a policy patronized the worst wine while competition produced the best. Thackeray made it an example of the pottering pomposity of George the Third that he wanted to have a finger in the literary pie as well as in the legendary dumpling. He chaffed the poor old patron of letters for having tried to found a sort of Literary Academy of his own— an Order of Minerva with a yellow ribbon, which

SOME FELLOWS

is not, so far as I know, among the insignia worn by the members of our own body. Thackeray demanded derisively what such a Tory organization would have done with Keats. But it is doubtful if things would have been any better though the ribbon had been a red ribbon or the academy a French academy newly inspired by the French Revolution. It is even more doubtful whether they would have been any better under the practical and public tests in which Macaulay and Thackeray believed. They assumed that a literary man need only be an honest tradesman appealing to the public, by which they always meant only the prosperous middle class. He would write for the papers, be reviewed by the papers, and so on. Patronage they regarded as a form of Protection and a blasphemy against Free Trade. But they did not see how they were answering their own argument about original genius and official mediocrity. It is not fair to pillory officials as slaves for neglecting what other people neglect even when they are free. Democracy, by its very virtues, would certainly have regarded Shelley with that hearty dislike which is not unfrequently the sentiment of democracy towards ideal democrats. Journalism did not exactly cover itself with glory in the episode of Keats. William Blake, enacting in his own back garden the part of the Image of God in its first innocence, was doubtless a highly unsuitable person to sit on the Academic Committee of the Royal Society of Literature, but not more unfitted to sit on the Committee than to walk down the street. The interesting papers in this collection have a certain common quality in the matter of answering his question. They all, in one way or another, throw light on the real answer and the reasonable defence of an academy. They all bear witness to the essential fact: that there are inevitably and in any case artists of a certain type or types, which cannot reasonably expect to be covered by the immediate comprehension either of academic judges or of anybody else. Their academic judges are no more to blame than their friends and neighbours, no more to blame than their fathers and mothers; last but not least, no more to blame than themselves. No theologian has claimed inspiration or even infallibility for the English Academy, or even the French Academy. And nothing short of Divine omniscience would enable academies, or patrons, or newspapers, or the public or anything else to discover every unique mind in every obscure or remote situation. It is as much as we can expect if a number of human beings will devote themselves to the study of such unique minds after they are discovered, if it be only after they are dead. It is as much as we can expect, in other words, if such unique minds, in spite of their oddity or obscurity, are seriously and sympathetically studied as they are studied in this book. Here many men are praised who might never have been patronized, never have been popularized, never under commercial competition perhaps even printed; but that is not the fault of the academies, but of the accidents and varieties of the human lot.

Of all this, Mrs. Margaret L. Woods offers a lucid and even radiant symbol in the figure of the old ballad-maker, in her graceful and wisely balanced essay upon Ballads. As she points out, poetry can be communal in the sense that the general movement of dance and chorus is communal, but a fine poem cannot be literally communal, in the sense of a hundred people writing it at once or composing it as a mosaic by each contributing a word. A poem requires a poet; and a poem like *Sir Patrick Spens* or the Northumbrain ballad of Edward requires a very fine poet. Yet it would obviously be unjust to blame the central authorities of that presumably feudal period because a natural genius existed in Northumbria or Lothian, while only Petrarch received the crown of laurel or only Chaucer received the butt of sack. The localism of feudal life, the slowness of communications on the marches and a thousand other things made it impossible for any prince or patron to pretend he had an exact mental map of the whole world with the undiscovered peaks drawn to scale. And the same difficulty, in a more modern form, is illustrated in all the literary problems treated here. Miss Evelyn Underhill deals with a type of medieval poet who, unlike the ballad-maker, did really have a chance and did really gain a reputation. The Franciscan troubadour Jacopone da Todi, living in the centre of religious culture and playing a part in a great social movement, was of the sort to be noticed in his own time, but also of the sort to be neglected at a later time. And yet he does not deserve to be neglected at any time. It was part of the anti-academic cant to dwell incessantly on the tragedy of a man despised during his life and only praised by posterity after his death. And it is part of the reasonable case for academies that the flat contrary is very often the case. Not only bad writers, but good writers, are often an inspiration to their contemporaries and only a puzzle to posterity. Jacopone da Todi is not praised by posterity, but by Miss Evelyn Underhill. It needs a critic of her delicate veracity and deep reading of the logic of the mystics to appreciate such a historic figure; and that appreciation is much more likely to be academic than commercial. She herself gives a good example in the

SOME FELLOWS

phrase that the modern world would imagine to be a piece of nonsense out of Lear or Lewis Carroll, but which she traces back to a profound truth of St. Augustine; the saying that the Catholic system is a thing in which an elephant could swim and a lamb could wade.

The other papers offer many examples of subjects not thus remote in time, but equally remote in essence. The Professorial Lecture itself, by Mr. Walter de la Mare, is a patient and penetrating study of Christina Rossetti, who was emphatically, if we may use the term, a very private person. It would be silly to explain at length why Christina Rossetti could never be a centre of artistic gossip like Dante Gabriel Rossetti or a centre of political excitement like William Michael Rossetti. It is unlikely that she would be offered a seat on any committee, but equally unlikely that she would be given a booth in any market—even a goblin market. The truth is better expressed in a more poetical form, by saying that Mr. de la Mare is the sort of troubadour who can be imagined as wandering at twilight and finding the lonely turret in which some veiled princess, with averted face, sings her rare and solitary songs. But the practical, if less actual, way of stating it is to say that Christina Rossetti is just the kind of person who is liable to be much too much neglected by posterity unless there is a more concentrated tradition of culture to preserve her name. Something of the sort is equally true, if in a lesser degree, of a rather elusive person like Baudelaire, and a simple yet rather self-deceiving person like Swinburne, as treated in the apt and accurate analysis of Mr. Nicolson. Swinburne was a nine years' wonder and Baudelaire might well be a nine hundred years' mystery; but the peculiar political and philosophical enthusiasms which supported Swinburne are now rather more remote from us than those which supported Jacopone da Todi. At least the secularist republicans of *Songs Before Sunrise* would be considerably surprised at the sun that has actually risen, and would have been quite as much prepared for a Franciscan as for a Fascist. To study that sort of enthusiasm, to be just to it, to compare it as Mr. Nicolson does with the isolated and inverted asceticism of Baudelaire, requires a criticism akin to scholarship.

A still stronger example can be found in the thoughtful study of the whole nature of biography by the late Dr. A. C. Benson. He notes that among the very best biographies of literary men is that of a man who really produced no literature. Carlyle's portrait of Sterling is all the more vivid to us because it is all that is left of Sterling. He was, as the critic notes, exactly one of those men who can only live in memory, but who in memory are very living. The preservation of that sort of portrait, like the preservation of fine works belonging to dead fashions or forgotten movements, must, in its nature, be the work of a group standing somewhat apart. Such a group will not pretend to catch every such personality as it flashes past; but it will profess to be more interested in them than most other people are after they have flashed past. And it will bring to its task, let us hope, a healthy humility about the rapidity with which most of us flash past, if we ever have the good fortune to flash at all. That humility is the burden of the very modest and dignified fragment of eloquence which Mr. Rudyard Kipling contributed to the records of this Society, which was delivered when he was awarded the Gold Medal of that body, and with which this volume closes. It has already become something of a journalistic joke that he said that a handful of men only had gained immortality; but no journalist like myself is quite so deficient in the apprehension of a joke as to suppose that any of us fancy ourselves in such a company. It is not we but the word that is winged and is immortal; and our only ambition is to help the Divine gift of language and letters to outlive us all.

RHYMES FOR CHILDREN[1]

THIS old-fashioned school of poetry for children has long been derided in essays and articles written by adults. Children do not write essays or articles. Or at least as only a few of them have yet been encouraged to write novels and books of verse, we may hope that the day of solid sociological studies and scientific volumes of history, written by our smaller infants, is still some way off. There are more ways than one of committing infanticide; and one way is to murder the infancy without murdering the infant. I am far from saying that some of our large educational experiments may not effect a sweeping change on a scale that would satisfy King Herod. But speaking generally, it is still true that the normal child, as distinct from the precocious child, has little or no opportunities of recording what he really likes in any permanent critical form. Children cannot ask for what they really want, as distinct from what they are supposed to want. If they could,

[1] *Grandmamma's Book of Rhymes*, by Elizabeth Turner. The Oxford University Press, 1927.

RHYMES FOR CHILDREN

the adult satirists would be surprised. For they would probably discover that these old moral rhymes were far more like the mind of a child than anything that has been written since.

First of all, they are in a technical sense exactly adapted to their end. Somebody said that when we distinguish between poetry and verse, we must still go on to distinguish between good verse and bad verse. Nobody will pretend that these narratives are poetry; but it is true that they are models of good verse:

> 'Yesterday Rebecca Mason
> In the parlour by herself
> Broke a handsome china basin
> Placed upon the mantel-shelf.'

That is a model of a mere rhyme. The china basin itself was not more smooth or more rounded. Half-way through we seem to feel prophetically that all the syllables will exactly fall and fit into their places. And this always gives an air of ease which is never achieved by mere laxity. The thing does what free verse never does; it flows freely. It fills the mouth and the memory like something friendly and familiar; something in which we are not likely to go wrong. At any rate it answers exactly to what a child means by a rhyme to be repeated; or rather a rhyme that repeats itself. So a hoop seems to run of itself, or a top seems to spin of itself, after the first impulsion from without; because they are both smooth and round and of a simple shape. There may be a new and more mathematical pastime, consisting of bowling hoops of an oval or elliptical pattern and noting the angles of reaction or rebound; but it can hardly be so soothing a pastime. There may be tops that spin on some unexpected or paradoxical principle, according to a paper of instructions by Professor Einstein; but anyone spinning them must be a little more self-conscious. Rhymes that go round and round without a jolt, like hoops and tops that go round and round without a stagger, satisfy something subconscious in all children and most normal adults; even if the thing of which these are broken rhythms is but a mighty lullaby.

Indeed it is upon the moral rather than the metrical side that the modern attack is generally delivered; and I need not say that these verses are generally attacked for being moral, in the sense of moralizing. Certainly it cannot be denied that they do moralize, as we should say in the most pompous and priggish and censorious fashion. But even here there is a great deal more to be said than the modern satirists have allowed for. For various reasons, most of us nowadays do not like literature to be quite so moral and didactic. But there is scarcely a grain of evidence to show that *children* do not like literature to be moral and didactic. And the truth is that they like it very much. Nobody has ever told stories to children without realizing how very particular they are about poetical justice and a sort of domestic day of judgment. They insist, entirely of their own motion, not only that the good should be rescued, not even that the good should be rewarded, but especially that the wicked should be punished. I remember telling a tiny little boy the whole story of Roncesvaux and the rear-guard of Charlemagne; of how Roland blew his horn in vain and Ganelon the traitor, riding by the king, told him it was but the cry of a bird; so that the king's army turned back too late and found Roland dead, and could only avenge him with victory after victory, with which rousing prospect my narrative ended. But the little boy was not to be carried away by that cavalry charge or led on triumphant into Spain. He said, with an innocent intensity and eagerness straight out of his unspoilt self: 'What did they do to Ganelon?'

The incidents recorded in these rhymes will not immediately recall the crags of the Pyrenees or the crown and sword of Charlemagne. But the moral of the tales is there because writers as well as readers were childlike, not because they were unchildlike; and because justice is still as simple as the Song of Roland. That a great many grown-up people do not find justice quite so simple does not even prove that they are right; far less does it prove that they are more fitted to write songs for children. The truth is that we are wrong to bring our doubts into this matter of childish literature, even when we ourselves have some excuse for them. The dislike of moralizing is entirely a mature or adult dislike. It comes from certain complexities that we know better than children do; but which we are not necessarily the better for knowing. For instance, we are acquainted with hypocrisy. We have been sickened of certain moral sentiments because we know they are used for immoral objects; by politicians who betray their country or philanthropists who oppress the poor. But a child knows nothing about hypocrisy. For him the moral terms mean simply and solely what they say; and what they say is perfectly true. A child has not had the English language spoilt for him by American journalism or German philosophy. A child has not seen words cheapened by stunts and slogans and the sophistries of snobs and time-servers. To him breaking a promise is something as definite as breaking a dish; not to be explained away like the promises of great statesmen. To him helping 'a poor lame man' really is helping a poor lame man; and not either investigating a 'case' (presumed to be that of a liar and a fraud) or getting a secretarial salary for organizing a hundred lame men to walk in a row. The child knows nothing of how vicious a thing we have made out of virtue; or how much evil we do by doing good.

To some extent, of course, it is true that changing manners put these particular Early Victorian childish pictures out of fashion. If a child finds it rather harder to remain childish, in the present ugly and uncomfortable social transition, it is also true, no doubt, that even a simple child might now find some of these things rather crude than simple. That amount of archaism clings inevitably to any transition in human history. The costumes of the children would alone be at once a delight and a derision. Even here perhaps the comicality of the contrast cuts both ways. Our ancestors dressed up children in antiquated bonnets and gowns and trousers, but they allowed them the happiness of having immature minds. There is such a thing as a modern household where the child is dressed as a new-born fairy fresh from an opening flower and treated as a sophisticated hedonist weary of all dissipations except the divorce court. But the quaint costume and setting of these tales serves admirably the artistic purpose of making a sort of new elf-land. Indeed, strangely enough, it is not very far from the borders of the very newest elf-lands. It is a case where extremes meet; and this simplification has been sought by some who are accused of the very extreme of sophistication. We know that it has been one of the most adventurous of the movements of the Later Georgian to restore the credit of the Early Victorian. There is a poem of Miss Edith Sitwell's about a little girl walking beside a donkey with panniers that might have been written to illustrate one of these verses; or rather to illustrate one of their illustrations. It would be rather entertaining to go through one of these poems word by word, altering the adjectives to suit the Sitwell muse or giving such a turn to the imagery as might further accentuate the quaintness of the landscape. The lines that run:

'They quickly tied their hats, and talked
Of yellow lilac, pink and green,'

seems to me essentially very Sitwellian; like the row of paints while still in the paint-box and before they are so boldly scattered over earth and sky. 'John White flew his kite on a boisterous day' seems to me quite promising, if the epithet were a little more boisterous than 'boisterous', and if the flowers and clouds were compared to coloured paper by a natural association of ideas. For I have a suspicion that Miss Sitwell and her friends are only trying, by rather rambling and mazy paths, to find that forgotten corner of the garden where these children are at play.

THE ENGLISH PEASANT [1]

MR. HESELTINE here speaks with authority, though certainly not with arrogance; and perhaps the writer of a preface may for once justify his existence by saying this of the author more definitely than he can say it of himself. He has practised what he preached; or rather (for there is a fine and not merely fanciful distinction) he has preached what he practised. He is not like some pedant who first draws up a plan on paper and then long afterwards is induced to let it be carried out in bricks and mortar, or more probably in plaster and stucco. He is not like some aged professor eventually visiting the South Sea Islands to test a theory thrown out in a Cambridge Common Room. The sense of private life and practical action comes very much first with him; and he is expounding realities which he knows from the inside to be real. He has known all the difficulties and disadvantages of trying to live the

[1] *The Change: Essays on the Land*, by G. C. Heseltine. Messrs. Sheed & Ward, 1927.

true life of a peasant in a diseased industrial society. We can teach him nothing about those disadvantages and difficulties, and he can teach us a great deal about the advantages and the virtues.

The general moral of all these studies can hardly be missed though it may in some quarters be misrepresented. But it can be represented rightly under a great many different figures or formulas. One way of stating it is this: that the writer fills up with solid stuff the rather empty outline left by that attenuated and starved and grossly ill-treated word Culture. He makes us understand how a word that sounds so bookish is nevertheless an integral part of words like agriculture and horticulture. Matthew Arnold, with excellent intentions, probably did a good deal to uphold this urban fallacy when he connected culture chiefly with literature; so that it has come to survive in the libraries of an utterly uncultured person like Andrew Carnegie rather than in the workshops of a really cultured person like William Morris. Books can be ordered wholesale like bottles of beer; and if they are consumed more slowly, it is sometimes because they are not consumed at all. But arts must be learnt individually, and taught individually, because they are creative even in their humblest or most limited form. Therefore a man can impose education without having it himself. But a man cannot hand on tradition without having it himself. In modern times we have had a vast increase in the sort of education that the ignorant can impose and a vast decrease in the sort of instruction that only the instructed can provide. The politician, who merely declares that so many thousand copies of such and such standard works shall be distributed to such and such schools, is in that exact sense an ignorant man. The agricultural labourer, who shows his son how to use a pruning-hook, is in that exact sense a learned man. And if we ask how this obvious truth came to be neglected at the end of the nineteenth century, the answer is that the commercial spirit overshadowed a number of people not at all consciously commercial. Matthew Arnold would have been very much horrified at being thus associated with Carnegie and his libraries; he would have been quite capable of appreciating the superiority of Morris and his crafts. Nevertheless, the germ of the error does lie in that definition of Culture which he thought so comprehensive, knowing the best that has been said and thought on this or that subject. It is a good definition within the field of literature; but the field of culture is much wider than the field of literature. And what is much worse, the definition leaves out the whole of that field which is the most fruitful of all. Culture is not only knowing the best that has been said; it is also knowing the best that has been done, and even doing our best to do it. Literature may be half creative and half critical; but there is a sort of creation which is entirely creative and in no sense critical. It is only by diversion, and in exceptional cases, that the agricultural labourer could be found criticizing his neighbour with a bill-hook. Even that is perhaps rather the difference between creation and destruction than between creation and criticism. But the agricultural labourer does make a hedge with a bill-hook as much as a sculptor makes a statue of Hercules with a chisel. In both cases there may be people to whom the act seems merely destructive or negative, the one producing only a litter of twigs and the other only a litter of chips. But that is only because there are people who do not know the hedge when they see it, and people who do not know the hero when they see him. In both cases a man knows how to make something; and therefore may be able to teach somebody else something about how it is made. But it must be taught by a man; it cannot be taught by a machine. It cannot be taught by a machinery for supplying people with books, any more than by a gigantic engine for pelting them with chisels. In this sense the agricultural

THE ENGLISH PEASANT

labours that Mr. Heseltine calls crafts are really and truly arts, whose generation is from artist to artist. You cannot teach a man broad-cast sowing by broadcasting lectures on the subject.

Mr. Heseltine, who actually begins with this example of the bill-hook, goes on to make very vivid notes of various other examples of the same thing. Thus, for instance, he takes the excellent example of thatching. Thatching has a thousand practical conveniences, as he points out; it probably also has a certain number of inconveniences; it is rather the way of things in this vale of tears. But the grotesque disproportion which has led to the destruction of so many useful things in the countryside can only be estimated by comparing them once again with the sort of things that come from the town to destroy them. For example, it is assumed suddenly and superficially, on the mere look of the thing, that thatch threatens a special danger from fire; though it does not really fulfil the threat any more than multitudes of other things. But imagine the same argument being employed to arrest the advance of the other things, especially the modern and mechanical things. Imagine forbidding houses to be supplied with gas; because gas poisons people and candles do not (even if you eat them), because gas acts like gunpowder and wax or tallow have no such expanding properties. Imagine a general veto at this moment on the use of petrol; because that witch's oil has always been recognized as inflammable and deadly, ever since it was hurled as Greek fire among the Crusaders and the Saracens. These things threaten danger far more obviously and immediately than thatch; but people take the risk because they want to run the race, especially with a very expensive racing-car. In other words, the purely practical objections to most of these old crafts and traditions are not practical objections at all. They are in the true sense theoretical objections; that is, they are examples offered as excuses for not accepting the theory on which the civilization of the peasant rests.

With that conception of the peasant, in the real sense of the peasant proprietor, Mr. Heseltine deals here in a series of articles which I had the great pleasure of publishing in a paper with which I am connected. With the theoretical side of it I have dealt in many other places, and with the practical side of it he is much more qualified to deal than I. But my justification in appearing for a moment in this place is not so much the opportunity of introducing him as the pleasure of thanking him for having brought so much new vigour and clarity of mind to the support of our common cause; to what is in strict truth the only human cure for that human evil: the separation of man from all that he makes, whether that separation be effected by a theory or a machine.

DICKENS'S FORSTER[1]

A GOOD book of biography is one in which the book vanishes and the man remains; not the man who wrote the book but the man about whom it was written. At the end of Forster's *Life of Dickens* we are admiring Dickens and not admiring Forster; and that alone is a good reason for Forster being admired. Most reasonable readers will agree that Forster does achieve this essential purpose of making Dickens visible and himself invisible; though in the real friendship of the two men the less famous man bulked large and was sometimes, it is said, even a shade too positive. It is this which makes Dickens's biography in some sense a fitting sequel to Dickens's books. The genius of Dickens has been very variously estimated and defined; but perhaps the best rough summary of it is this. He was a man whose imagination could draw other men out, in the sense of developing some germ of fun or folly in them which mere life

[1] *The Life of Charles Dickens*, by John Forster. Everyman's Library. Messrs. J. M. Dent & Sons, Ltd., 1927.

was not warm enough to germinate. He exaggerated them because they could not exaggerate themselves. Some small irony, some innocent inconsistency, some fortunately unfortunate phrase, had for him a principle of life in it which could be extended with living logic and varied with tropical exuberance. The bee in the bonnet or the maggot in the brain were insects which became gigantic as dragons, in his microscope. If anyone falls into the affected folly of despising this Dickensian art as 'mere caricature' there is only one answer to him, if indeed he is worth answering. Let him become a caricaturist. He will soon find out whether caricature is always crude and whether it is never subtle. Let any man do to his own friends what Dickens did to his. Let him take a trivial word and turn it into a man or even a monster. He will not do it; but the task will keep him quiet.

If it was the genius of Dickens to draw everybody out, it is only justice to say that it was the talent of Forster to draw Dickens out. He could not always draw him; even when as in the case of *Edwin Drood* (of which a word may be said presently) it is possible that he imagined that he had. Nor was the drawing out of that triumphant and almost faultless kind which exists in the great model of biography. He could not draw Dickens out as Boswell could draw Johnson out. He did not even attempt to do so in anything like the same series of ingenious interviews. But his own success was of the same essential sort; though he generally achieved it more by reporting correspondence than conversation. He understood that he had to deal with an individuality that was interesting not only in public but in private; though he observed a Victorian restraint (for which some will think none the worse of him) concerning the private things that can be public and the private things that had better be private. But the essentials of such a biographical success remain the same. In dealing with Dickens he was dealing not only with a creator but with a character; we might almost say with a Dickens character. Dickens must be encouraged to give himself away; as it is the essence of every Dickens character to give itself away. And in the case of Dickens, as of the Dickens characters, it is the very best of gifts. There was indeed a certain real reserve behind the external exuberance of Dickens's correspondence and conversation; but that is concerned with other private problems; and I am only speaking of the spontaneous effect of being introduced to a character, as in a club or an evening party. And this sense of a personality, or what is commonly called a portrait, does certainly emerge from the letters and memories preserved by Forster. Anybody who will try to make such a literary portrait of any one of his personal friends will soon find out how difficult is the achievement and how high is the praise. The life of Dickens is not like the life of the Victorian poet or politician; which was often not so much a matter of painting a portrait as of white-washing a portrait. We do receive a very vivid impression of a very vivacious person; we do feel that he is walking briskly about the street and not that he is lying in a coffin helpless under funeral orations; and that is victory in the arduous art of biography.

A biographical success of that sort must be judged as a whole. It is not reasonable to argue about every opinion of the biographer, so long as he has given us the material for forming our own opinion. It is not a question of everything that he thinks about Dickens; but of the fact that he has given us a Dickens to think about. We cannot even think about the whited sepulchre of the purely official biography. In the great model already mentioned, James Boswell as an individual utters many opinions that seem almost meant to make him look silly; and a few that seem almost meant to make his friend look silly. He was not perhaps competent to be the critic of Dr. Johnson. And yet he was competent to be the creator of Dr. Johnson. He made him over again as a great character in fiction is made; and that impression is a general impression, that has nothing to do with the accuracy of his own detached individual thoughts. But this principle of common sense, which has been commonly conceded in the case of Boswell, has occasionally been rather neglected in the case of Forster. A lady whose opinion has the highest authority in the matter has hinted that Forster as a friend took himself a little too seriously. Curiously enough, she seemed to give this as a reason for herself taking him almost equally seriously. She suggested that he was a little touchy and exacting in the matter of secrets being kept from him, and no doubt she was right; but it seems doubtful whether we can draw the inference that none were kept. And indeed, in the particular case at issue, it seems to me much more probable that the secrets were sometimes all the more carefully kept.

It is in the affair of *The Mystery of Edwin Drood* that this problem principally arises; and it may well serve as an example. Forster himself reports Dickens as saying that he had conceived a new and original idea for that story, an idea very difficult to work and one which must not be revealed beforehand, or the interest of the story would be gone. And yet, strangely enough, this is the very passage upon which many Dickensians base their insistence that the idea *was* revealed beforehand; so that the interest of the story presumably *was* gone, even before the story was begun. They base this inference on the fact that Forster, a few lines lower down, proceeds to say that the point of this crime story was to be the peculiar form taken by the confession of the criminal; that he was to tell his own story as if it were the story of another. Now it seems quite obvious to me that this is merely an example of one of those accidental confusions which may occur easily when a man does not very strictly connect the sentence he is writing with a sentence he wrote recently in another connexion. Forster does not mean that the mode of confession constituted the revelation of the great idea which Dickens admittedly refused to reveal. Obviously it could not be; the autobiographical antic of John Jasper could not *be* the mystery of Edwin Drood. He only means that this was to be the point of the confession scene, which Dickens had described as distinct from the main mystery which he had refused to describe. Forster only means that this was a very interesting feature of the scheme; and he leaves this slight ambiguity because he was a human being who had no call to be a faultless logician or a radiantly lucid literary man; but was simply a good biographer writing about a man he knew in a natural and ordinary way. But in this case critics have refused to allow poor Forster to write in a natural and ordinary way. They have not allowed him to have any accidental ambiguities. They have treated every line of a long and variegated biography as if it were a sworn affidavit examined by lawyers and corrected by logicians. They have cried aloud that we are calling Forster a liar or Dickens a hypocrite if we say there was an ambiguity; though Forster actually tells us that Dickens actually told him that there was meant to be an ambiguity. They regard Forster as infallible in everything except the one definite fact that he does definitely record; that Dickens refused to tell him the secret. Thus whenever anybody talks naturally of the 'murder' of a man whom the reader at least supposes to be murdered, they draw the strict logical inference that the victim could not possibly have escaped from the man who was trying to murder him. This is, under the circumstances, quite fantastically far-fetched. It does not allow for the ordinary elliptical way in which all men speak even about a story they know; let alone a story they do not know; a story which they have actually been prevented from knowing. Who would not naturally talk of the story of Bradley Headstone as the study of a murderer, although his victim does in fact recover? But what should we say if Dickens had deliberately hidden the story of

DICKENS'S FORSTER

Eugene Wrayburn and had only mentioned one aspect of Bradley's broodings to illustrate Bradley's character? Would any man in his senses infer from the phrase 'murder' being used at second-hand in such a vague forecast, that Lizzie Hexham could not possibly help her wounded lover to get well? Yet this is rigidly and relentlessly done in the case of the mystery of Edwin Drood, even when Forster has admitted that it was a mystery to him. He must be not only logically but literally exact. He must be literally exact not only in what he says, but in what can be indirectly and rather doubtfully inferred from what he says. Above all, he must be exact not only about what he says that he knows, but about what he distinctly says that he does not know. Assuredly it was not only John Forster who took John Forster too seriously.

As a matter of fact, his merits as much as his limitations make him the very last man in the world to be treated in this strict and stringent fashion. It is not the least virtue in the biography of the great Victorian novelist that it is itself a very Victorian book; full of that delightful air of ease and sanity and social comfort which is the lost secret of that historical interlude. In this sense the life of Dickens is less like a book of Dickens than like a book of Trollope. Forster gives us a hundred opportunities of getting to know the man; he is not intensely interested in intellectual things except as they affect a man. This is the last sort of spirit and atmosphere in which we should look for this sort of mathematical precision, or litigious vigilance. His chief charm is the air of amplitude and largesse with which he scatters before us the scraps and scribbles of a man of genius, the admirable letters of Dickens; and shows how much true creative literature there was in his post-bag and even his wastepaper basket.

A SHROPSHIRE LASS [1]

MANY of us can remember the revelation of poetical power given to the world with the songs of a Shropshire Lad. Much of the noble, though more neglected, work of Mary Webb might be called the prose poems of a Shropshire Lass. Most of them spoke in the spirit, and many through the mouth, of some young peasant woman in or near that western county which lies, romantic and rather mysterious, upon the marches of Wales. Such a Shropshire Lass was the narrator of *Precious Bane*; such a one is the heroine, and a very heroic heroine, of *The Golden Arrow*. But the comparison suggested above involves something more than the coincidence of a county and a social type. Those two writers of genius, devoted to the genius of Shropshire and the western shires, do really stand for two principles in all living literature to-day; and especially in all literature concerned with the very ancient but very modern

[1] *The Golden Arrow*, by Mary Webb. Messrs. Jonathan Cape, Ltd., 1928.

subject of the peasantry. I do not put them side by side here for comparison, in the paltry sense of competition. I have the strongest admiration for both literary styles and both literary achievements. But the comparison is perhaps the clearest and most rapid way of representing what is really peculiar to writers like Mary Webb and to books like *The Golden Arrow*.

There are two ways of dealing with the dignity, the pain, the prejudice or the rooted humour of the poor; especially of the rural poor. One of them is to see in their tragedy only a stark simplicity, like the outline of a rock; the other is to see in it an unfathomable though a savage complexity, like the labyrinthine complexity of a living forest. The Shropshire Lad threw on all objects of the landscape a hard light like that of morning, in which all things are angular and solid; but most of all the gravestone and the gallows. The light in the stories of the Shropshire Lass is a light not shining on things, but through them. It is that mysterious light in which solid things become semi-transparent; a diffused light which some call the twilight of superstition and some the ultimate violet ray of the sixth sense of man; but which the strictest rationalist will hardly deny to have been the luminous atmosphere of a great part of literature and legend. In one sense it is the light that never was on sea or land, and

A SHROPSHIRE LASS

in another sense the light without which sea and land are invisible; but at least it is certain that without that dark ray of mystery and superstition, there might never have been any love of the land or any songs of the sea. Nobody doubts that peasantries have in the past, as a matter of fact, been rooted in all sorts of strange tales and traditions, like the legend of The Golden Arrow. The only difference is between two ways of treating this fact in the two schools of rural romance or poetry. For the pessimist of the school of Housman or of Hardy, the grandeur of poverty is altogether in the pathos of it. He is only softened by hard facts; by the hard facts of life and death. The beliefs of the peasant are a mere tangle of weeds at the feet of the pessimist; it is only the unbelief of the peasant, the disillusion and despair of the peasant, which remind the pessimist of dignity and warm him with respect. There is nobility in the benighted darkness of the hero; but there is no light or enlightenment, except from the atheism of the author. The poor man is great in his sufferings; but not in anything for which he suffered. His traditions are a tangle of weeds; but his sorrows are a crown of thorns. Only there is no nimbus round the crown of thorns. There is no nimbus round anything. The pessimist sees nothing but nakedness and a certain grandeur in nakedness; and he sees the poor man as a man naked in the winter wind.

But the poor man does not see himself like that. He has always wrapped himself up in shreds and patches which, while they were as wild as rags, were as emblematic as vestments; rags of all colours that were worn even more for decoration than for comfort. In other words, he has had a mass of beliefs and half-beliefs, of ancestral ceremonies, of preternatural cures and preternatural consolations. It is amid this tangle of traditions that he has groped and not merely in a bleak vacuum of negation; it is in this enchanted forest that he has been lost so long, and not merely on the open moor; and it is in this rich confusion of mystical and material ideas that the rural characters of Mary Webb walk from the first page to the last.

Now we may well for the moment leave the controversy open, as to whether these works make the rustic too transcendental, or whether the works of the pessimists make him too pessimistic. But something like a serious historical answer can be found in the very existence of many of the rustic fables, or even of the rustic names. It is very difficult to believe that any people so brutal, so bitter, so stupid and stunted as the English rustics are sometimes represented in realistic literature could ever have invented, or even habitually used and lived in the atmosphere of, such things as the popular names for the country flowers, or the ordinary place names and topographical terms for the valleys and streams of England. It looks rather like bad psychology to believe that those who talked of traveller's joy were never joyful, that those who burdened their tongues with the title of love-lies-bleeding were never tender or romantic, or that the man who thought of some common green growth as Our Lady's bedstraw was incapable of chivalry or piety. The characters in the romances of Mary are the sort of rustics who might have invented such names. The Golden Arrow itself would be a name of exactly such a nature, whether it were invented by the natives or invented by the novelist. The legend of The Golden Arrow, which lovers went wandering to find, 'and went with apple-blow scent round 'em, and a mort o' bees, and warmship, and wanted nought of any man', is a myth bearing witness, as do all myths and mythologies, to the ancient beauty for which man was made, and which men are always unmaking. But this mystical or mythological sense would not be genuine, if it did not admit the presence of an evil as well as a good that is beyond the measure of man. One of the things that makes a myth so true is that it is always in black and white. And so its mysticism is always in black magic as well as white magic. It is never merely optimistic, like a new religion made to order. And just as in *Precious Bane*, the old necromancer was driven by an almost demoniac rage to raise up the ghost of the Pagan Goddess, so in *The Golden Arrow*, a man is lured into the ancient and mazy dance of madness by that heathen spirit of fear which inhabits the high places of the earth, and the peaks where the brain grows dizzy. These things in themselves might be as tragic as anything in the realistic tragedies; but the point to seize is the presence of something positive and sacramental on the other side; a heroism that is not negative but affirmative; a saintship with the power to cast out demons; expressed in that immemorial popular notion of an antidote to a poison and a counter-charm against a witch.

The characterization in *The Golden Arrow*, if rather less in scope than that in *Precious Bane*, is sometimes even more vivid within its limits. The difference between the two girls, brought up under the same limitations, observing the same strict rural conventions, feeling the same natural instincts in two ways which are ten thousand miles apart, is very skilfully achieved within the unities of a single dialect and a single scene. And through one of them there passes, once or twice, like the noise and rushing of the Golden

Arrow, that indescribable exaltation and breathing of the very air of better things; which, coming now and again in human books, can make literature more living than life.

SONGS FROM THE SPIRIT [1]

IT is usual, in writing such a preface as this, for the writer to commend the enclosed verses to the reader. In this particular case, however, such a form would fall short of truth. It would not in any case, perhaps, be wise to depreciate the reader. It would be less than tactful in the introducer to taunt and revile the reader, or the whole art of reading. The reader doubtless has his virtues; the quiet, laborious virtues of the student. Nevertheless, in the event of any arrogance, the reader must be firmly told that he is not the only pebble on the beach, or the only person in the world, and that these priceless words were not written for him alone. In a word, these songs are intended to be sung; and not merely, in a base and mechanical manner, to be read. The reader who is only a reader cannot truly be said even to have read them. The reader who does not, on beholding the first few lines, instantly burst into song or into some sort

[1] *Drinking Songs and Other Songs,* by W. R. Titterton. Cecil Palmer, 1928.

SONGS FROM THE SPIRIT

of loud bellowing noise, is devoid of critical delicacy and *finesse*. It is unfortunate that this test, which is the triumph and glory of the songs, is also the condemnation and complete extinction of the preface. Obviously, a thing meant to be sung ought to have no preface. Can we be sure that anyone, on reading these prose paragraphs of mine, will instantly carol them aloud to an impromptu or a popular air? Alas, it is by no means certain.

I know that these songs, especially those at the beginning of the book, are songs that can really be sung, because I have sung them myself; and a more complete proof of lyrical adaptability and the powerful contagion of melody could not be found. The author, who is an old friend of mine and an older friend of Fleet Street, has led these choruses in many companies that I remember with gratitude and entertainment; in many gatherings in the brave days of old, before some of the bravest left us for even better things. For the tradition of the festive chorus, which is one of the oldest things of human history, had descended to us by a tradition unconscious and unbroken; and the last men of Grub Street sang in their taverns as naturally as the first barbarians sang round their camp-fires. We did not have to be taught to do it. We did not call it Community Singing. We called it singing. Whether even that was not too friendly and favourable a description of it, we were in no mood so cold and unconvivial as to discuss. I hasten to say that I intend no aspersion of the Community Singing movement as a movement; I have no doubt it is an excellent and necessary movement. At least it is certainly excellent if it is necessary. But I cannot help mildly wondering why it should be necessary. I have no doubt that when the habit of human laughter has temporarily disappeared under the influence of Evolutionary Ethics and Uplift, it will be recovered by something called the Individual Mirth Movement; and I shall (with my dying breath) strongly approve of that movement. But I shall think it odd that men should have left off laughing in the middle of the twentieth century, as I do that they left off singing in the middle of the nineteenth. I am all the more proud of sharing in a custom that bridged the abyss of the industrial anarchy, in which so many bridges were broken.

For the rest, if songs that can really be sung are not meant merely to be read, still less are they meant merely to be reviewed. To weigh down the wings of these soaring lyrics with a load of commentary would be equally incongruous whether it were compliment or criticism. The writer of these songs has very definite ideals and principles of his own, for which he has sacrificed much in his time; but it is only very indirectly that they are indicated in the sort of levities which the serious, who are shallow but not light, may read in a more literal fashion. For that quality in certain modern intellectuals, by which they do not sing when they sing, is the same by which they do not think when they think, or pray when they pray, or fight when they fight, or define when they define. All that ought to be made clear and decisive they leave loose and vague; all that ought to be loose and vague, like songs and lighter memories, they would probably explore and correct with a pedantic pen. To such we need offer no defence or explanation, save in a most general fashion; leaving them to ponder on our inexplicable cheerfulness and to call a parody a paradox. It will be enough to inform them gravely that we do not offer the poem about King Solomon as a contribution to the Higher Criticism of the Hebrew Scriptures, or to the solution of the Sex Problem in modern fiction. Nor do we account the lines upon the town of Ickenham a complete sociological survey of the merits of that suburb; or as any kind of substitute for a reliable Fabian tract on the expansion of the modern town. Mr. Titterton and I have been engaged for many years past in fighting for what I will not call a forlorn hope; for I think that our demeanour at least has been rather hopeful than forlorn. We have indeed had various things to say about these serious matters; about Fabianism, or suburbs, or sex problems, or the Higher Criticism. We have been engaged in urging what we regard as the return to a more normal human society; which, instead of following the Capitalists to the last extreme of their modern mania for concentration, should rather reverse the process and return to a reasonable equality of distribution. In that sense, if any malicious person likes to take advantage of the confession, we have sometimes been serious. In that sense, if any enemy would press the charge home, we have been intermittently guilty of public spirit. But the enemy will look in vain, through many pages of verse here provided for him, for any definite details of the crime. These songs have nothing to do with the Distributist State, except that in the Distributist State men may perhaps be happy enough to sing them.

THE CURÉ D'ARS [1]

THE Catholic Church is much too universal to be called international, for she is older than all the nations. She is not some sort of new bridge to be built between these separated islands; she is the very earth and ocean-bed on which they are built. Nevertheless, as she has always been able to work through variety as well as uniformity, she is now able to appeal to the nations as nations, but to appeal to them rather to learn from each other than to lie about each other. The Catholic nations are very national; but each has specialized in some spiritual truth, rather as each of the Catholic Guilds specialized in some technical trade. So the fullness and kindliness of the Faith has abounded in Flemish art and folk-lore; so the fire and chivalry of it in Polish history and tradition. The Spaniard has splendidly maintained in poverty that human dignity which he never wholly lost even under the load of wealth. The Irish have kept a

[1] *The Secret of the Curé d'Ars* (translated by F. J. Sheed), by Henri Ghéon. Messrs. Sheed & Ward, 1929.

clear space for that strange purity of the mind, in which even hatred has become something clean and translucent, compared with the loves of other lands. In the same fashion, French Catholicism gathers up and gives expression to the vital virtues of France, of which (needless to say) it was the creator in the dim and turbulent age when Gauls and Franks became a nation. And it is of the very nature of France that the French Catholic should emphasize the fact that the Church is a challenge.

In this case we feel at its worst the weakening of the word 'apologetics' for the defence of Christian dogma, and the verbal degeneration by which the defiant thing once called an apologia has dwindled to the feeble thing called an apology. In fact, of course, an apologia is almost the opposite of an apology. But it is true, and it may in some cases even be fortunate, that men of a somewhat milder type or tradition have often defended Christianity, and even Catholicism, in a tone that was deprecating and tactful, and might have seemed to some to be apologetic. There is nothing of this sort about the typical French Catholic. There is nothing of this sort about M. Henri Ghéon. There was nothing of this sort about the Curé d'Ars. The first fact that will strike anyone outside the Catholic Church, and even a good many people inside it, in the attitude both

THE CURÉ D'ARS

of the author and the subject of this book is that a Frenchman of this sort is essentially militant. There is nothing apologetic about his apologetics. He is not only propagandist but provocative. It is a quality which can, of course, take bad as well as good forms; just as it can be put at the service of bad as well as good causes. But there has always been apparent on both sides of the French religious quarrel a certain insistent and irritant character. I have heard that a sceptical mayor of some French town was not content with taking the metal of certain church bells, but cast it into a statue of Zola. He did the most annoying thing he could possibly think of. I believe that a statue of a great French freethinker, honoured in foreign countries as a great scholar and man of letters, was set up to be a glory to his own village; and the villagers instantly battered it to pieces with stones. Try to imagine villagers in Surrey doing this to a statue of George Meredith, because he was an agnostic. To put this aspect of French Catholicism in a word, in France the defence is not merely defensive. It is, in the honourable and soldierly sense of the word, offensive. As Mr. Belloc has remarked somewhere, 'the French do not fight with reluctance.'

This book is the story of a humble and saintly parish priest, who lived a quiet life in a rustic corner. It is natural to think first of him as gentle and pacific; and in one sense, like all such men, he was very gentle and very pacific. But he was, above all things, challenging. If I might so express it, he was above all things exasperating. He was a walking contradiction; he cut across the whole trend of his time at right angles; quite content to know that the angle was right. Nearly all people of the other race or temper, like so many English and some German people, take their divergence in a sort of curve, feeling the forces round them as things that can be partially followed, if they are ultimately left behind. But M. Ghéon sees M. Vianney primarily as a protest and a denial; a denial of all the things which were at his moment most confidently affirmed. M. Vianney appeared in history at the supreme moment of the French Revolution, when it was proclaiming both tremendous truths and tremendous falsehoods as with the trumpets of the Apocalypse. And in the midst of all those thunders the Curé d'Ars stood calmly talking about something totally different. He was talking exactly as he would have talked if he had been a Celtic hermit of the Dark Ages talking to a savage tribe of Picts. At the very moment when the human world seemed to have been enlarged beyond all limits for all to see, he declared it to be quite small as compared with things that hardly anybody could see. At the moment when

THE CURÉ D'ARS

thousands thought they were reading a radiant and self-evident philosophy, proved quite clearly in black and white, he calmly called its black white and its white black. For us who live at the end of the rationalist and republican epoch, it is difficult to measure how hopeful was the beginning of it, and how hopeless seemed the contradiction of it. For already the curve of the world has begun to creep backwards a little nearer to the mysticism of such a saint; though, alas, the modern mind has more often change negatively by disillusion than positively by enthusiasm. But in the atmosphere of his own age, he was like a man dug up out of some other aeon or flung from some other planet. And indeed the quarrel of the world about such a man must always be, in a deeper sense, on whether he has risen from the Stone Age or fallen from the stars.

M. Ghéon, the author of so many striking dramas, sees here chiefly the drama of such a defiance. Sometimes, I am tempted to fancy, he even exaggerates the contrast, not so much between the saint and the period as between the saint and the ordinary life. But I recognize in that the fighting French exaggeration; such as appears in Wilfrid Ward's life of his father, touching the parallel between the French and English reaction. While Newman was rationalizing against rationalism in *The Grammar of Assent*, Veuillot was hurling Holy Water in the faces of the French rationalists, as the thing that would exasperate them most. And there is in fact a vital value in emphasizing the contrast, as a part of the controversy that concerns everybody. The critics of the Church are notably unlucky in hitting on the charge that she belongs to a feudal world or particular periods of the past. They are driven to call so many modern things medieval, that it is at last apparent that she is no more medieval than she is modern. It was in the dull daylight of the manufacturing and materialistic nineteenth century that the unearthly light shone from the cavern of Lourdes. And it was in the full sunrise of the secular age of reason introduced by the eighteenth century that a nimbus not of that age or of this world could be seen round the head of the Curé d'Ars.

APOLOGIA [1], [2]

AS a variant on the popular advice to give a dog a bad name and hang him, I propose to give this paper an exceedingly bad name and hang on to it. When it was first suggested to me that I should use my own initials in the title, I regarded the proposal with a horror which has since softened into loathing. It is due to the reader to state very briefly the reasons that have led me at last to accept this description; and the chief reason is that, owing to rather peculiar circumstances, it is very difficult to find any other. It is true that journalistic titles are often strangely unsuitable. The paper called the *Daily Herald* is not likely to show a special tenderness for heraldry. The paper called the *Nation* has always shown a special hostility to nationality. Some might even say that the organ of the Guilds, which was called the *New Age*, ought rather to

[1] The opening article in the (advance) specimen number of *G. K.'s Weekly*, November 8, 1924.
[2] Chronologically this paper should appear earlier; but here it probably makes a good end.

be called the *Middle Ages*. But there is something in our particular position which differs from all these papers; and it is no mere vanity to say that it is at once more universal and more unique.

I desire this paper to stand for certain very normal and human ideas. But though they are very normal and very human, it is the cold and literal fact that they will not be printed in any other paper except this one. They are not fads; they are only human traditions that are treated as negligible while fads are welcomed as fashionable. They are not eccentricities; they are only the central ideas of civilization that are forgotten in a welter of eccentricity. But because they are neglected they are new, and because they are forgotten elsewhere they will only be found here. They are simply common sense in a world where sense is no longer common.

I will take as the chief example the present problem of poverty and wealth. In itself my position would seem singularly simple. It is simply that I am heartily opposed to Bolshevism and heartily opposed to Trusts. I believe it is possible to restore and perpetuate a reasonable just distribution of private property; and I will give my reasons for thinking so in this paper. But the point for the moment is this. No other paper in this country can be *heartily* opposed both to Bolshevism and to Trusts. For it is the

APOLOGIA

whole point of a paper like the *Daily Mail* that we must tolerate more or less in the way of Trusts, because the only alternative is Bolshevism. And it is the whole point of a paper like the *Daily Herald* that we must accept more or less in the way of Bolshevism, because the only alternative is Trusts. The *Daily Mail* cannot really try to destroy Trusts; for it is itself a part of a Trust. The *Daily Herald* cannot really try to defeat Bolshevism, for its most sincere backing is among Bolshevists. For them there are only two alternative courses, on which they take two opposite sides. But for me there is a third course: and no other paper will defend or even discuss it.

This third course has been called 'Distributism', signifying that it hopes to distribute private property more equally. But if I were to call this paper 'The Distributive Review' (as has been suggested) it would produce exactly the impression I desire to avoid. It would suggest that a Distributist is something like a Socialist; a crank, a pedant, a person with a new theory of human nature. It is my whole point that my solution is simply human, and it is the other solutions that are dehumanized. It is my whole point that to say we must have Socialism or Capitalism is like saying we must choose between all men going into monasteries and a few men having harems. If I denied such a sexual alternative,

I should not need to call myself a monogamist; I should be content to call myself a man. I should appeal to the whole of our own normal and national tradition of manhood. If I started a paper denying that alternative, I should not want to call it 'The Monogamous Review'. And if I did, nine people out of ten would get the impression that I was some other and slightly differentiated sort of crank. They would get a vague impression that a Monogamist was as mad as a Mormon. The parallel in this case happens to be pretty close. For the Great Trust has no more right to absorb all private fortunes into a monopoly, and say it is defending the institution of property, than the Grand Turk has to kidnap all women into a seraglio and say he is defending the sanctity of marriage. But almost any other parallel would do as well, so far as the point about the insane dilemma and the sane alternative is concerned; indeed the more fantastic were the parallel the more exactly it would fit the fact. If all the newspapers had impressed upon the public mind that we must choose between being vegetarians and being cannibals, we might need a newspaper to point out that the alternative was all nonsense. But we should not show a very bright journalistic instinct if we called the paper 'The Anti-Anthropophagous Carnivore'. It is a strictly correct description of our normal habit

APOLOGIA

of eating mutton but drawing the line at eating men. It is a barbarous mixture of Greek and Latin; but it is all the more like a real scientific word for that. And logically if not linguistically it is perfectly accurate. But though we are most of us anti-anthropophagous carnivores, we do not often mention the fact, especially when we wish to convince our neighbours that we are only ordinary sensible people—as we really are. The difficulty is, therefore, that any title defining our doctrine makes it look doctrinaire. The truth is that the true idea of private property has been so long neglected in England that there is no easy and popular phraseology attached to it. It has to invent its own terms and they are inevitably lumbering and elaborate terms; it is so old that it has become new. At the same time I want a title that does suggest that the paper is controversial and that this is the general trend of its controversy. I want something that will be recognized as a flag, however fantastic and ridiculous, that will be in some sense a challenge even if the challenge be received only with genial derision. I do not want a colourless name; and the nearest I can get to something like a symbol is merely to fly my own colours.

For instance, the first proof that a thing is familiar is that it is funny. There are jokes about the Profiteer. There are jokes about the Socialist.

But there are no jokes about the Distributist. Anybody can draw a conventional caricature of a Socialist by adorning him with long hair, or colour it by giving him a red tie. But nobody can draw a caricature of a believer in small and well distributed private property; because nobody has any familiarity with the theory or the type. No visionary can venture to imagine what would be the condition of the Distributist's hair. No poet, dipping his brush in hues of earthquake and eclipse, can give a colour to the Distributist's tie. There is therefore no familiar image that we can call up, to remind our friends and foes of the sort of thing we mean. But while there are no jokes against small property, there are jokes against me. They range from the ancient but admirable story that my old-world chivalry prompted me to give up my seat to three ladies to the more recent and realistic anecdote, which tells how my neighbours remonstrated with a noisy local factory, pleading that 'Mr. Chesterton can't write', and received the serene reply 'Yes. We were aware of that'. Nobody whose notoriety is based on such legends is likely to feel any very solemn arrogance in connexion with it. I do not say that my journalistic reputation is particularly dignified; but I am bound to admit that it is probably more familiar than my opinions about economic distribution. So blindly and blankly has this natural social ideal been ignored in England, that I really do believe it to be true that my normal ideal is less known than my name. I am therefore driven to use the name as the only familiar introduction to the ideal.

But I live in hopes of seeing this relation to things reversed. I shall work upon this paper in the hope that familiarity with the name may be allowed to fade as familiarity with the cause increases; and that that will increase and I shall decrease. Then perhaps a happier generation, living under a healthier social order, may be completely puzzled by the initials that stand at the head of this page. Learned professors will ponder upon what the hieroglyphic of 'G.K.' can possibly have signified; those holding the barbaric theory of the twentieth century interpreting it as 'Good Killing', while those with a more pious idealization of the past translate it as 'Greater Knowledge'. Students of contemporary literature may suppose it to be a sort of monogram of God and Kipling or possibly Kipps, while dynastic historians prove that it was but a ceremonial inversion of King George. But I shall not care very much what they say, so long as they say it in a free country where men can own once more.

For there is no nobler fate than to be forgotten as the foe of a forgotten heresy and no better success than to become superfluous; it is well with him who can see his paradox planted anew as a platitude or his fancy shed like a feather when nations renew their youth like the eagles: and when it is no longer thought amusing to say that a farm should belong to a farmer and no longer called brilliant to suggest that a human being might live in his own house as in his own hat, then indeed the trumpets of a final triumph will tell us we are needed no more.

*Commentary
on the Essays
by Arthur Livingston*

BOSWELL

CHESTERTON'S principal themes in this introduction to an abridgment of Boswell's *Johnson* is his admirable defense of the very idea of abridging classic works, even when they need such pruning as to be palatable to modern tastes. Not only does he defend abridgement, he goes so far as to delight in the love of dipping into books for the sheer love of serendipity (or is that serene dipping?). These ideas have long been anathema to the fastidious literati, as if snatching enjoyment is the refuge of the gauche. If we are unable to endure every syllable of, say, Proust's *magnum opus,* then one has permitted a blindfold for his execution. What nonsense, and Chesterton says as much.

Boswell was all GKC claimed for him and he is doubtless correct in declaring that Boswell records two great men, thee good doctor himself—and Boswell, too. Johnson in the pages of the Scotsman's biography becomes as memorable as any character in any imaginative work of English literature. The elaborate scrapbook of table talk is an endless joy to read, skim, or ponder. Johnson springing to life in those pages is the model of extraordinary detail, as if (often noted) Boswell had taken down everything Johnson said and (less noted) that he chose the right stories to select for posterity. The method has been standard for literary biography ever since.

Boswell, however, does have one flaw he seemingly repeats *ad nauseum,* Chesterton would most likely have said something were the selections to also mar this abridgement. When we read the complete life of Johnson, we can quickly learn to skip those passages when they come rather predictably. After letting some bit of Johnson's conversation entrance us, Boswell will undercut it with a lengthy explanation and interpretation of what calls for little comment because Johnson whenever engaged in words is a lucid as anyone who ever spoke or wrote the language. On these occasions, Boswell is as tedious as a typical MLA conference, rare sense and much droning on. One hopes that Banks and Higgins struck these offending passages, because otherwise few books of English prose match Boswell's *Johnson.* Criticism may not have been Boswell's long suit, but recording loving detail and recreating happy discussion were. This he has done as well as anyone. Ever.

OLIVER WENDELL HOLMES

MOST contemporary readers associate the name of Oliver Wendell Holmes with the *son* of the subject of this biographer. This subject is not the infamous jurist who defended eugenics through judicial enforcement, and who said famously, "Three generations of idiots is enough." The subject rather is the altogether more agreeable father of the Supreme Court justice. The elder Holmes was a journalist and controversialist and, in that way, is not unlike GKC himself. What they had in common was a rather specialized kind of journalism because these kinds of author, many of whom consider their columns ephemeral, nevertheless become *belle lettrists*—but only when some acclaim deems such work worthy of preservation. This tradition dates from at least the time of Addison and Steele and, like them, many such essayists published their work in their own little papers like *The Spectator* or Samuel Johnson's *The Rambler.*

Holmes, particularly in *The Autocrat of the Breakfast Table,* stands out in this field like no one else in

American letters until at least the turn of the twentieth century. Neither Holmes nor Chesterton ever poked his nose much into stories detailing the whos, whats, wheres, whys, and hows of the news story. Instead they wrote graceful essays, sometimes on a daily basis. Most work is quickly gone. How many today can relate to us the political positions of the once highly influential Westbrook Pegler? *Sic transit Gloria.*

Chesterton is a just critic of Holmes and justly notes his limitations. In preparing these remarks, I discovered s painful detail, which is a comment on the times, not on Holmes. The ubiquitous *Norton Anthology of American Literature* no longer even mentions Holmes anywhere either in even one essay, nor does he even get one reference in its dreary pages of what passes for English scholarship nowadays. Nowhere can it editors find room for the one journalist this country has produced in its early days who consistently maintains a balance of wit, style, elegance, and the long-lost patience that overtakes writing that can justly be called gentlemanly. The may not be, as GKC points out, the highest combination of literary virtues, but we are hard pressed to think of anyone today in our newspapers who rises to anything even approaching this level of civilized thought.

MATTHEW ARNOLD

ONE'S first instinct would be to laugh upon being told that the highest virtues of Matthew Arnold are those matching the best of antiquity. We think of him first, if we still think of him at all, as that man with his "singular whiskers" who wrote a handful of memorable poems verging on despair; but, as Chesterton makes clear in his essay, Arnold's work was not despairing, but rather "cold humility," an attempt to get the dirt from one's own soul so that real virtue can be embraced. A thirst for this kind of goodness the classical world bequeathed us as absorbed by Christianity. Nineteenth century England had, Arnold believed, repudiated that kind of Socratic humility (which was never pretense even in Socrates), and had fallen into a morass of commercialism and rapacious monetary speculation.

Each epoch requires not only virtuous people, but also, and even more to the point, the courageous lovers of rectitude whose most conspicuous demonstrations of righteousness contradict the besetting sins of the zeitgeist. As Chesterton mentions,

Arnold remind the mid-Victorians of their crassness and almost bewildering philistinism, and because of this quixotic venture, segments of respectable society either scorned him, or ignored him altogether. His career acted as a kind of purgative with a desired medicinal effect of health in the English soul and strength of character rather than the constant pendulum swings from dour piety to lip-smacking profligacy that had plagued the nation since the time of Henry VIII.

Some who listened too closely to Arnold's message yielded to the temptation and took his medicine in toxic doses and thus became the aesthetes—those who scorned the Good and True wherever they could not detect the Beauty. Curiously, nearly every one of the major aesthetes that followed in the train of Arnold and Pater converted to Catholicism after seeing first hand Arnold's core ideas of culture were in dire need of its own corrective, for unfortunately Beauty too often transformed into most unbeautiful vice. Arnold's true contribution to culture was that of a sensitive soul who tearfully cannot enter into faith, but cannot let loose of her gifts; but he led the way for the reconciliations of men like Wilde, Dowson, and even the author of the Yellow Book himself, J.K. Huysmanns, who began as a near diabolist and ended his life a monk.

LITERARY LONDON

WHAT Chesterton says about London is true of every town everywhere. People generally do not see what is in front of them and Chesterton's preface to Miss Lang's now obscure book can be instructive for anybody who wishes to become observant of his surroundings. The old saw that man made the city but God made the country is in its way true; but God made mankind in His image, and part of that image is his desire to create. GKC provides a few examples of the London lurking right outside his window; but the gist of his essay is that any of us who live in town can be what Tolkien would later call a sub-creator and we can participate in the history of the place where we find ourselves, no matter where it may be.

An objection might be raised that London is a city teeming with history. As I look up from where I write in Chicago, I see a street sign named for a local newspaper publisher (Joseph Medill), who suggested the name Republican for his political party. I was raised, on further reflection, a short walk from the office where L. Frank Baum first saw the letters OZ on a filing cabinet drawer. History is all around us.

Augie Alexis, the proprietor of Centuries and Sleuths Bookstore, where the flagship group of American Chestertonians meet each month, recently compiled a collection of stories of famous or otherwise fascinating folk who are all buried in a local cemetery located in Forest Park, Illinois. He uncovered enough riveting information that Alexis mounted a production of short dramatic monologues about these people patterned on the model of the *Spoon River Anthology*. Here we find stories of Ernest Hemingway's mother being offered a chance to sing at the Met; we find as well voices from both sides of those who died in the Haymarket Riots.

The next person we will meet has a good or bad (though we hope not the latter) story to tell us were all truth known as it someday will be; and many of them make artifacts. Even something as humble as a railway crossing sign reveals the traces of mankind's visit. If we ask the question "why" repeatedly and with the insistence of an average five year old, within a minute or two we will be asking that which should make us fall on our knees in worship; and we learn of such things first from that which we see around us.

THE BOOK OF JOB

"THE riddles of God are more satisfying than the solutions of man. This sentence bedecks almost all collections of Chesterton's aphorisms, and rightly so, but when viewed in light of its context, as commentary on the book of Job, its profundity trebles. As simply a truism it is a slightly more religious sentiment of the kind of table talk made most famous by Oscar Wilde. The quip satisfies, but then, when applied to Job, man's solution takes on a proper subordination when we recall the spiritual discomfort Job's comforters supply, and the shrewish heckling of his most liberated wife. God Himself stands up to Job's most just questions by offering a series of riddles unanswerable by anybody who had not himself laid the foundations of the world. A telling point is that Job never points out God's logical fallacy, "But you didn't answer my question". God's riddles are all we get.

Chesterton tosses off profound comments in nearly every paragraph of this essay, a model of how to think Biblically and how theological truth works within this one book in particular that his remarks amplify. Here are just a few of the concepts lightly touched upon in its few pages: That the final text Job may have been shaped by using ancient methods of composition in no way challenges any belief in its divine inspiration; those who attack the morality of the Patriarchs do so by anachronistically reading developed Christian moral theology as the standard for those who had not yet received it; that God is perhaps the only real character in the Old Testament and all the people are his tools and weapons; that what makes the book of Job different is that it asks not what God is doing to His creation, but asks the Creator a reason for what He does; that the riddle of God's answer is not sidestepping Job's question, but is the strictly logical result of the finite questioning the Infinite; and that among many other precepts, whenever we (like Job) create or state our rationally formed opinion, we enter the cosmic realm, as did Job. We also ask these questions of God.

THE MAN IN THE FIELD

TWO years after writing this essay, Chesterton became part of a group of writers in England who consciously inaugurated a social movement with the most unmusical name of *distributism,* an awkward appellation to be sure, but no one yet can find a better word for the thing. The distributists were to become a serious, even influential political movement, although the number of its membership was somewhat small. Reduced to a bumper sticker, they believed in "the widest possible distribution of private property". This would of course pull down the wrath of both major political parties in both the U.K. and the U.S.A., whether in Chesterton's time or in ours. A neo-distributist, Philip Blond, is an advisor to the current Prime Minister as this is being written. The cumbersome name refers to distributive justice, i.e. how can social justice be achieved by as just a way as is humanly possible, and by honorable means. The League's latter day distractors insist on speaking as if their ideas are quixotic, ignorant, or both. A few did behave somewhat like the self-dubbed knight of La Mancha when they decided prematurely to form a political party, over Chesterton's objections; but their ideas have helped shape much political action throughout various corners of the world, such as Mohandas Gandhi learning from Chesterton that a truly independent India must spring from Indian roots to Michael Collins carrying a volume of Chesterton with him into battle.

The root of the distributist ideal that the English people be given back their land is diametrically opposed to what is now called socialism. The book GKC prefaces is long forgotten, but it is apparent that it gave pictures of rosy old English cottages, although England has now only a tiny remaining number of rosy cottages. One feels Chesterton's indignation seething from the page.

Although a towering and robust figure in English thought and letters (literally), Chesterton is not infallible and, like Homer, sometimes naps. He was wrong about the French Revolution, and his misunderstanding of its essential anti-Christianity will remain a blot on his record, and it should be pointed out now and then. The kind of people for whom he fought all his life, the peasantry of the Vendee, were the victims of the first modern genocide, when the revolutionaries slaughtered 300,000-500,000 people in the name of the People; but this is in no way a blot on the Chestertonian ideal, but more likely not being fully informed of the facts. When was the War in the Vendee taught us in school or anywhere else without a long search?

A LETTER TO A CHILD

A much reprinted photograph offers an unforgettable image of the enormous bulk of Chesterton reaching out either to offer to or to receive from a little girl some small gift—a most touching moment in itself, but it captures an aspect of the man seldom glimpsed in his public life. Although filled with that scintillating wit that most often kept an adult audience thinking while laughing, he was just as well known by the children in his Beaconsfield's neighborhood as the adult who liked giving parties; by all accounts, the fat man was popular with them and also funny. He loved to throw buns in the air and catch them in his mouth.

Still only twenty-seven, GKC in 1901 went so far as to offer an essay in defense of "baby worship". In that essay, Chesterton had this to say about small children: "Their top-heavy dignity is more touching than any humility; their solemnity gives us more hope for all things than a thousand carnivals of optimism . . . "

Mary Arendt is no longer read much and is one

of many figures discussed in *G.K.C. As M.C.* who deserves wider recognition, as does Chesterton's note to her daughter reprinted here. Subsequent horrors in the past century with its death toll in the hundreds of million of people have made most of us at least somewhat jaundiced. The battlefield of France to a degree found its way into Tolkien's Mordor and good readers respond to its dangers; but have we lost the ability to read verse as being enjoyable in the nursery? Perhaps so. Even if she never seems trite, many of her poems may seem exercises in sentimentality, which was probably not the case to her original audience, in the nursery and out, which is a shame. We are no longer innocent enough.

When she turns to the subject of Fairies, even these poems written for a four year old seem almost like Walter de la Mere had he restricted his vocabulary:

> Along this shining way
> Bright winged creatures stray,
> From realms of purple space
> They wander to this place
> Paved for celestial feet
> Where Earth and heaven meet.

Surely there is a place in the canon of children's poetry for a poet who writes this well. This project is primarily concerned with making available some rare Chesterton essays; but the secondary role of reprinting this book is that we meet some people worth meeting who only a few the public at large has encountered in many decades and we are first really meeting them through Chesterton's eyes. Introducing forgotten figures has an importance of its own, which gives this venture an added dimension, one, which, by itself, would have been a worthwhile undertaking.

DR. JOHNSON

A photograph survives of Chesterton dressed either for a party or, more likely, for some presentation made while in character in the guise of Dr. Samuel Johnson, periwig and all. GKC resembled him remarkably, especially the scowl, which in both cases may be a sign of myopia. This was certainly true of Chesterton. If he did not identify with him, Chesterton certainly felt a great affinity toward the man and even wrote one of his four full length plays about him, *The Judgment of Dr. Johnson.*

Chesterton begins here with a serviceable thumbnail sketch of Johnson worthy as an entry in any of the shorter encyclopedias, although probably rating *The Rambler* and *The Idler* somewhat below their deserts. His essay takes wing when the topic moves from Johnson's writing (which he enjoys and respects) to his table talk, which almost invariably holds the first rank in the opinion of Johnson's admirers. If this preface or the anthology itself moved anyone to dip into the sea of Johnson stories, Chesterton and the compiler would have accomplished much. The names of GKC and Alice Meynell on such a collection of extracts assures that each dip is refreshing.

Unfortunately, Alice Meynell nowadays is only recalled, if she ever is recalled, for tangential biographical reasons, because she and her husband took Francis Thompson, who had been living out of trash cans on the street, and gave him a home. The exclusion of her poetry in the canon of approved literature once again calls into question those who devise the canon. In his autobiography Chesterton, who saved her for best and last of the literary figures he had met says of her:

"...There was nothing about her that can decay. The thrust of life in her was like that of a slender tree with flowers and fruits for all seasons; and there was no drying up of the sap of her spirit, which was in ideas. She could always find things to think about Even on a sickbed in a darkened room, where a shadow of a bird on the blind was more than the bird itself. She said, because it was a message from the sun . . . [Her own] presence had indeed something of the fugitive accident of a bird. I know now that she was not fugitive and not shadowy. She was a message from the sun."

THACKERAY AND THE BOOK OF SNOBS

IN 1911 Chesterton could write with great assurance that everyone knows *The Book of Snobs*. In our time that sentence sounds as if it came from a book of snobbery, but Chesterton was right. Those who read popular magazines knew of this work that first appeared in the pages of that periodical, the paragon of English humor, *Punch*. Thackeray's book was almost as popular in North America as it was in England. In that same year, the famous eleventh volume of the Encyclopedia Britannica boldly tells us in its article on Dr. Johnson that his Jacobite sympathies are well known. Whether or not either Chesterton or the encyclopedia were correct about their readership's knowledge of earlier literary figures, what is important to note is the level of literacy expect from the reading public.

In the twenty-first century, *The Book of Snobs* is kept alive, although just barely, by two types—by academic specialists in university English departments selecting their niche, and by common readers who have probably read *Vanity Fair*, perhaps *Henry Esmond*, or even have given a whirl at *Barry Lyndon* after watching Stanley Kubrick's film, and venture to try something more by Thackeray in that vein. If he never again will be as popular as Dickens, he also does not have the kind of devotees who relish Trollope.

The Book of Snobs, as a survey of any random assortment of contemporary readers will testify, is at best an acquired taste. Nothing can date more quickly than humor, especially satire because what is being satirized dwindles and disappears from living memory. George S. Kaufman was a man whose plays audiences of my generation thought hilarious, but I question if most of them would resonate with those born after 1970. Kaufman may have made the *mots justes* on this very subject. When asked for a definition of satire, he opined, "That which closes on Friday".

Topical humor tends to wither on the vine. Parts of Thackeray's book can still be read with some pleasure, but the necessity to research topical references at almost every turn makes even the lightly smiling humor more of a chore than a pleasure. We can, however, delight in Chesterton's own delight in these *Punch* articles. A man whose book has at least bequeathed us with the useful word *snob* has about it an infectious quality that can make us perhaps some day give another try to this volume, one that begs for a decent annotator.

AESOP

BECAUSE all our information about the historical Aesop is entirely legendary, Chesterton jumps at the chance of wedding paradoxical comments and stresses that whether or not an Aesop actually lived, the fables certainly do live, and the more anonymous they are, the more appropriate. Trying to sort out biographical matters about Aesop make us feel a shroud of mystery as deep as the pronouncements from the oracle of Delphi, but the fables themselves are plain and popular. Some of the best of them remain proverbial whether in the story itself like "The Tortoise and the Hare" or as part of a proverb like "sour grapes", a phrase many use without knowing "The Fox and the Grapes". Chesterton observes a rightness of the actors of the tales all being animals, except that in his evident rush to meet a deadline (so typical of him), he sometime forgets a lesser truth. "The Boy Who Cried Wolf" was more about the boy than the wolf. One can almost hear GKC defending himself by replying that in the fable the boy had acted like an animal, an exception proving the rule. Sometimes our pets can act like the boy. If accidentally trained to do so, a dog might reenact the last scene of *Camille* if one comes within a foot of tramping on its paw if this tragic scene results in a dog biscuit. The boy behaved like an acting spaniel.

If few read *The Book of Snobs* because its satire has become obsolete, then fewer readers pick up Aesop than once upon a time, probably because so many people think they find morality obsolete, and because every detail of each fable leads us inexorably to a moral such as "Slow and steady wins the race." Rooting for the underdog make have kept this particular fable popular, but not for its *raison d'etre*. It can be taken for a spirit of modern revolution unknown to Aesop whether he existed or not, which makes some love the tale and despise the hare not because he is a blowhard, but because he is fast. This is envy of anything superior to oneself; and how many people even remember the moral of the story?

DICKENS AS SANTA CLAUS

CHESTERTON wrote what is surely his most popular, and perhaps best, study of another author in *Charles Dickens, Last of the Great Men*. Dickens comes alive in its pages, as alive as Mr. Pickwick or Pip. Five years later, in 1911, the publishing house of Dent commissioned Chesterton to write prefaces to each volume in its Everyman's Library set of the complete works of Dickens. These essays Dent then collected and published as *Appreciations and Criticisms of Charles Dickens,* thus making that author the only person about whom Chesterton wrote two books. The former volume is about the man and the man in his writing; the later focuses as much as Chesterton ever did on the works themselves.

The essay we are considering is a topic that Chesterton addressed in numerous places either in a complete piece or in passing reference—a defense of the Dickensian Christmas. Christmas has been for anyone in living memory so trivialized by a floodtide of commercial kitsch that many folks, especially Christians of all denominations, yield to GKC's arguments, while the world in their immediate experience could well present nearly insurmountable obstacles to appreciating the good of Dickens on Christmas. Look closely at what Chesterton attacks. That same commercialism which forever infects the house of Scrooge and Marley before the latter's repentance fairly represents the nadir of Christmas celebration during the sad days when utilitarian liberalism reached its peak. Doing away with a wicked disdain for celebration and ushering in the fresh air that comes from a hearty relishing in Christ's birth was largely the work of Charles Dickens—at least in England. We owe him a debt of thanks. He can hardly help it, after all, if the same kind of people now instead infect us the last quarter of each year with a jingle bell rock we may hardily wish were a rock from a left hook and a little drummer boy we wish to beat about the head with his own sticks. As long as the cash register opens, the heirs of capitalism (and its close buddy socialism) Chesterton everywhere condemns—these predators are happy. Were he writing 150 years later, he would still defend the outpouring of goodwill and the joy that is the overflowing in the cosmic significance of Christ's birth, and the exuberance those who participate in it enjoy. That is what the Dickensian spirit is about, even if Dickens only half understood it. With the One who made the blind men see and lame men walk; but with all the indignation he could muster, he would pit himself against anyone who would try to kill Christmas by selling it or by trying to prohibit our shouting from the rooftops our celebration of the Lord's birth.

HILAIRE BELLOC

GEORGE Bernard Shaw, a friend of both Chesterton and Hilaire Belloc, deemed in the early 1900s that a two-headed beast stalked the streets of London, a quadruped to be dubbed the "Chesterbelloc". Sadly, Belloc in these times is nearly a forgotten figure except among those who are his fierce champions. His intense, even aggressive, Roman Catholicism has made him a picture turned to the wall in many circles, many of them nominally Catholic.

The difference between the two men can easily be observed in a necessarily apocryphal tale concerning a conversation the two were having with H.G. Wells, who proffered a comment insulting Chesterton. As the story goes, Chesterton immediately challenged Wells to a debate; Belloc challenged him to a duel. The Catholic Church automatically excommunicates anybody who participates in a duel on any level, but the story does capture the uniqueness of each man. Whereas almost all who were in contact with him revered Chesterton, his most powerful literary ally met his enemies in the literary equivalent of back alley brawls. I do not mean that as a negative statement.

Any number of readers initially comes to Belloc expecting perhaps a lesser version of Chesterton and leaves disappointed. Whereas Chesterton dashes about verbally with light-hearted wit laced with paradox no matter how serious the subject, Belloc bludgeons the reader with straightforward truths presented with relentless logic and a cocky satisfaction in the faith, not minding whether or not he is abrasive when he believes the opposition deserves a stinging barb.

The first two sentences of the preface under consideration has often appeared in blurbs on reprints of Belloc's many books or in secondary sources about him. Henry James visited the Chestertons while he was in England, as GKC recalled in his autobiography. While James had steered the subject to his beloved topic of English refinement, Chesterton heard a voice from around the corner shouting, "Gilbert! Gilbert!" The voice was discovered to be coming from Belloc, fresh off the road from some strenuous hike, with several days' growth of beard, and in need of a bath "bellowing for bacon and beer". We can almost hear Chesterton's chuckle in the book as he tells us that Belloc at that moment represented all that was best in England.

WILLIAM COBBETT

CONTEMPORARIES must bear in mind several almost conflicting elements in William Cobbett to understand fully why the Chesterbelloc found him not only one of the greatest of English authors, but one of its major heroes. To comprehend the reason why Chesterton especially so revered Cobbett, one must first get past the half-truths written of him, and the arguments that he participated in the French Revolution and that he was also a major influence on Karl Marx. The real truth is that Cobbett arrived in France, choosing it as a temporary refuge from certain prosecution because of his vociferous attack in print against the wretched conditions of the British soldier; he reached Paris in 1792 just in time for the Terror and fled almost immediately to the United States. Marx does quote him, but any reading of Cobbett in context reveals a thinker far removed from what we call socialism today, by which we mean a state-controlled socialism Cobbett would have found anathema.

Cobbett was a journalist and pamphleteer (whose

pamphlets could reach 400 pages) while presenting his ideas in one of the liveliest styles of any English author, and was so outspoken, he was in constant danger of imprisonment, usually for printing bald truths. For instance, he served two years in Newgate Prison for having protested the public flogging of militiamen.

The enemy he fought with every ounce of energy, however, was that same enemy Chesterton and his circle fought all during their careers, whether that thing be called Hanoverian, Whiggish, Capitalist, Socialist, or Fascist; or, after 1910, Parliamentarian, because the founders of the distributist movement believed firmly that the party system is hopelessly corrupt and a tool of those they fought. Nowhere in their writings is this point so graphically portrayed as in Chesterton's outline of what he thought of "left" and "right" in the political arena. In *What's Wrong With the World,* he called them Hudge and Gudge, each holding on to one half of a false debate and keeping the sinking ship afloat with policies that hurt real people. Chesterton wrote one of his best studies in 1925, a book simply entitled *William Cobbett. Cottage Economy,* the book Chesterton discusses here, is a self-help book on bread baking and raising livestock, among other topics; in other words, a book about becoming as self-sufficient as possible, something admired at least a goal by all distributists. Why Cobbett? In all his work, he was a guide for living a sustainable human existence and an inspiration for those who admire resistance to unjust restraint.

ERIN GO BRAGH

AMONG Chesterton's less famous, but no less noteworthy, achievements are the longish pamphlet called *Christendom in Dublin* and the short book, *Irish Impressions,* both about the then topical subject in England of what to make of the Irish and their revolutions. Those writings, as well as this essay and the appended book, were issues during the times of trouble. Michael Collins on more than one occasion carried into battle among his paraphernalia a book or two by Chesterton. When advisors prepped Lloyd George on strategy for presenting his fatal offer of compromise to Collins, it is reported that the prime minister spent some long hours boning up on Chesterton. The same shortsighted pragmatism that prevailed at Versailles and had covered up the Marconi Scandal (which had implicated Lloyd George) succeeded in its negotiations because poor Collins thought he was dealing with a man of honor, much to England's shame. In retrospect, Versailles virtually assured another world war just as the hush-hush dealings of the backroom created the atmosphere surrounding the outbreak of the Irish Civil War, thereby proving everything the Chesterton brothers and Belloc had said all along about the reigning government. One can dream of what might have been had Collins consulted Belloc first; it is not outside the realm of possibility that Ireland would have been spared that last tragedy.

Chesterton thoroughly despised the way the English had treated the Irish from the Elizabethan plundering until his own time. In Ireland probably most of all, he said repeatedly, all the wicked doctrines of Whiggish philosophy had been played out in full; what horrid thinkers like Ricardo and Malthus scribbled became grim reality that played out among the Irish dead. The casual acceptance in England of brutal policies helped make a war criminal like Edmund Spenser a revered poet throughout the land; his verse is magnificent so long as it is read on a literal level. The blasphemous portrayal of Elizabeth as Gloria proves that the real Archimago was Spenser himself—lies presented in sugared words. Chesterton doubtless agreed with the democratic inclination that spurred the local Irish population to burn down Spenser's house. One shudders to think of his thoughts about those whose practice accords with the intentional neglect of those who withheld aid to the starving Irish during the great potato blight and the consequent famine. Maybe the essential difference between a modern revolutionary and Chesterton reacting to such unspeakable indifference is that he was a Christian man with only the power of the pen. He consistently kept his mind on sacred theology by trying to evangelize his contemporaries and constantly kept in mind before the British public his vision of restoring small property and the real self-reliance that follows from it.

CECIL CHESTERTON

WE can almost feel G.K. Chesterton restraining his rhetoric to an extraordinary degree whenever he mentions his younger brother. Had Cecil Chesterton survived the world war, in all likelihood we would know him today as something more than a footnote to Gilbert's career. Shaw's picture of the Chesterbelloc would make plain sense were the Chesterton portion of the monster Cecil. It was he, far more than G.K., who was a convert from socialism to the political philosophy we call distributism, and was of all the early distributists the one we now would call an activist. After Belloc refused to stand for parliament again in 1910 because of the corruption in the parties, he collaborated on his findings with Cecil in that most informative of books *The Party System,* mostly written by Cecil. That little volume, along with Belloc's *The Servile State* and G.K.C.'s *What's Wrong With the World* (all published in 1911) really established what burgeoned into a large audience for those who both advocated widely distributed property and who opposed front bench corruption.

Reduced to a sentence one can put on a slogan, that odd mode American use for proclaiming their philosophy of life, distributism is the belief that private property should be spread to as many people who both want and can sustain it. Just as important, however, is the belief in what later was to be called *subsidiarity*. The family is the essential element of society and solutions to problems begin quite literally at home. Whatever of importance the family alone cannot do because it needs greater social organization should be accomplished at the most local level possible. This is a social doctrine that calls for political decentralization wherever it can be achieved.

The next year Belloc began a newspaper called *The Eye Witness,* with Cecil as second in command. A year later, Belloc withdrew and Cecil became editor-in-chief of *The New Witness.* And he continued to run it until entering the army late in the war. Cecil died of trench fever in late 1917. Just before the war broke out, Cecil had his finest moment. He face squarely the stringent British libel laws and for all practical purposes uncovered a scheme within the Liberal Party that today we would call insider trading; some M.P.s were apparently investing in shares of the Marconi wireless concern and then granting them a monopoly. What sometimes looks like a tangled tale when we read now of the Marconi Scandal was real a quite simple matter. Cecil was put in the dock for what he uncovered, but the truth was not a defense; he was, however, only given a fine. Because Cecil could have been sent to prison, the Chesterton entourage burst out in cheers in the courtroom.

After Cecil's death, G.K. took over the paper and edited it for the rest of his life. His friends persuaded him in 1925 to change the name to *G.K.'s Weekly,* a move made solely to keep the paper afloat by dealing in Gilbert's name. He always thought that the paper should survive both on its own merits and as a memorial to Cecil.

BERNARD CAPES

IN a paradox he himself would have appreciated, GKC almost never becomes obscure when he writes as a topical journalist; but as the decades roll by, some topics become obscure. To paraphrase Oscar Wilde, one should not be too modern; one is apt to become old fashioned quite suddenly. Only when he refers to the latest news does Chesterton become antiquated.

The prolific and popular author, Bernard Capes, has now been reduced to little more than an occasional footnote about this once famous literary figure, which is most unfortunate. He created over forty books, many crying for rediscovery. The present writer recalls several ghost stories fondly as well as the consequent goose bumps, especially the ones that were of the same kidney as Robert Louis Stevenson. Werewolves, suicides, and pure horror occupy hundreds of his pages. His detective stories, also, were in those days of yore among the most read by the British public.

C.S. Lewis once remarked that when he read William Morris' *The Roots of the Mountain* that he felt a numinous longing from the title that no tale could equal. Chesterton reports in his essay that identical chords were struck in him by Capes' title *The Lake of Wine*. *The House of Many Voices* is another that can occasion a few shivers.

Did it not already denote something common, *The Skeleton Key* could possibly have the same effect, and Capes, who had died in the 1918 influenza pandemic, did not live to see this detective tale reach the press. Chesterton's praise is always high for those who achieve anything equivalent to what he had accomplished in his own Fr. Brown tales—the elevation of a popular genre into enduring literature. What Chesterton refrains from telling us here, but does often elsewhere, is that he would be just as satisfied with a "dead Eyed Dick" story. His defense of the penny-dreadful and popular literature in general was not a pose of any kind. He never posed, which many then as now refuse to understand. He invariably meant exactly what he said, especially when he said it smiling.

MY NAME VILLAGE

J.P. Fonseka clearly recognized the essential element separating the quality of Chesterton's preface from the body of M.E. Moncton's otherwise justly forgotten potboiler *Life in Old Cambridge*. Almost as an afterthought GKC chimes in with a paragraph running close to two pages dealing with *Magna Carta* and its resultant consequences; but the lasting reason for selecting this essay for *GCK As MC* is that arresting image of Chesterton fearing to visit the town of Chesterton because he was afraid that he might fulfill a prophecy. This sentence is vintage Chesterton and he repeated this sentiment almost verbatim in his 1935 *Autobiography*.

Some superficially astute theological students may take from this observation, which he took pains to repeat in the summation of his own life, that he is in this instance guilty of superstition, but that would be to miss his larger meaning. Although he, alas, lacked the gift to craft lasting mythopoeic literature himself (no human being can excel at everything), nevertheless he repeatedly returned to myth and fairy tales as nearly the ideal form of creating, whether it be in traditional tales like "Jack the Giant Killer," or in the Curdie books of George Macdonald—of whom more anon.

Anyone who allows Chesterton's magic to work will realize all his most important themes present themselves in these stories, and that he really would not be surprised were he to see a mermaid before his eyes. The more we read Chesterton, the more aware we are of a man thankful to God for his own existence. Myth at its best is awful in the original sense of sparking a sense of awe in the observer. We even have a little verse, a prayer actually, in which he expresses gratitude for the day that has just passed and quietly asks his Maker, "Why am I granted another?"

He also concludes the remarkable opening paragraph of the essay under consideration with some well-aimed barbs at academic historians.

Chesterton is almost always suspicious, and often downright hostile, to "experts" whose minds are narrowed by their own professionalism. Here he reveals a defense of the kind of writing he preferred—the loving discoveries of the gifted amateur, amateur in the sense of someone who does what he does for the love of the thing itself, an avocation and not for his livelihood.

THE HUMOUR OF H.M. BATEMAN

MOST Americans, even those who enjoy what an earlier generation called the "funny papers," will today likely find H.M. Bateman's drawings only mildly amusing, if that; but the more discerning will still be able to appreciate his extraordinary draftsmanship and what Chesterton calls in the opening phrase of his essay Bateman's "wild exactitude." Because his precise pictures of English life in the early twentieth century require Americans, before they can interpret the majority of his work, first to reference their knowledge of a culture both foreign and long gone, what still can be appreciated is that Bateman almost invariably captures the still comic emotional attitude about his subjects, especially in his series "The Man Who..." With such titles as "The Umpire Who Confessed He Wasn't Looking" or "The Cad Who Was Improperly Dressed on the Lido", Bateman in his line makes us recognize the type even if we have never met him— in these cases the befuddlement of the one and the effete superciliousness of the other.

Although we may no longer guffaw at Bateman's cartoon strips, we can still appreciate that "exactitude", which is the hallmark of any good illustrator of human foibles. Bateman's work was an obvious influence on Harvey Kurtzman who in turn was one of the most important and influential comic artists the United States has produced. That somewhat wavy line in his caricatures of the human form clearly owes much to Bateman. In truth, only to a lesser extent, Bateman often echoes Chesterton's own illustrations, sometimes to an easily noticeable extent. When the Kurtzman elements gets added to the mixture, we can draw a straight line from Chesterton to Bateman to the man whose cartoons became the foundational work for *Mad,* the comic book, which became *Mad Magazine.* Evidentially, draftsmanship, like politics, makes strange bedfellows.

JANE AUSTEN

CHESTERTON'S literary criticism resembles that of C.S. Lewis, in one aspect, often noticed of Lewis, but rarely observed in Chesterton. They both illuminate their subject, which is hardly news to anyone who has read either author. Lewis wrote a perceptive essay on Austen, which is, as one might expect, a delight to read, its prose as pellucid as a glass of water; but when the clichés begin flying, a sniping attitude affects the dilettantes as we read the standard comments on GKC's criticism and biographies, far too often taking something of the following line: "Chesterton's book on Topbottom tells us more about Chesterton than it does about Topbottom," as if that were not also true of any criticism worthy of the name in what is a most Chestertonian paradox. The reality is that his critics (to use the expression in its loosest meaning) chatter about his manner, especially the real truth that he never provides footnotes and that he often misquotes from memory. Lewis was an Oxford (and later Cambridge) don, where meticulous scholarship is the order of the day. Chesterton was a product of Fleet Street, where daily deadlines come with the morning milk. Chesterton often writes in a rush, but this does not have the slightest bearing on his substance. At all times, and this is part of what makes him masterful, a mystical logic is working hard. If a pragmatist is a person who believes all truth is merely relative, then a mystic is a person who believes all truths are relative to one central truth—God. Everything else we can know radiates from that central fact, and any subject can lead to any other subject. Assuming the writer has assimilated essential truths, scurrying about the library to marshal facts is a waste of time. No matter where we start, we end with the central truth of God.

Even in this short essay, introducing the juvenilia of Jane Austen, Chesterton penetrates into the heart of what makes Austen so beloved and worthy of a reader's love. As a writer she was herself like a Dickensian character in that she always appears to us supremely as herself. She assumes no airs and her prose itself, like Mrs. Gummidge in the corner crying she is a poor lorn creature, and the words feel as we read them that they have always been and yet were not written by a turn of the eighteenth century lady. "Jane Austen was not inflamed or inspired or even moved to be a genius; she simply was a genius."

JANE AUSTEN

All but the most ardent devotees of Austen's *Love and Freindship* instinctively desire to right her title's half-sunk ship of spelling, but that would be akin to the misguided lucubration of the previously noted choir of Chesterton's antagonistic audience who read him with half their wits. GKC's judicious choice of quotation, even with the occasional comma out of place, is almost always the hallmark of the sympathetic critic, which he believed the only kind worth writing or reading.

DICKENS' 'CHRISTMAS CAROL'

IN yet another essay on Dickens' most popular work, Chesterton hits a note that may strike many Christian ears in our time as sour. We have become accustomed to nearly two months of our lives each year of being unable to go about our business without being bombarded by the kitschy blare of "Rudolph, the Red Nosed Reindeer" snorting from public electronic devices. This perversion of a sacred day had become so corrupt that even the most festive among us may be inclined to think the Puritans might have had a point when they tried to ban the feast. Today one must make a concerted effort to celebrate two possible Christmases—the real Dickensian Christmas and the real Christmas, which *begins* on December 25 with the celebration of the birth of Jesus Christ.

When Chesterton wrote this essay in 1922, the American commercialization of Christ was in its infancy; and what he notes is that eighty years before him one single work saved the traditional celebration of joy that attends the birth of our Lord. Tom Lehrer, who penned many impressive and funny songs, tells us in his Christmas anthem that it is time to "drag out the Dickens". Christmas as the time of year that is Yule log, grog, and roast hog—the celebration of love of neighbor as well as God—was dying, dying in the 1840s because England was fast becoming in the nineteenth century progressively more like Ebenezer Scrooge and less like nephew Fred. Dickens, who was then at the height of his fame, decided to do what could be done to remedy this dreadful situation.

GKC rightly compares Scrooge to Gradgrind. Whereas *Hard Times* was a frontal assault on the "individualists", all of them seeming much alike, "A Christmas Carol" was an impassioned plea for their conversion. Although it is doubtful Dickens was what some people would call a Christian, he was a cultural Christian *in toto,* even letting Tiny Tim tell us that Christmas must ultimately be about Christ. He also wrote a book for his children in which he consistently refers to Christ as "Our Lord". If we are right to celebrate the Incarnation born, Dickens and Chesterton both remind us if it is not fitting that we do so at least partly in the spirit of the party at Fred's, a place where the spirit of Malthus and Ricardo have no place, and where forever Uncle Scrooge contritely begs admission to the dance.

UTOPIAS

MANY decades ago a wise professor encouraged his students, myself among them, to compare and contrast two Utopian novels in a paper for his course in modern history. I chose Edward Bellamy's *Looking Backward* as one of them (the second is lost in a time tunnel somewhere), but found the same basic pattern in all of them for which Bellamy's polemic (it is barely offered as imaginative literature) will stand for the lot. The unsuspecting reader is guided along to gape in wonder at the imagined future state of mankind, where the poor are no longer with us and the race of humans is no longer greedy. I also noticed, especially in Bellamy, probably because he wrote better than the others, that this world lacked anything that smacks of the real humanity any of us has ever met, the one where the really holy people call themselves sinners. And I also realized that anyone who lived in one of these Utopias would be facing hell on earth.

These people live in a state that provides for all their material needs and each adult works only a few hours a week, which could happen perhaps, but that is not the point. Placing humanity in such a Paradise would satisfy the present human condition as much as did the original, at its best possibly a kind of Limbo like Dante's first circle of hell. Better in this context may be Solzhenitsyn's depiction of what happens to anyone not joining in the cheers for the workers' paradise, *The First Circle*. We get such inklings of unavoidable doom in Chesterton's essay in regard to bureaucracies, which design everybody's affairs to suit the bureaucrats, and no one else; and they invariably rule these monstrosities. Chesterton understood this thoroughly.

Those with a shallow understanding of its oeuvre, however, have too often accused GKC himself of being a Utopian. True, he wished to see a society transformed into something substantially different from what it was then (and is even more so now); but even a nodding acquaintance with his ideas, will know that distributism, as this social philosophy is clumsily designated, is if anything anti-Utopian, and is reactionary in the most literal sense. Distributism is the belief that private property is so good that it should be promoted as such, and should be as widely distributed among the population as is practicable. (Not everyone wishes to be self-employed." Not everyone wishes to own his own land. Whatever may be right, some will wish to do otherwise.) The small farmer, the small shop, the small businessman—as discussed by the Chesterbelloc advocacy of smallness (beginning with the family and only from there working out to any form of a state)—this smallness is the essential feature of the distributist social ideal; but this is not idealism in the negative sense. All they desired is that the English lands be restored to the English people. This can only begin with people desiring the restoration of property.

GEORGE MACDONALD

THE pervading influence of the saintly Scottish novelist and short story writer George Macdonald is hardly a secret. Lewis routinely referred to Macdonald as his master, compiled a book of excerpts from his writings (especially his sermons), and even allotted him the role of guide through heaven in *The Great Divorce*. Less often noted is that G.K. Chesterton, if only less frequently, paints in his essays a portrait of Macdonald and his world in equally rapturous hues; Chesterton reserves a special space of memory for the ecstatic effect *The Princess and the Goblin* produced in him when he was a child. GKC, unlike Lewis, wrote hardly any mythopoeic works himself, but the entire atmosphere of Chesterton is one permeated with a wafting of breeze from the uncharted and charmed air of Fairieland, as if brought on the same puff of wind that brought *Lilith* to our shores.

In much of Chesterton's work, one finds "The Ethics of Elfland" being played out as fare for reading in the morning newspaper. Sometimes those who know

Chesterton only from bound books forget that the great bulk of his essays appeared in papers like the *Daily News* or in magazines like the *Illustrated London News*. The famous cartoon of the enormous bulk of Chesterton seated on a horse and plunging into battle is a fitting picture of at least how his mind worked habitually. Fairy stories teach headlong that dragons exist, which would catapult any soul to despair did he not also believe that St. George can kill that dragon—an image of redemption. Fat GKC on a charger is funny, but each Christian is made for battle with the equipment given him by God. That is Chesterton's deeper theological point and why fairy stories are essential reading for all of us. He even goes Lewis one better in his admiration of Macdonald by calling commendable the older writer's "Realistic novels, at least many of them, almost mythopoeic in tone, if not quite in substance".

If Rasputin had the eyes of a saint rather than those that produce a shudder in any sane man, he would have looked something like George Macdonald. And Lewis Carroll's photographs of him are themselves masterpieces of their kind. Certainly in those eyes Carroll captures something in the expression for anyone touched by the Curdie books and "The Golden Key", something that can only be called holiness.

Those eyes take on the aura of the halo as artists employed it in painting until recent times. Greville Macdonald's official biography of his father captures his awe at having been raised in the household of such a man. One could get a Ph.D. in English literature without once hearing the name of George Macdonald, and that is shame on those who devise the English canon. Come to think of it, the same could be said for G.K. Chesterton.

ON DETECTIVE STORIES

APART from any literary merits of an individual detective story, the love for the genre dictates its form, no matter how much other qualities may be desired. As C.S. Lewis stated about fairy tales, so in the classical story of sleuthing, the artistic merits remain secondary for a significant number of the audience and a close reading in this essay finds Chesterton depicting the desire of the reader to be beguiled and speaks to a sense of mystification that the beguiler finally dispels. That desire for beguilement is identical to the expectations while watching a stage magician. Although some readers (and a portion of the prestidigitator's viewers) simply will be vaguely aware of the craft of misdirection, this is incidental to the unveiling of the murderer or the rabbit popping out of the hat.

Some, however, will try to figure out the tricks and guess how the illusion was concocted. Why is it we never suspected the butler? How did he get the bunny get in the topper or escape the locked trunk? Thus the creator of Fr. Brown, the fictional detective only slightly less well known than his compeer who lived in Baker Street, delights in this preface that he was baffled when reading Walter S. Masterman's long forgotten novel, *The Wrong Letter*. Evidently the moment of revelation caught GKC off-guard because he saw the solution as akin to what would happen had he been told young Hamlet killed old Hamlet. Here Chesterton provides a stellar example himself of what he maintains is the whole point of good criticism. The good critic expresses joy in what he has read, provides insights that elucidate, and instills in his own readers a desire to seek out the considered work.

Chesterton also offers a quick summary list of the dos and don'ts of writing. The dos will cost any aspiring author little time and, perhaps, save him from misadventure, a handsome payout. The third-rate hacks (that is not redundant) Chesterton paints sharply in his don'ts. On the other hand, the first-raters in England about this same time formed their own Detection Club. Chosen as the first president of that who's who of august sleuth word magicians was, fittingly, G.K. Chesterton.

A STORY FROM THE GOTHIC

LOVE of medieval culture ran deep in Chesterton, but his understanding of its daily operations, its love of church and guild, the rich and poor hobnobbing together, influenced his social thought as profoundly as did the *Rerum Novarum*. Emblematic of those beliefs was his oft-expressed passion for gothic architecture, especially the great cathedrals with their wild pointed arches and flying buttresses and the even wilder gargoyles where goblins perched on high rather than down below. All in them that modernity had so wantonly rejected, he delighted in as part of his embrace of "topsyturvydom". Even a twenty-page excursion into a Chesterton novel makes clear what he meant and he would have said of it that the last shall be first as well as the bottom shall be top. Yet, all that wildness in the gothic, as wild as anything in Wonderland, is also as ordered as an encyclopedia, but presented with the sense of play that had in the high Middle Ages transformed travelers' tales of the rhinoceros into the altogether more agreeable (not be mention believable) spark of imagination that invented the unicorn. Presumably the travelers left out the more disagreeable features of the beast they reported.

But what makes the medieval period so congenial to Chesterton is that in the secular sphere, and as a natural result of its belief in Christianity, it had achieved something far superior to the absentminded cruelties of pagan antiquity or to the more calculating cruelties of the modern world. If Christianity cannot have a Golden Age this side of the second coming because all history is a struggle against each age, Christian cultures may have Golden Ages— and those in strict proportion to how its acts on its Christian faith.

Whenever such cultures assert themselves, the secular world moves slowly but surely from slavery to serfdom to freeholder. The modern world had reintroduced slavery almost as soon as Christendom was torn apart and certainly, the Chesterbelloc will trumpet in many places that the faith itself disappeared as the focal point of English life descended into the anti-Christianity of the Whigs, the Enlightenment, and the worship of progress. These made Chesterton and Belloc thunder whenever they entered the discussion. Alexandre Arnoux 's Abishag, as GKC indicates, deserves revival, but eighty-nine years after this essay, even greater obstacles stand in the way of its proper reception than in 1929, were that possible. Chesterton and his great compeer believed that proper understanding of what medievalism offered could lead to a real evangelization of the modern world were it only to have an unbiased hearing. On their lips the word "modern" was not far removed from "barbarous".

FRIENDS, ROMANS, COUNTRYMEN

HAD de Fonseka not reprinted this little essay, perhaps no one would have come upon it, except that indefatigable Chestertonian bibliographical hound of heaven, Geir Hasnes. That tireless man has assigned himself the more than daunting task— and probably a mountain not scalable to its pinnacle—of compiling a complete Chesterton bibliography. When Ignatius Press initially undertook publishing GKC's complete works back in the mid-80s, it had projected thirty-seven volumes averaging over 700 pages of fairly small type. Many of these have yet to be printed.

Almost day by day, somebody (especially Hasnes) seems to unearth a piece scholars had not previously known because Gilbert gave them away generously to ephemeral magazines, or in some place sure to become obscure. His preface to the 1925 edition of *The Catholic's Who's Who and Yearbook* is a good example of the latter kind. Indeed, the best portion of this little gem is given over to the idea that he expected no one to read it. Were it not for the volume we here reprint, he may have been right. How many people ever bother to read the preface to a reference work, except for a handful of librarians trying it grasp its scope?

In the last paragraphs, Chesterton allows himself (maybe because he thinks he is talking to himself) for one of the few times, to discuss matters internal to Catholics of his time. The fruits of the Catholic revival, both literary and otherwise, flowing as they did from the conversion of John Henry Newman in 1845, had grown steadily, until it reached its full flowering between the world wars, although it never completely entered the full mainstream of English life. Chesterton here, sadly, anticipated a much larger growth to come than ever did, nor could he envision a post-war revival, which now has left a remnant only in England, although a fighting one. In 1925, *The New Witness* became *G.K.'s Weekly*, which was read by many who had also read his columns in *The Illustrated London News* ever since 1905. From all over England, followers of the Chesterbelloc formed the Distributist League, a small sign of a way out of anti-Christian modernism by embracing Christian social principles. This essay is almost a clearing of his throat for the adventure he was about to undertake.

GILBERT AND SULLIVAN

CHESTERTON'S first published volume, *Greybeards at Play* (1900) was a collection of nonsense verse, which owed much to that mad, funny topsyturvydom whose king is W.S. Gilbert, GKC's closest literary associate Hilaire Belloc. That one-man assault team in words is remembered grudgingly, even by many who otherwise hold in abhorrence *The Servile State*, and, treat him as a kind of literary leper, still do laugh heartily at the *Cautionary Tales* and *A Bad Child's Book of Beasts*.

Gilbert's world of pure nonsense equals, and often excels, all others in the field. Lewis Carroll is the only other author whose name in this field has captured the public imagination as completely, although a few votes may come from intrepid admirers of Edward Lear. Although many images of Carroll mark themselves on the memory, relatively little of it is in verse. Gilbert gave us thirteen full-scale mock-dramatic plays, one shorter one, as well as the riches of that treasure house of nonsense, *Bab Ballads*.

Unlike the Chesterbelloc, Carroll, or Lear, W.S. Gilbert had the financial backing of Sir Richard d'Olye Carte, who, having yoked him musically, dramatically, and professionally with Sir Arthur Sullivan, brought out the best in the saturnine humorist and linked his mad world together with a master musical magician possessing a rare light touch. Sometimes forgotten in the fun is that just as the audience for one of these confections adjusts itself to the magnificently silly idea of a roving troubadour in feudal Japan, Gilbert and Sullivan insert as fine a ballad as any produced in the nineteenth century, "A Wandering Minstrel, I." Not only that, but the barbs against innocent people in *The Mikado* and in other productions are gentle, if not entirely innocent, and, fortunately, were well taken by those barbed.

The aesthetes in *Patience* act as they do to entrance young women, which may have even been true in 1881. Even today, that odd couple of the British stage can easily subvert the young viewer in his regard of ten or so various professions, so skewered were they. Can anyone see *Trial By Jury* and not forever feel a suppressed giggle in any courtroom where one is not the defendant? Or take with full seriousness the goings on in legislative chambers after watching *Iolanthe,* in which the entire House of Lords become transformed into fairies? Not taking the world too seriously is always good for the soul; which Gilbert and Sullivan can teach a grim world.

RASSELAS

DOES anybody read *Rasselas* anymore except as a school assignment? Probably not, and more's the pity. In addition to the unmistakable aura of melancholia adding real bite to his prose that hangs over almost everything Dr. Johnson wrote when he does anything other than crack a joke, we also sense the wisdom of one who had surveyed all, "from China to Peru." Any astute reader will detect real profundity in *Rasselas,* certainly as compared to the superficiality of Voltaire's *Candide,* which appeared at about the same time. Where Johnson takes his reader by the hand to let him share vicariously in the suffering of life, Voltaire ultimately sneers at everything including his own story, the tending of his own garden to be done by someone who does not care for gardens.

Chesterton's comment that Johnson wrote everything in black and white is just, but that was true of all neo-classical English writers of any quality and, as GKC also points out, this fact is both his strength and his weakness. We are just close enough in time and language to authors who flourished between the Restoration and the Romantic explosion that we sometimes believe we understand them completely. Johnson must be understood in the same spirit that he "writ," and we must bear in mind that he still looked upon an ordered universe where all exists in the "Great Chain of Being." A.O. Lovejoy"s *The Great Chain of Being* is still the indispensable volume for understanding this image of the universe. He accomplished for the neo-classical world what C.S. Lewis had for the medieval synthesis in *The Discarded Image*. In our essay, Chesterton does preliminary spadework, especially in his penultimate paragraph, in which he writes, " . . . Johnson never forgets that he is writing a certain type of tale, with certain conventions and certain licenses that are real conventions [themselves]". Sometimes the best scholarship is work that itself is a delight. Lovejoy and Chesterton are each good, readable guides to take with us on a journey with Rasselas.

THE MAN WHO WAS THURSDAY

GEORGE Bernard Shaw, as Chesterton often noted, was seldom right about anything, which is partially why the two men spent so much time in public debate, Shaw being even in those days the almost only one who could sometimes parry GKC's wit with a few *bon mots* of his own. Shaw was absolutely correct, however, about one matter: Chesterton should have written more for the stage. As good as his novels are, and they are imaginative accomplishments of a high order, they would have been even better plays (or films). At this writing, an excellent film production of Chesterton's novel *Manalive* is still looking for a major distributor. The popular comedy movie *Passport to Pimlico* was a watered down plot similar to *The Napoleon of Notting Hill*. Dialogue often carries much of the rising action in a Chesterton story and most of the physical action is realizable on stage, although such events in *The Man Who Was Thursday* require stage directions to accommodate some approaching elephants.

Shaw even wrote a series of letters stating that unless GK wrote a play he would do handstands in front of his wife and torture Belloc. After a good six years of being hectored, Chesterton wrote a three-act play, *Magic,* a delightful romp with serious implications about a prestidigitator who performed no tricks. He was a real magician. To say more would spoil the play. Unfortunately, he wrote only two other full plays, both among his best work. The most famous is his posthumous work *The Surprise,* which is available on DVD, any rightly understood tells us what we need to know about Chesterton's belief in free will and the need for salvation. The other play is the seldom revived, *The Judgment of Dr. Johnson.* The chances are that few want to take a chance with a play requiring a little, but just a little, familiarity with Samuel Johnson. Do we live in an age where mentioning his name will produce nothing but blank stares? As Dr. Kirke in the Narnian stories would say, "What do they teach them in these schools?"

Along the way, he also adapted his novel *The Flying Inn,* which certainly is better as a comic play because those character scream for incarnation. Mrs. Cecil Chesterton, GKC's sister-in-law was a journalist who wrote under the name of Ada Jones; she also sponsored a number of homes for wayward memory named, after her husband's memory, Cecil Houses. Her book *The Chestertons* is somewhat notorious for its unfounded smear of Mrs. Gilbert Chesterton, Frances. In an interview with this author in 1979 Frank Sheed believed she strayed into libelous territory, but matters must have been comparatively pacific in this edition Gilbert of TMWWT published fourteen years before Jones' errant memories led to bad feelings that can still be felt in Chestertonian circles.

A version of this story removing its cosmic significance was staged in Chicago several years ago and was instructive. Remove the metaphysical order that informs the story and the play became a piece of diabolism. One needed a long, cold shower after seeing it. Orson Welles' radio production broadcast in 1938, five weeks before his infamous *War of the Worlds,* remains the best dramatic version available. Ada Jones could write well when she was something other than prickly. Perhaps her version will be made available some day soon.

WOMEN IN DICKENS

CHESTERTON really does commit the scholarly *sin* his enemies and other unobservant readers sometimes lay at his door. He says almost nothing about the nominal topic, in this case the argument of Mr. Charles (which GKC sidesteps casually), or about any of the women in Dickens, which is less forgivable because we would like to encounter a few of them here.

Because Chesterton put down enough on paper to help deforest England, he, like Homer, sometimes naps, but even so, he makes us listen even when he talks in his sleep. What he does say here is true, especially his comments that "people who like Dickens like talking about Dickens and like the people who will talk about him". Although it is also true about some other authors (have you ever spent the evening with people who know every blade of grass in Tolkien's invented world?), this is not true for many writers placed high in the accepted canon. Can you imagine a society devising contests and fancy dress balls to supply the best ending for Byron's *Don Juan*?

Although, farfetched, we shall doubtless hear soon of just such an undertaking; but it seems absurd in any case. Although Byron provides many possible emotional reactions a spontaneous overflow of popular elation is hardly one of them. He may excite his readers' curiosity, but it takes an author with a lighter touch (lighter even than Byron's) to create characters as beloved as Dan Peggotty.

The Sherlock Holmes stories have this quality, as does the Stevenson of the adventure stories. Dickens had this elusive touch in almost every piece of fiction he wrote from Pickwick to Edwin Drood. A teaching colleague told me recently that American college students have a hard time reading Dickens today. If true, this is a cause for weeping. I understand they may require some guidance in understanding Sam Weller's dialect, but not to be able to ride the roads of England with the Pickwickians, to joy in hoping something will turn up for Mr. Macawber, or to cringe at Nancy's murder—this is a road leading from fellowship to indifference and then to barbarism.

SOME FELLOWS

UNLIKE the French, the English have ever resisted the idea of an official academy of language or literature. Chesterton might have said (and may well have said) the idea of such an institution speaks to the fierce and relentless logic of the French. (He would also have meant that as a compliment.) For whatever reasons, the French language is comparatively self-contained, whereas the history of the English language consists of layer upon layer of infusions from the various cultures that settled or conquered that area called England. The word "bard" can be traced to Celtic roots. As GKC also said, the island (south of Hadrian's wall) was Roman before it was English after Julius Caesar came, saw, and conquered; only then came the Angles and Saxons and a new language to dominate the land; but it has always since been open to change from other cultures, particularly from the French. Only in the eighteenth century did English have formal grammar imposed on it in a major way, and then it was the foreign grammar of Latin, which has since that epoch not allowed us to quietly split our infinitives or to uses prepositions to end sentences with. This is why even the literate, maybe even especially the literate struggle with English grammar so.

One of Chesterton's most strongly believed prejudices was against the specialist dictating to all and sundry, those narrowly educated babblers (especially modern philosophers) who think it their role in life to be as nannies for the rest of us. After all, he went to art school and not university, which means he understood the posturing of art critics as well as anyone could, probably better than he wished he could; but he did understand the real need for some kind of patronage, even if only because the artist must eat.

From what GKC says, the Royal Society of Literature made something of a comeback in his day after a long period of eclipse; and he found commendable any organization that offered lectures by such eminent literary figures as Evelyn Underhill, Walter de la Mare, and Rudyard Kipling; and he would also applaud any lecture that concerned itself with that most democratic (always a term of approbation in Chesterton) of forms, the popular ballad.

He also could not forbear mentioning why the Society had previously fallen into eclipse in the Utopian era of the 1800s. It was the period when the triumph of utilitarianism, or extreme individualism, based on the rather cocksure arguments from highly promoted economics and the practical commercial exploitation, which was self-evident to all but those who had blinded themselves against Christian charity, stultified English life. Nor could Chesterton refrain from swiping at the most self-consciously "artistic" of the authors' discussed, Algernon Swinburne. Chesterton's taste ran more to the Franciscan troubadour, Jacopone de Todo than to the modern decadent, because the friar's verse, like all the best poetry, makes us want to lift a glass with friends, pray, or both at once; such as these Chesterton celebrates.

RHYMES FOR CHILDREN

CHESTERTON is lauded correctly for many outstanding accomplishments in his thirty-six year career; but among the children of his own neighborhood we hear numerous accounts of the portly gentleman who staged parties for the young, entertaining them with his toy theatre, not to mention his tossing buns into the air and catching them in his mouth. Whenever he addresses the mind of the child, we sense his real understanding, especially of the very small child, and it is completely free of sentimental treacle, although we can hope he served that unjustly maligned dish as part of the fun at the parties.

He insists correctly that children themselves have no use for sentimentality; it is a self-indulgence of grown ups that is rightfully resented by the young. They normally have a taste for that which is strictly true and (above all) just. They have a positive thirst for justice and fairness, mostly lost later when sin or a sense of sin makes us yearn rather for mercy. We all remember the cry on the playground of that greatest of all iniquities—unfairness. One could argue, and some do, that this strict rule by which children live is a sign of immaturity, but is it perhaps also an echo of something prelapsarian the jaded adult loses?

Such purity may also be found in the child's love of primary colors. If these and other observable, primal facts define the child, we can observe as corollaries, one of which is love for the most elementary rhythms in song and verse. Wherever well-treated (and even some not so well-treated) children congregate, we will note simple rhyming games and chant, often of a quality that makes condescension impossible except to the obtuse. They also understand that red causes wonder and joy simply because it is red and peaches being purely peach is peachy; but never forget that bad people do bad things and deserve punishment. Black is never white, nor vice versa. This may be the real reason children cannot sit on juries; they are too just. Chesterton, in this essay, celebrates those beings who exemplify such common sense and even suggests that such sense is often woefully lacking in some who masquerade as really being the thing behind the uniform, whereas the child, far more clearly, realizes he is only wearing a costume; to wear one is customary. We may learn much from looking at the behavior of children. It has been said, I believe, that Someone once said we should become like them.

THE ENGLISH PEASANT

SMALL is beautiful was a rallying cry of a vocal minority in the United States in the 1970s and 1980s. The phrase derives from a collection of essays with that title and was written by E.F. Schumacher. One central essay is entitled "Buddhist Economics". When asked why he chose Buddhism as a model for his theories, he replied, "If I called it Christian Economics, no one would have listened". How true that statement is.

Chesterton has once more become among the most quoted of authors; scarcely a day goes by without a reader being brought up short by meeting GKC even in the daily press. Perhaps a miracle accounts for the restoration he had made from the deliberate silence that reigned from shortly after his death, when all England knew him, until the revival, which has continually gained strength over these past few decades.

The majority of his books are now in print, or at least readily available. Yet, surprisingly, comparatively few even dedicated Chestertonians could articulate

THE ENGLISH PEASANT 351

his social beliefs clearly, and they are most often caricatured badly, and, even when partially understood, many modern readers are baffled because they do not take his presuppositions into account. Many take as an historical accurate summary of those beliefs the joking current among his friends "Three acres and a cow". That was pub talk, not distributism, although it could be a fit emblem. An emblem is not an argument, however. To Americans, that slogans smacks of General Sherman's infamous field order that the freedmen were to have forty acres and a mule. Pipe dream, those who dismiss it say, but press someone who speaks against distributism this way, and chances are that its opponents could not articulate what the distributists believed either.

Although they do believe that a society works best if its *tone* is agricultural, they by no means wish everyone to return to the land. Forcing people to do so is the way of such as Pol Pot, and scratch the surface of someone arguing against Catholic social theorists (for that is what they are), Distributism is all about restoration of individual private property. *Peasant* in the true meaning of the word is a good thing, salt of the earth, and those who even think of the word as a pejorative need a good talking to. Therein lies a root presupposition—those who are self-sustaining and part of a family form the backbone of any society worthy of the name. We are talking not only of people on land, but also the small craftsman or the small shop owner. The best circumstance would be a fully self-sustaining family who owned productive property and used it well. As to enterprises too large for one family, we may need the introduction of guilds. A term, coined by the distributists, is now in the catechism of the Catholic Church. That word is *subsidiarity*. Understand the term, understand the concept.

They offered no set program. Indeed, Chesterton in *The Outline of Sanity* threw out six practical programs that could be started in England as he wrote in 1926. These people were not Utopians like the communists. They believed in community and abhorred communes.

DICKEN"S FORSTER

ALTHOUGH John Forster never reaches the heights of biographical literary excellence that James Boswell achieves, nevertheless he belongs in that rare category of being the first important biographer whose work is still wisely read more than a century afterwards. That is no mean feat. Usually early biographies are merely provisional portraiture, although the biographer either was of his circle or had possession of surviving manuscripts and the like. This is almost especially true when the biographer was a close friend of the subject, as Forster was to Dickens. Forster's situation has a close parallel with Maisie Ward, close to G.K. and Frances Chesterton, who wrote his first full biography, and whose work has yet to be excelled. In both cases, Dickens and Chesterton, only materials subsequently made available make another work necessary, although that has not stopped many from trying their hands at their subjects. Maisie Ward, though, found sufficient material for a book of addenda to her biography, *Return to Chesterton* that is nearly as long as her first volume.

In his last paragraph of his preface to Forster, GKC touches on the one reservation some readers in subsequent generations have felt about Forster's book—that it is Victorian in the mere parochial sense of being simply in its time and not greater than its time, and that Dickens requires something more universal where Forster is sometimes humdrum. That disappointment is one that anybody could feel about any biography written by a contemporary of a major literary figure; but do we require a Boswell to a Samuel Johnson? Do we demand a Ben Jonson for a Shakespeare? If that were true, we would probably know nothing about Shakespeare except from a few stray legal documents. We would have nothing of what our own contemporaries like Peter Milward have been able to detect, and we would be the poorer for it. Forster was of Dickens' time in a way Dickens was not. The world of Dickens is populated by archetypal figures that could exist only in that timeless universe. But Forster provided yeoman's service in ordering the events of Dickens' life as it was played out in the prosaic world about him. Sometimes, as any modern biography rich in investigative detail will teach us, Dickens could have used some thrashing, but, in Forster, we meet the nineteenth century man as the nineteenth century experienced his presence.

A SHROPSHIRE LASS

TWO kinds of people found no sympathy for Chesterton—optimists and pessimists. He even went so far as to turn one of his stories on the despair that lurked behind a perpetually smiling philanthropist who, as we later discover, only succeeded in committing suicide on his third consecutive attempt. So much for optimists.

He was even harder, if it is possible, on pessimists. GKC famously called Thomas Hardy the "village atheist brooding and blaspheming over the village idiot". Truly no one was more the professional sourpuss than Hardy although A.E. Housman in *A Shropshire Lad* could run him a close second. Houseman's attitude toward English letters was so morose that among his papers discovered after his death was a small collection of scurrilous book reviews with only blanks left to fill in the names of the books.

The Shropshire lass of the title, *Mary Webb*, were a far different case. She was to live only two years after the publication of her 1916 novel *The Golden Arrow*, which appeared with G.K.'s preface. Here he speaks warmly of her novels. Her characters are kin to all those rural, unsung peasants who populate the poetry of William Wordsworth. Some cynical city types denigrate country people who, if they among the few that depict them at all, turn them into L'il Abner types, loveable, but stupid; or, worse, into degenerate killers of the kind one tries to avoid seeing in such fare as *The Texas Chainsaw Massacre*. Even when a transcendentally beautiful English film about such folk was brought to the United States, in a Michael Powell production no less, the release prints of *Gone to Earth* was unbearably hacked (although it has since been resurrected).

Webb's other work remains largely unknown on this side of the Atlantic. Simply imagine good-hearted protagonists who encounter the kinds of problems those bordering on sanctity undergo anywhere. This is the landscape of her books and hers is a reputation too long floundering in obscurity. Her work demands republication.

SONGS FROM THE SPIRIT

PERHAPS only one of a hundred readers who have savored the prose and poetry of G.K. Chesterton have ever remembered as being part of his world the flamboyant figure of W.R. Titterton, which is shameful. Perhaps the identical melody of their last names may have caused some of the problem. Oddly enough, that melody sounds as if a hurried journalist were clicking off the name on an old typewriter. Whatever the reason, he is forgotten as is the Devereaux pub where the Distributist League met. For some years, Titterton served as Chesterton's man Friday at the *New Witness*, and then held the same post at *G.K.'s Weekly*. By all accounts, his wit sparkled, yet he realized which of them was the writer for the ages. That is real humility shining beneath the comic exterior of the man, and his own book on Chesterton is a minor treasure.

He ran the Distributist League meetings as well. Here he is on the subject:

"The formal business of the [Distributist] League was followed by after-meetings in the general bar of the Devereux, where an account by one of the members describes pint pots banging on the tables and members "shouting texts of St. Thomas at each other, calling on the people of England for the overthrow of their taskmasters, and a return to the religion of their forefathers."

"There was also much singing. I have always regarded this singing as an essential part of Distributism."

The collection of songs Chesterton discusses is mostly rollicking bar room ballads, with much of the musical notation included. The melodies are most important because the lyrics alone do not convey the humor. What is funny about saying, "Let's all get drunk today?" This is a similar problem to some of Burns' drinking songs extolling the virtues of usquebaugh. To hear the melody completes the lyric and vice versa. They are little without the other, but together form a complete comic ballad. Finding his drinking songs and learning to sing them is rewarding even for those who do not drink. For good reasons the distributists were called by someone "The Maddest, Merriest Political Party in All England". W.R. Titterton had much to do with directing that spirit, probably even more than did his boss.

THE CURE d'ARS

ALTHOUGH at this writing a movement is formally underway to canonize Chesterton, only a relatively small amount of his work, even after his conversion to Roman Catholicism in 1922, addresses matter of differences between Catholics and Protestants. *The Thing* is his masterpiece of specifically Catholic apologetics and forms a kind of third part of a trilogy with *Orthodoxy* and *The Everlasting Man*. His other two books specifically Catholic, *The Catholic Church and Conversion* and *The Well and the Shallows,* are by comparison attendant lords to that towering and densely constructed model for apologetic argument

He would also dash off articles in his latter years for Catholic publications, and one of them is reprinted here. St. John Vianney is one of those Catholic saints not known much beyond the Church and, in these days, not even to the broad Catholic public. Often referred to only as "the cure d'Ars", he flourished at the time of the extreme persecution of the Church by the French revolutionaries. By this time, the revolution had committed the first of many modern genocidal slaughters. After putting down the War against the Enlightenment government in the Vendee and other western provinces, the enlightened one murdered 300,000-500,000 peasants in the name of *the People*.

Vianney became a priest shortly after the Church was reestablished. Henri Gheon proves the cure in biographically good hands as he recounts the priest's many adventures, and brings the deft touch of a playwright to Vianney's riveting story. The deep historical fact is that, because of the revolution, the French had become poorly catechized, as happens in any country where secular revolution has taken hold. His work helped restore religious practices and proper altar worship as well as organizing religious education. His influence was so powerful that, in 1855, the number of pilgrims who came to d'Ars to be shriven had grown to an estimated 20,000 per year with Vianney often in the confessional over sixteen hours a day. He is, since 1929, remembered as the patron saint of parish priests. Gheon wrote his book for that occasion. Even for those who do not share the Roman Catholic faith, one cannot help but be struck by his Godly goodness; all Christian can learn much from his sanctity.

APOLOGIA

WHENEVER the topic arises, one senses Chesterton's annoyance at fellow distributists who talked him into using his name as the selling point of the magazine he edited and one can almost feel his blush when he explains why he allowed it. He replied with his customary penchant for striking at the heart of a problem, but concedes that all alternative remedies make their movement sound as if it were simply another cranky fad like nudism or vegetarianism. Perhaps a current online magazine called *The Distributist Review* has made a strategic mistake in its title, one that by no means affect the plain horse sense of that organ of sane social thought. At best, labeling something as distributist today wither (as GKC himself notes) makes any essays that flower from its name reside in one small corner of the map of −isms, something to take as seriously as a military threat from Lichtenstein. At best, those who do know the terms set in this remote corner of debate will tend to preach to the choir while others have found read to hand a reason to pigeonhole one's thoughts and disregard it. This was also why Chesterton did not wish the Distributist League to form a political party; they would be perceived as cranks, and they might become so. The failure of the party broke the political hope of many of the original distributists, but GKC warned them from the beginning that such was possible.

Even Chesterton was at a loss to finding a better name to suit the vision, probably because the theory describes only what is sane, and his volume on the subject is called *The Outline of Sanity*. Once at a crowded wedding feast with many Chesterton Society members in attendance, the table where I sat was at the opposite end of the hall from the group's president, Dale Ahlquist. Somebody at the table nearest me must have misunderstood some random comment of mine. In the middle of the main course, Dale came up and asked for the name I have found for the thing. He really looked disappointed when I came up empty. Bad things have taken all the good names. One proposal offered Chesterton had rejected outright. He refused to reside over anything called "The League of Little People". Even a lapse of taste that lets us imagine Chesterton as an overripe leprechaun cannot be ignored entirely, but still the search for a good name goes on.

I have long thought "Auburnism" has a good ring

to it, but it is too literary and too remote for modern folk. Auburn was the name of the village of good old England, the same whose abbey received faint hints in Shakespeare's "bare ruined choirs". That was the place of the once and future England, and what was lost first fully described as lost in that Oliver Goldsmith masterpiece, "The Deserted Village."

To conclude with a glimpse into that older lost world is one Chesterton would have applauded. Someone said that if Chesterton has been so often proven right in his conclusions, his premises must also be true, which is correct, but behind premises are axioms, and nothing is more axiomatic to Chesterton than a vision of Englishmen owning their own property in a land where the family is the bulwark against the state. If that ideal looks even more impractical in our day, and seems "irrelevant" in the cant phrase, that is a comment on our age, not on Chesterton's thought. Adam Wayne may yet take Notting Hill and the ideal attitude is still *The Return of Don Quixote.*

BIBLIOGRAPHICAL NOTE

The following is a list of introductions contributed by G. K. Chesterton not included in this volume:

1902. Carlyle, *Past and Present.* Oxford University Press.
1904. Carlyle, *Sartor Resartus.* Cassell's National Library.
      Bunyan, *Pilgrim's Progress.* Cassell's National Library.
1905. Maxim Gorki, *Creatures that Once were Men.* Alston Rivers.
1906 and onwards. Introductions to the works of Dickens in Dent's Everyman's Library, collected in one volume entitled *Criticisms and Appreciations of Charles Dickens's Works* (Dent, 1911).
1907. George Haw, *Life of Will Crooks, M.P.* Cassell.
1908. Ruskin, *Poems.* Routledge.
1908. Darrell Figgis, *A Vision of Life.* Lane.
1910. Thackeray, *Selections.* Geo. Bell.
      Eyes of Youth. Herbert & Daniel.
1912. *Famous Paintings in Colour.* Cassell.
      A. H. Baverstock, *The English Agricultural Labourer.* Fifield.
1915. *Bohemia's Claim for Freedom.* Chatto & Windus.
      Theodore Maynard, *Laughs and Whifts of Song.* Erskine Macdonald.
1916. H. N. Maitra, *Hinduism.* Cecil Palmer.
      L. J. McQuilland, *Song of the Open Road.* Heath Cranton.
1917. S. Nordentoft, *Practical Pacifism.* Geo. Allen & Unwin.
1918. Sybil Bristowe, *Provocations.* Erskine Macdonald.
      Will Dyson, *Australia at War.* Cecil Palmer.
      Leonard Merrick, *House of Lynch.* Hodder & Stoughton.
1921. Vivienne Dayrell, *Little Wings.* Blackwell.
1922. A. J. Penty, *Post-Industrialism.* Geo. Allen & Unwin.
1923. Irene Hernaman, *Child Mediums.* St. Dominic's Press.
      O. R. Vassall-Philips, *The Mustard Tree.* Burns, Oates & Washbourne.
1924. *Catholic Who's Who.* Burns, Oates & Washbourne.
      P. M. Wright, *Purple Hours.* Gay & Hancock.
      J. T. Grein, *The New World of the Theatre.* Hopkinson.
1925. F. J. Sheen, *God and Intelligence.* Longmans Green.
1926. L. de G. Sieveking, *Bats in the Belfry.* Routledge.
1927. H. Massis, *Defence of the West.* Faber & Faber.
      Franciscan Studies (published at Crackow).

ACKNOWLEDGEMENT

THE editor of this volume wishes to express Mr. G. K. Chesterton's and his own obligation to the courtesy of the authors and publishers, who gave full permission for the majority of the prefaces in this collection to be extracted from their respective places, and to the co-operation of the publishers in the few cases where an arrangement was necessary. Particulars of the book introduced and the names of author and publisher have been given in a footnote to each introduction.

www.ingramcontent.com/pod-product-compliance
Lightning Source LLC
Chambersburg PA
CBHW071231290426
44108CB00013B/1364